Praise for *Indigenous: Growing Up Californian*

"Cris Mazza is well known for her witty and irreverent experimentation in fiction, so she might be expected to fool around in telling her own story. But this collection of essays is rooted, courageous, and breathtakingly near the bone. Though her memoir has its exotic elements—an ancestor shipwrecked as an infant, a Swedenborgian uncle, work as convalescent hospital aide, symphony sidekick, and intensive dog trainer—she sets herself in the context of familiar Americana. Her head-on dealing with madness, illness, blood, anxiety, sexual dysfunction, and death speak to the drama of our ordinary lives." — Janet Burroway, author of *Embalming Mom*

"In *Indigenous*, Cris Mazza shows us the beauty of the paradox. A girl plays the trombone in a marching band in the heat of Southern California, making the rigorous discipline look and sound like the most natural form of grace. A young woman trains her obedience show dogs by teaching them the joy of playing—a quality that is both natural and learned. A middle-class physics professor's family lives off the land of Southern California, fishing in its streams, hunting small game in the various terrains, raising animals that become food. The details of this memoir are beautiful and yet gritty and real, like the cloth-napkins-and-silver Sunday dinners of the narrator's childhood, with the delicate meat of mourning doves floating in tomato sauce, or the Waldorf salad in which persimmons take the place of the predictable apples. Writing with lyricism and honesty, Mazza covers a wide range of topics from family history and the geography of Southern California, gender politics, astute observations about the generation that came of age in the 1960's and 70's, lores of dog training and outdoor life—

always returning to a vision of life as rich, complex, and nourishing as the landscape of her childhood. The result, her "particular rendition of the real thing," is a solo piece in which we hear the grandeur of the symphony." — Kyoko Mori, author of *Polite Lies*

"These personal essays shine with a hard-won honesty and emotional clarity. You can trust Cris Mazza to level with you and entertain you with her stylish prose; this is an engaging collection." — Phillip Lopate, editor of *Writing New York: A Literary Anthology*

"Cris Mazza's stunning memoir, *Indigenous*, worries the notions of belonging, of be-longing for a place and of longing for the memories of same. Her tales of her native California expertly excavate an always surprising and always rewarding experience cache. It is a book about scourging, scouring, and scoring (in the musical sense) the stuff, the scraps that make up the worlds we remember and the worlds we inherit." — Michael Martone, author of *The Flatness and Other Landscapes*

"Cris Mazza's autobiographical landscape — in a now nearly vanished California — is rendered so vividly that I closed my eyes and heard our past: the owls, coyotes, and the shrill, joyous cries of wild childhood." — Susan Straight, author of *Highwire Moon*

indigenous

GROWING UP
CALIFORNIAN

Cris Mazza

**CITY LIGHTS
SAN FRANCISCO**

Cover design by Victor Mingovits
Cover photo by Elinore Mazza
Book design by Elaine Katzenberger
Typography by Harvest Graphics

Library of Congress Cataloging-in-Publication Data

Mazza, Cris.

   Indigenous : growing up Californian / by Cris Mazza.
      p.   cm.
   ISBN 0-87286-422-7
   1. Mazza, Cris—Homes and haunts—California.   2. Authors,
American—20th century—Biography.   3. California—Social life and
customs.   4. Mazza, Cris—Childhood and youth.   5. Family—
California.   I. Title.

   PS3563.A988 Z467 2003
   813'.54—dc21   2002041269

Visit our web site: www.citylights.com

CITY LIGHTS BOOKS are edited by Lawrence Ferlinghetti and Nancy J.
Peters and published at the City Lights Bookstore, 261 Columbus Avenue,
San Francisco, CA 94133

Acknowledgments are made to the following publications in which these
essays or excerpts first appeared:

The San Diego Reader for "Homeland"
The San Diego Reader for "A Girl Among Trombonists"
The San Diego Reader for "Land of Make Believe" (published as "What
    Happened to Marie?")
The San Diego Reader for Symphony Ex, Ex-Symphony" (published as "The
    Ex Mrs. Symphony")
The Milk of Almonds (Feminist Press, 2002) for portions of "Homeland"
    (published as "Our Father")
In the Middle of the Midwest (Indiana University Press, 2003) for "Displaced"
High Plains Literary Review for "Waterbaby"
High Plains Literary Review for "To Ashes" from "Withstanding the Elements"
Sycamore Review for "Displaced"
RiverSedge (The University Press, Univ. of Texas-Pan American) for "Let it
    Snow" from "Withstanding the Elements"
Another Chicago Magazine for "Tell Me"

Photo Credits:

photo on page 108 is by John Stubbs
photos on pages 16, 182, and 226 are by Cris Mazza
photos on pages i, viii, 1, 2, 28, 181 and 216 are by Elinore Mazza
photos on pages 42, 252 and 294 are by Ralph Mazza

for my parents, sisters, and brothers

CONTENTS

Displaced, *an introduction*   xi

PART ONE: HOMELAND   1

Homeland   3

Waterbaby   43

A Girl Among Trombonists   87

Exemplary Lives   109

Land of Make-Believe   141

PART TWO: HOW FAR SHE CAME   181

Symphony Ex, Ex-Symphony   183

How Far She Came   217

Withstanding the Elements   227

Tell Me   253

DISPLACED

an introduction

O n a snowy January evening in Elmhurst, a far western suburb of Chicago, I watched an A&E documentary called "California and the Dream Seekers." But I didn't need to be reminded that the world reflects on California from the perspective of those who yearned to be there. California's history is a linear succession of great migrations: conquistadors and Franciscan missionaries, gold-rush prospectors, Chinese laborers escaping their country's exhausted resources, midwestern dust bowl farmers fleeing both environmental and financial ruin, movie star pipe-dreamers, and contemporary migrant agricultural workers. The state's growth into a region with the world's eighth-largest economy is credited to those and other pilgrim castle builders who came to it as a place of unbounded possibilities. Over nearly a century and a half, hundreds of thousands of people elected to turn toward California for what they wanted or who they aspired to be.

But what of those who were born there? Jostling for space with the transplants and snowbirds and immigrants and "zonies" (a special word for those escaping Arizona's heat), we haven't really known a *wow-look-where-I-am* wonderment, an *I'm-lucky-to-be-here* glow. We're there because we've always been there. Media's depiction of the place may engulf or dupe us; but for many natives, it does not.

We scoff at, even rebel against the notion of California as land of the ocean-view condo, land of the forever-young Coppertone beach-baby, land of the year-round after-work buffed-out executive surfer, land of the sunglassed convertible-driving blond aerobics instructor, land of the cult-of-the-month, of palm-treed boulevards made just for rollerbladers, of psychedelic black-lit drug parties begun in the sixties that have never ended, of drive-in churches and drive-through espresso bars, of crystalline blue cloudless skies sailed ever-lastingly by a hang-glider (and his dog), a vegetation restaurant on every block, a guru on every corner, a Lana Turner on every drug-store stool. But if we didn't *choose* this enchanted place to live out or chase our visions, if we are a generation or two removed from those that dared to hunt a dream, does it mean we *don't* dream? Or don't have the same quality of dream? Or don't have the same fortitude because we're not *required* to uproot and resettle in this unique region in order to help make our dreams possible? Does it mean California, either the real or the fanciful, doesn't influence or put its distinct mythic stamp on our dreams—and on who we become?

IN AUGUST 1993, a moving van left a small postwar slab house in east San Diego, followed by my white Mazda pickup, its aluminum shell packed to the roof. I was moving to Illinois. My fourth book of fiction had just been released and I'd accepted a position as an assistant professor at the University of Illinois at Chicago.

I'd left California before, always for temporary stints, for a second graduate degree in Brooklyn, as a writer-in-residence in Tennessee and then Pennsylvania. At one time the reasons for these ventures, including the latest, had caused a bitter sentiment for my own state: off to Brooklyn because, advisers told me, I couldn't be well-rounded if my education was concentrated in Southern California. To Tennessee and Pennsylvania and now Illinois because California had become so accustomed to being the aspired-for destination of so many, the state had developed a sweeping attitude that jobs could be filled with the highest caliber candidate only when *not* filled by a native. "No man can be a prophet in his own land," someone advised, and it seemed especially true of California. It looked as if one had to either be educated elsewhere and/or gain experience elsewhere before expecting to come home and be given credit for accomplishments. Or just *go* elsewhere. Southern California and San Diego in particular—beneficiaries (or victims) of a literal flood of "new blood" that hasn't abated since the depression—didn't give me a second look. There were so many exotic nonlocals to choose from! But should my bitterness have been aimed at California, or the *people* who'd moved there *then* turned it into their icon of Land of Banished Free-Thinkers-from-Elsewhere? Wasn't there another California that had, after all, given me a more subtle and priceless endowment?

Free-thinkers-from-elsewhere. Hadn't another population of indigenous people endured this kind of guest (who never went home)? I recall hearing of the Native Americans who once populated San Diego County as culturally uninspiring, "merely" nomadic gatherers without the imagination of more sublime native peoples who built pueblos or hunted bison. Was a new breed of "natives" now doomed to carry this mantle as well—had each passing generation's energy and hope and inspiration somehow been diluted? I don't know how this perception of the original people of California came about, but I can guess: it seemed the natives docilely accepted the new order imposed by Franciscan missionaries, became virtual slaves in the mission compounds, and, except for minor uprisings and skirmishes, were basically easily subjugated. Simply put, the native people didn't have an organized enough society to wage a *war*. Thus they have been generally regarded as fundamentally uninteresting, and were even classified as such by European anthropologists of the era.

WHEN I ARRIVED at Brooklyn College in the early eighties, a fellow student, upon hearing I was from California, responded: "Oh, California? Isn't everything really *laid back* there?"

Laid back? Of course I'd heard the term. But I had never been asked to apply it to myself or my experience, or even to give a particular example of its manifestation. *Laid back:* chill-out, mellow-out, everything's-cool, go-with-the-flow, whatever-makes-you-happy, have-a-nice-day, find-yourself, get-in-touch-with-the-inner-child, take-it-easy, I'd-rather-be-surfing, hey-dude-whatever. Did my life fit on a bumper sticker? Was it laid-back to plug my ears during the detonation of the shotgun but keep my eyes trained on the falling bird so I could retrieve it, decapitate it, and drain the blood? To take away the hammer and hand my father the knife after he'd cracked a rabbit's skull? To throw not just balls, but sticks by the thousands and even rocks into the tumbleweedy, foxtail-filled canyon to be retrieved by a pedigreed dog whose ancestors had strutted in dog show rings? To spend teenaged afternoons marching with a trombone under an oppressive glare of sunshine, and spend teenaged weekends doing the same in full dress wool uniform being judged on musical and military precision? To participate in family outings gathering the rejects of a farmer's harvest that's been dumped behind the trucking docks? To earn minimum wage spoonfeeding pureed spinach into a profoundly handicapped imbecile's mouth after you've changed his diapers? To hike miles up and down a Sierra creekbed with a rod and reel, engrossed body-and-mind solely in a contest with wily native trout? To watch your husband, dressed in white tie and black tails, pace in a picket line outside Symphony Hall? To see the clear ripples of heat in the air, watch the rain of ashes, and stand in the current of fleeing grasshoppers as the yearly brushfire thunders up the hill toward our property line? To have your grandmother drown in a swimming pool? To sit like a stone during sex therapy while a charlatan pigeonholes you as a puritan? To time and again attempt to make pets of lizards, craw-dads, snakes, frogs, tortoises, horned toads, and other indigenous things that slithered through seasonal run-off creeks or crawled through the brush of the arid coastal scrub which the rest of the world doesn't seem to know *isn't* a lush, palm-treed tropical paradise?

I was, at first, dismayed that my state citizenship had been called to the test, and that I would fail, right out of the gate, to *really* be what the world seemed to hold so dear: a Californian.

I would evolve to realize that my non-laid-back experience has, in fact, been a variation of—my particular rendition of—the real thing.

DURING THE 1998 World Series between San Diego and New York, the predictable scorn reigned forth from the "superior" metropolis toward the one on the West Coast. New York newspa-per columnists alleged that San Diego has no image and has noth-ing to offer but weather. They claimed that everyone except New Yorkers shops only in malls and considers Denny's to be fine din-ing, that everyone except New Yorkers smiles too much, and that San Diego doesn't even have enough infamy to make the city inter-esting or the citizens "smart." At once boasting of New York's diversity then slamming a place that chooses to neither compete with nor emulate it. One columnist spoke of *our* jealousy that we don't live in New York. Don't bullies pick on other kids because they themselves feel uncertain? Would a truly superior place speak with such venom against another if it didn't feel some insecurity?

Moving to Chicago in 1993, I was not-too-obliquely informed that displaced Californians are presumed to be ashamed of where we've come from, and should only admit to missing the weather. During my interview, I was asked if I would "be able to" leave San Diego's weather. Eight months later, at a department reception dur-ing the first week of my first semester in Chicago, a senior member of my department sidled up to me to make introductory small-talk. She politely asked where I'd chosen to live. With only slightly guarded verve, I informed her I'd found a one-bedroom cottage with a big yard in Elmhurst, eighteen miles west of the loop.

"Why *there?*" she responded, not bothering or unable to conceal her disgust, "there's nothing *there* you couldn't find in Southern California."

Ouch . . . in one breath she'd cast aspersions on not only where I was living but where I came from as well. Long after my stammered response (something about my dogs needing space), I realized that this person, who obviously had the stock intellectual's intolerant view of Chicago's suburbs, had an even dimmer stereotyped opinion of Southern California. Looking askance at the suburbs might come naturally for an academic in Chicago, but where might her view of California have come from? What sources *are* there except inane TV shows, magazines, and slick popular novels that depict Southern California as either a witless wasteland or a vast tract of bland white middle-class with no deeper thought than what color stucco should houses in the community be made of, and no nobler pursuit than getting a tan during lunch hours? If this college professor seemed to actually hold pop media's shallow view, what does it reveal about *her* and all the tens of thousands like her: What must she have been reading or watching in order to develop such a view?

This attitude continues to be displayed in my presence. At a meeting where the business at hand was devising a flier to promote the department, someone described a circular they'd received from the University of California at Santa Barbara. Not only was it a slick, four-color brochure, but it dared to contain photographs of the coast. This information immediately won scoffs and laughter from several of the professors around the table, as well as a comment that Santa Barbara's faculty was likely out surfing. Our discussion, meanwhile, had determined that our brochure should show some kind of cityscape, to promote the fact that the university is in Chicago. There is no doubt that the city of Chicago with all its resources is one of the advantages of an education at the University of Illinois at Chicago. But why is admitting (or promoting) that your university exists in a coastal landscape automatically denotative of low intellect while a cityscape is indicative of important serious thought? Perhaps we should consider that the existence of the coastline so near the University of California speaks highly of its scholars' intellectual abilities, if they don't need to be locked inside a winter-bound city of concrete, steel, and glass in order to produce music, art, literature, scientific breakthroughs, or academic research of the same caliber as work completed in Chicago.

What indeed does Southern California possess that either isn't found in greater Chicago and/or could be worthy of notice by an educated person—and could I possibly miss anything other than the weather? That's how shallow Californians presumably are: *Oh, dude, where's my sunshine?* (Admittedly a small sampling, but among the people I know, the only "California-beachy" types are non-natives.) So I must be just slightly more profound than that mythical Californian. Among the things I miss are canyons, hills, bluffs, and mountains, a soft tawny color most of the year, until days after a rainfall when a tint of fuzzy green begins to pervade, then overwhelms the brown. I miss the sharp scent and graceful silhouette of eucalyptus trees and the midnight caterwaul of a coyote pack making a kill. I miss ranch houses with walls of picture windows overlooking valleys or canyons or with views of hazy hills. I miss college campuses and museums built in red-roofed Spanish style architecture, the dry furor of Santa Ana winds, and the zinging white streak over green grass of another Tony Gwynn opposite-field single.

Many of Chicago's suburbs, mine included, have maintained a small-town charm, with tree-lined streets, a town square, and storefront village shops—hardware, bakery, bookstore, jeweler, drug-store, shoe repair, library, town museum, and more. The suburbs shoulder the burden of their negative reputation among the city's "intellectuals"—called yuppie sprawl or plastic mommyhoods— by ignoring it. If *I* were in charge of boosting the image of these boroughs, I would eliminate the word *suburb* from colloquial speech. In San Diego, probably in all of Southern California, the vernacular doesn't use the word *suburbs*. In the city's vast geological area (in square mileage, San Diego has 320 to Chicago's 228), there are, as in Chicago, *neighborhoods*. The regions within the metropolitan area, but outside the city limits, are referred to as *North County, East County,* and the *South Bay,* even though it's all one big county. The word *county* in these cases is like *country,* a place you used to be able to keep livestock and poultry, even slaughter your own domestic rabbits in the backyard. At least until the little municipalities in the county began incorporating themselves into cities.

OF COURSE I love my home state. But I love a different state than the image-hologramed place I left. And a different state than the one now being covered on every available flat place, and some not so flat, with big boxy houses, nearly shoulder-to-shoulder, or condos crusted like barnacles on sandstone bluffs. My feelings are for the state whose indigenous people were "a disappointment" because they didn't declare war over proprietorship of the fragile yet durable landscape. The state where you might have to go outside to get warm in December because the night's chill has refrigerated little slab houses without central heat. A state whose seasons are named *fire* and *rain*. The state in which there are parcels of land that were originally a "throw in" free offer for anyone who bought a dictionary or encyclopedia from a depression-era door-to-door salesman somewhere in the East. A place where the real value is a little harder to see.

A&E's "California and the Dream Seekers" said California is best represented and characterized by visionaries who had the boldness, vigor, and imagination to pioneer what would become great industries, great movements, great development, or just greatness. But that idea only seems to consider what it meant, 50 to 200 years ago, to *become* a Californian or for California to *become* what the world thinks it is. And, of course, there's even a substantial amount of truth — truth that admittedly feels good — in the observation that no other place on earth has inspired so many different migrations of people seeking a better life. So maybe there's something to the Conquistador legend that said there was no other alloy there but gold.

For those of us who didn't have to *become* but *are,* understanding the state is not a task of expressing enough aggrandizement, but of locating the words at all, a delicate endeavor to extract the state *we* know from the romance and hoopla. Perhaps the indigenous people, overwhelmed with the pomposity of the Spanish explorers and missionaries, would agree.

I can't begrudge California to those who sought it as a source of hope, as the last romance of the last western frontier, or simply for its unrivaled resources from agriculture to precious metals to recreation. After all, if my parents hadn't come — one with a family reeling from the depression, the other as an implicit gesture of postwar personal independence for women — I wouldn't've been one of the fortunate, one of the upshots of someone's flight of fancy: to be born there.

But like those who have left hometowns and home states and now call themselves Californians — those who sit in the stadium in San Diego and cheer for the Chicago Cubs or New York Mets; those who dock their sailboats at Quivera Basin, De Anza Cove, or Shelter Island and send yearly contributions to orchestras or museums back East, tsk-tsking the bankruptcy of the symphony in San Diego — like *their* life-long allegiances to other "more worthy" places, no matter where else I am, I'll not ever *not* be a Californian.

Part 1

HOMELAND

HOMELAND

L ike (too) many other Californians, I have (a few) photographs of myself sunning on the beach. Like many (fewer)
natives of Southern California, my mother has old
Kodachrome slides of a smaller me sunning a lot more of myself on
the beach. But, natives know, sometimes the beach is gloomy.
There's one slide in particular where I'd be a better poster child for
an orphan-rescue fund than for Coppertone. It's a tear-swollen,
puffy-eyed, baby's-been-crying face. But it's not the lack of sun that
makes me sad. It's because I'm sitting on the sand beside my father's
head. I can't remember what I must've witnessed in terror that day.
The next slide in the carousel, a wider angle shot, shows that behind
my father's head stands a gaggle of lanky teenage boys.

"He was their senior class adviser," my mother explains, "this was
the beach party after graduation. For their class gag they dug a hole
then they all surrounded him, grabbed him, put him in, and buried
him up to his shoulders. It scared you!"

I maintained my fear of beaches and teenage boys for years.

Recently, as my mother showed me her latest batch of snapshots,
another photo caught my eye: my father, in his seventies—the same
smile and laughing, crinkled eyes as when his head sat on the beach
sand, but with less hair—surrounded by what seemed to be titanic

tall men, most of them also sans hair, in their sixties. "Who's this midget?" I asked.

"That's your father."

"I know *that*, who're these gigantic men?"

"They were his students. He was their class adviser. We went up to Chadwick last month for their fortieth reunion."

"*These* are the kids who buried dad?"

"Oh yeah, I guess they did."

Wow, I had always thought it must've taken an army to get my powerful father (all five foot four of him) buried up to his neck in sand. He's five foot two now, but he's still climbing to the roof to cut the wisteria and prune the bougainvillea, still digging renegade palm trees from his vegetable gardens, still making rock walls. More important (for me), he's half my DNA.

The head-spinning odds against being alive can be astronomical. Not only do we spend our lives evading insidious viruses and microbes, war, crime, car accidents, cholesterol, and general stupidity, but any individual's chance at being conceived in the first place is equally outrageous. The odds are even more enormous considering we're all made up of the specific DNA of *only* our parents. Those two parents had to not only meet, but perhaps fall in love (at least decide to have sex, or at least *one* of them had to decide). At that point the other numbers on the conception roulette had to fall into place in order for any individual to now be walking around on earth griping about how their mother didn't hug them enough or their dad wouldn't play catch.

My fascination involves the utter unlikeliness that my parents — an Italian boy in a Brooklyn family brought to its knees by the depression, and a middle-class girl from a professional family in Boston — would meet in on the Palos Verdes peninsula, twenty miles south of Los Angeles.

The story of *how* my parents managed to be in the same place at the same time starts even further back. But looking back to find the *how*, I discover the object of my search isn't the most interesting story. It's only an instigator for a variety of other discoveries that involve being native to a place where so many others have relocated to realize their fantasies: from an insight into my family's hunter-gatherer-scavenger way of life to a realization that the state famous for the Beach Boys, the Summer of Love, drive-in churches, and ballpark sushi vendors also nurtured this quaintly sane family.

OURS WASN'T A family in public housing, not on welfare, not living in an urban war zone. No encounters with gangs or guns or any crime more dramatic than shoplifting at Disneyland (I confess). Also not a destitute farm family who'd migrated from Oklahoma's dust bowl or a flooded plain beside the Mississippi. This isn't a story about victimization and deliverance. It's about a middle-class California family that didn't realize it was middle-class, in any sense of the word. We just didn't know any better: that middle-class families ordinarily don't cull the rejected vegetables left in a farmer's harvested field nor eat what the fish store sells as bait.

I would never claim that a family living in a three-bedroom home in a semi-rural county, whose main source of income was a father employed as a community college professor, was suffering or merely surviving. Even if the family numbered five kids. Even if a community college professor only made around $10,000 in the sixties. Even if new school clothes meant sneakers from FedCo plus bundles of hand-me-downs from cousins and friends. Even if going to the movies meant the drive-in with five kids in the back of a station wagon, or the occasional Saturday matinee at the Quonset-hut one-screen Helix Theater. (One time we sat in the dusty purple velvet seats of the old vaudevillian Fox Theater and saw *Mary Poppins*. Years later I had a weekly ticket to the same theater to hear my then-husband play in the San Diego Symphony.) When the neighbor kids outgrew their bicycles, we used Brasso to make the chrome fenders and wheel rims sparkle (but still lusted for an Orange Crate Special model Stingray bike with hot-rod–style gearshift). There were new toys—at Christmas and birthdays, never in between—Monopoly, Parcheesi, knock-off Barbie or troll dolls that wore the same size clothes. We always had books to read thanks to library cards and our uncle's bookstore. Of course the living room housed a B&W TV, until it broke down and wasn't replaced for over a year. (Didn't matter, we could only watch if Dad turned it on, and then could only watch what he chose.) We had to ask permission to open the refrigerator, seldom knew the (coveted) joy of individual chip bags or Twinkies in our school lunches. We were required to split cans of generic-brand pop between two of us, a process that involved intricate measuring to make the split equal.

But ours was not a family in poverty. Not in distress. Not in trouble. Just an ordinary family like millions of others, where dad had a job and mom was the Girl Scout leader, a family that might've eaten hamburger and tuna seven days a week without feeling deprived. Instead we dined on quail, rabbit, albacore, calamari, duck, eggplant, squash blossoms, artichokes, figs, olives, natural honey in the comb, persimmons, even quail eggs. What might've seemed, had we recited our activities to a school psychiatrist, like an indigent family *scavenging*—going on weekend outings to gather abandoned or discarded, still living, freshly killed, or already *dead* food from the countryside—was actually just a way of life, a deep relationship with landscape and region, something tacitly handed down from an Old World father to son.

IT STARTS, OF course, with an immigrant. Rather than the archetype ignorant peasant fleeing destitution in the southern regions of a newly unified Italy, bringing with him a family of uneducated children, Crescenzo Mazza (Grandpa) came to the United States around the turn of the century, after he finished his high school education in Naples, Italy. He came with his brothers, their wives, and his parents, and they all had money in their pockets as his father had recently sold the family's two Mediterranean shipping vessels. Eventually Grandpa was working in Manhattan as a salesman for three or four Italian jewelry importers. He was married to Anna Capriglione (Nana), a girl who'd come to the United States when she was two, spoke English with a Brooklyn accent, understood and spoke Italian, and had worked since finishing sixth grade in various factories, particularly lace piecework and a shoe assembly plant.

With five children plus various extended family members, Grandpa and Nana lived rather well in a multistory house in the Flatbush district of Brooklyn. The first-generation kids were supposed to be *American*—the boys had been given American names, and they were not expected or encouraged to speak any language but English. But Dad learned Italian while sitting with his grandfather, listening to the old sea captain tell stories of life on the Mediterranean. For nearly fifteen years Dad had the quintessential Brooklyn pre-Depression life. He played stickball in the street, delivered prescriptions by bicycle from the neighborhood pharmacy, rode the streetcar to Coney Island, and got walloped for staying out late fishing and clamming near Flatlands Bay. The family then feasted on seafood cioppino.

As it would for so many others, everything changed in 1929, when Dad was nine years old. The stock market plunged and my grandparents lost everything, including Grandpa's livelihood, so he went to California to hawk trinkets at the California-Pacific International Exposition in San Diego's Balboa Park. Dad was the eldest child, so responsibility for supporting the family trickled down to include him. He finished ninth grade in Brooklyn then quit school when the whole family left New York and moved west, stopping for almost a year to sell baubles and pennants at the Texas Centennial in 1936. But California was their intended destination, and later in 1936—like tens of thousands of others in one of the biggest voluntary migrations in history—they arrived "home."

Our grandfather had brought enough left-over stock with him to open a jewelry shop in Long Beach's now extinct waterfront amusement zone called "The Pike," a rinky-dink version of Coney Island. While the younger children attended school, Dad worked in the store. When (serendipitously) the store failed, Grandpa was offered the opportunity to manage an Anaheim fish market owned by the DiMassas of the L.A. Fish & Oyster Company. This gave Nana the opportunity to prevail in her determination that Dad's education should resume, even though Grandpa was not happy at losing full-time assistance from the family's eldest son.

The Mazzas' San Pedro home was across the street from the temporary quarters of a private academy called Chadwick School, where Dad worked part-time as a janitor, earning twenty-five cents an hour—all went directly to the family's budget. Mrs. Chadwick, the founder and headmistress of the academy, was more than merely satisfied with Dad's work cleaning the floors, chalkboards, and rest rooms. After inquiring, she discovered he was also a stellar student at San Pedro High School, even though he'd missed two years of formal education. The fledgling Chadwick School was striving for state accreditation and would need its first graduates to begin attending college immediately. So when her most advanced students were juniors, Mrs. Chadwick invited Dad to be part of Chadwick School's first graduating class. Then when the school relocated to its permanent (and present) site on the Palos Verdes peninsula, Dad went along to board there with the other students, grades K-12, who lived on campus. The former janitor was two years older than his classmates, but was now set to graduate from an exclusive private boarding school.

Chadwick School would later become home to the children of celebrities and movie stars. Among others, Jack Benny, Dean

Martin, Edward G. Robinson, Jascha Heifetz, George Burns, and Joan Crawford sent their children to Chadwick. High school scenes from *Mommy Dearest* take place at Chadwick School, (my parents both taught there at that time). Liza Minelli attended classes at Chadwick, as did Jack Jones. Mrs. Chadwick's concern was that these privileged children might not be anxious to attend college, and with an inaugural gradating class numbering a dozen, she wanted to ensure at least one college graduate. That was Dad's role.

Meanwhile, Grandpa bought the fish market as well as the two other storefronts in the building, and he moved the rest of the family to a house he'd purchased in Orange County for around $2,400. Vine Street, where the house was located, was one block long, surrounded mostly by orange groves. The region—divided occasionally by long rows of huge, old eucalyptus trees—also contained farm fields with lima beans, bell peppers, green beans, tomatoes, strawberries, and other produce. Every Saturday in the fish market Grandpa would prepare a big bowl of raw fish, and the field workers—Mexican and Japanese—would come to get supplies for weekend festivities. Grandpa was not only acquainted with many of the farm workers, he also knew the owners of the produce fields. They gave him permission to come any time to pick his own produce.

Dad's education at the University of California was partially sponsored by another of Chadwick School's founders. He helped support his schooling by again working as a janitor, this time in a sorority house. Before he could finish his degree, however, Dad's progress through college was interrupted by World War II. Four years later the new G.I. Bill allowed him to finish his education at San Francisco State. Then—partially out of gratitude—he went back to Chadwick School as the chemistry teacher, and there he met my mother, a new phys. ed. instructor fresh out of Boston University. My sisters and I spent our early childhood on the

Chadwick School grounds on the still agrarian, somewhat feral Palos Verdes peninsula. The campus shared the peninsula with an all-glass chapel. Couples came from Los Angeles to be married on the cliffs over spectacular ocean waves. And there was a pioneer theme park called Marineland headlining a pilot whale named Bubbles. There was little else: tumbleweeds, rattlesnakes, coyote, small produce farms, and shepherds with dogs pushing flocks of black sheep across the round, often brown hills.

OUR PARENTS' LITTLE stucco bungalow on the campus of Chadwick School was rent-free and we were given complimentary admission to the school, but monthly teaching salaries were approximately $250 in the years around 1953–1958. When our mother had a fourth child, the house threatened to rupture.

But our parents' bigger concern was that growing up with movie stars' children as classmates would give us a distorted view of the world. So they decided to leave Palos Verdes in 1959. Dad was hired by San Diego City College as a physics professor. By 1963 the community college district's second campus, Mesa College, opened its doors, and Dad was among the inaugural group of professors who moved over to staff the new campus. That same year he relocated his (still growing) family to semi-rural Spring Valley, to three-quarters of an acre and a ranch house that we immediately mistook for a ranch.

WHEN THEY BOUGHT it, our parents' property had only the long house built on the slope of the hill. The front lawn and back lawn on a lower level were both horizontal, but the rest of the property sloped downhill at about a thirty-degree slant. From the edge of the back lawn down to the property line, and continuing from there down to the bottom of the hill, it was all natural terrain of tumbleweeds, rocks, lizards, wasps' nests, rattlesnakes, wild cucumbers, buckwheat, cacti, and nonindigenous rippling wild oats, possibly descendants from failed wheat farms in the late 1800s. Dad looked around at his property and announced, "There's ten years of work here." Forty years later, he's still at work.

It started with dynamiters who leveled out a place in the volcanic rock for an above-ground swimming pool. Then for several months Dad (with a wheelbarrow), Mom, and all five of us (ages three to thirteen) picked up the rubble and made rock piles around the perimeter of the property. With these rocks, over the past four decades, Dad constructed walls. Some as thick as two feet, ranging in height from two to six feet, these walls terrace the entire property into multiple levels. He searched through the rocks for those with flat surfaces, saved them in a special pile, and fitted them like puzzle pieces, glued together with concrete, to make the tops of the walls flat. He can walk around his terraces on the flat paths made by the tops of the walls.

These terraced levels have become home to a wide variety of fruit trees, including fig, persimmon, tangerine, lime, several varieties of orange, grapefruit, quince, avocado, loquat, pomegranate, plum, nectarine, peach, banana, apricot, and certain kinds of apple—almost any kind of fruit tree that does not need a frost. Plus there are beds of rotating seasonal vegetables: lettuce, cabbage, brussels sprouts, broccoli, asparagus, onions, garlic, herbs of all kinds, radishes, carrots, squash, pumpkins, artichoke, eggplant, spinach, Swiss chard, rhubarb, bell peppers, several varieties of tomato, green beans, strawberries, boysenberries, raspberries, and more. The property came equipped with two full-sized olive trees, so Dad also cures olives in several different ways—green, black, and Italian salt-method. Mom cans and preserves everything from strawberry, peach, plum, and boysenberry jam and mint jelly, quince sauce (like applesauce), tomato sauce, and boysenberry and pomegranate syrup. When we were young there were also rabbits, and under the rabbit hutches in the steady, always-ready supply of nitrogen-rich fertilizer, Dad raised worms for freshwater fishing and to aid in composting and aerating the garden. We kept beehives for honey, chickens in a ten-foot-square coop, and quail in their own smaller coop—not for meat, just for the tiny eggs.

Backyard chicken coops are nothing new, but they're probably more popular than advantageous. Well-kept chickens are no longer cost-effective. Feed is expensive and, unless poultry are kept in small cages artificially lit to create longer "days," hens don't lay an egg every day. More like five out of seven days for the best laying breeds. Some banty hens will go "broody" after laying eggs every other day for three weeks. That means no more eggs for a while, they just want to sit and incubate. I used to feel sorry for them when they got this way and gave them avocado seeds to sit on and satisfy their urges. Their broodiness could be broken if I dipped their undersides in water several times a day. But if I needed fresh stock, I could wait for a banty hen to go broody, then purchase chicks from the feed store. At night I would slip into the chicken coop and, taking one chick at a time, reach into the dark nesting box and nestle the day-old baby under the broody hen. In the morning the hen got up, clucking with pride, and led her new brood into the yard to teach them to scratch. Three weeks later the babies had outgrown their mother (because commercial breeds are so much bigger than banties), but were still trying to find security under their mother's feathers. She would be sitting with wings raised over her head to allow one or two huge, gawky "babies" underneath.

It was even funnier when the banties were used to raise quail. The Asian quail were for eggs only—little delicacies smaller than the end of a thumb—but these birds didn't have parenting instincts. They didn't even lay eggs in nest boxes, just left them lying around, and were never interested in sitting on their eggs. Dad made an incubator to try hatching quail eggs, but the percentage of successful hatchings was very low that way. It takes constant surveillance, turning the eggs, making sure the heat and humidity are consistent. So we decided to let a broody banty hen hatch the quail eggs. Trust nature: she hatched every one of the eggs we gave her, probably more than a dozen because so many little eggs could fit under her. The quail chicks were yellow and black, no bigger than bumblebees. But this method had problems too. The hen took the tiny quail chicks out in the yard and tried to show them how to scratch for food. But the eager little chicks would themselves be scratched out from underneath their mother's feet like pebbles. Several were mortally injured, so the rest had to grow up motherless in the incubator.

Except for living in a coop, my poultry had "pet" status, including a duck who thought she was a chicken—her name was Chickie. All of my birds were individuals with personalities, living lives fraught with interpersonal connections, complex unfolding scenarios, and drama. I had a turbulent love-hate relationship with a rooster named Clarence. Clarence had been raised by a hen, whereas his predecessor, Eugene, was hand-raised in a lightbulb-heated birdcage in my bedroom. Eugene had followed me, danced courtship dances around my feet, allowed himself to be picked up and cuddled, even relaxed when I held him with one hand on his back. When Clarence came of age, he had two-inch-long horny spurs growing from the backs of his legs. With a flapping frenzy he would hurl his body at my shins, spurs-up, with a force that felt like being hit with the claw end of a hammer. By the time he established his supremacy over the hens in his domain, he was positive I was a hired assassin. When I came through the door with a pail of grain and mash to pour into the feeding trough, I had to bring a broomstick. This allowed us a terse cease-fire. Keeping the blunt end gently touching Clarence's breastbone, we stayed four feet apart

13

as I emptied feed for the clamoring hens. After I cleaned the water bowls, I could sit back on my heels—my protective weapon lowered but still in hand, extending in front of my feet—and watch my flock bicker, cajole, and flirt. Often Clarence wouldn't eat as long as I was there. He strutted in slow motion, puffed up and vigilant, never taking his orange eye off me.

He waited, and he got his chance. One day when I was distracted, he placed a well-timed attack past my momentarily unprepared defense. Not only did he manage to pound me with his sharp spurs, he got in a few snaps of his beak as well. But any pain I felt was compounded by fury, the indignation of being bested by a foe with whom there's been a long standoff. I stood, held the broomstick like a baseball bat, and swung, cracking it into the side of Clarence's head.

Clarence went down, a flopping pile of harmless feathers. Time—which a moment ago had condensed his attack and my response into a pinprick instant—now thudded. Each second seemed like more than an hour. Dropping the stick, and all fear of him, I fell to my knees beside him in the rank henyard dust. He was flopping crazily in a circle until I held him still. When I rubbed his waddle between thumb and fingers and saw blood on my hand, my throat closed off, tears blinding me, until I realized it was *my* blood from where his beak had gashed a cuticle. I held him, patted him, apologized to him over and over, gently pressed his extraordinarily hot head against my cheek. It was the most I'd touched him since I'd bought him as a day-old chick and slipped him under his adoptive mother. When I stood him up, he stayed that way. When I picked up the broomstick and backed out of the coop, he was still standing, beginning to strut, in slower-than-usual underwater movements, muttering in his throat. I waited hours to hear his first crow. He lived out the rest of his life with no long-term effects of his convulsions, and I began entering the coop with not just a stick but the complete broom, using the bristle end to sustain our new, permanent stand-off.

TWICE I USED our rabbits for school assignments. For a high school chemistry project, I tanned the hides of a litter of rabbits. Usually we dried the hides on stretching racks and traded them for bags of rabbit feed. My tanned hides weren't going to be worth even a handful of rabbit feed, weren't exactly soft, didn't exactly smell great, but they *were* preserved! I did not earn an A on the project, yet the only criticism I received was when the teacher said she couldn't stand the idea that the skins came from rabbits I'd helped slaughter. Later, in a college photography class, I did a photo series of the wordless slaughter-choreography my father and I knew by heart.

After helping him hang a live rabbit by the hind feet, I turned away while he dispatched a blow with a hammer to the base of its skull. Slaughtering was done in silence except the grunt in Dad's chest as he hit the rabbit behind the ears. The impact had to be clean — breaking the animal's neck instantly — or the rabbit would scream, but my ears couldn't be plugged because as soon as the hammer hit and the bones cracked, the assistant had to be ready to take the hammer and hand him a knife. As soon as the rabbit was dead or unconscious, Dad decapitated the rabbit and let the blood drain from the twitching body into a bucket placed directly below. He then cut through the hide, down to the bone, in a ring around each ankle. The knife now held in his mouth by the handle, he began the removal of the hide. Since handing him the knife, I'd done nothing except to get one of the hide-stretching racks from where I'd hung them in the grape arbor before we started. Slaughtering took place in the shade of the arbor, surrounded on two sides by the rabbit hutches. One of the hutches held the eight-week-old litter now being processed, so it was convenient to not have to move them. But this meant that not only those destined for the meat freezer, but the adult breeding stock were witnesses.

Meanwhile, Dad would be peeling the hide down the two legs. When the hide had rolled as far as the tail, he needed the knife again, one quick cut across the crotch. The knife back in his mouth, both hands back to gripping the slippery inside-out skin, he could now peel the hide quickly, in one motion, the rest of the way from the body. It made a long sucking sound. Curiously, the hide would "pop" free of the front feet, leaving them still covered with fur, without further assistance from the knife. Dad held up the inverted tube of hide while I threaded the stretching rack through it, fixed the hide with clothespins to the rack, then let it spring open and tight. It would hang in the basement to cure until the next litter of rabbits was ready for slaughter.

Dressing the carcass required one more slit from the knife, diaphragm to neck hole, then I took the knife and set it on top of a hutch with the blade touching nothing but air. Next he needed the first cooking pot. This pot would catch the heart and liver as Dad separated them from the viscera. Lid clamped on, that pot was quickly exchanged for the other in time for him to drop the lungs and kidneys there. Those were for the dog. So now the carcass was empty, closely resembling a skinned cat. Once more with the knife, Dad cut the front paws off and let them fall into the bloody bucket, then cut the body free of the back feet and slid it into a different bucket of clean salted water. Once each session, without saying anything, he would hold out his palm for me to see the small heart still beating there. This was our proof of how quickly we were working, how quickly it would soon be over. How nothing was suffering.

I didn't enjoy killing rabbits. But the distasteful part of the process was, somehow, disconnected from enjoyment of rabbit for dinner. It was disconnected from the sublime phenomenon of the half-pound, pink, blind babies that would appear, without anyone's help, the morning after the doe had lined her nest box with fine white fur. It was disconnected from blithe sunny mornings playing with six or eight softball-sized bunnies on the lawn. The slaughtering was somehow so disconnected from all the other care of the rabbits, that I felt true sorrow and distress when roaming stray dogs came and bloodied the adult rabbits' feet through the bottoms of the cages. And another, more horrible time when the bees in the nearby hives became angered and attacked the first animals they found—the rabbits in their wire hutches. Filling their vulnerable ears with stings, the bees killed two adult rabbits. Rage at the bees and the dogs was useless—bees attack their enemies and dogs hunt in packs, and people all over the world raise their own food. Skeptics ask how could I do it? I don't have an answer that anyone without similar experience finds satisfactory.

HALFWAY DOWN HARTZEL Hill, not far below the house, is a road named Lakeview. It snakes, slightly downhill, from the east side of the hill to the west. Now lined with big custom-made houses, Lakeview was, the first ten years we lived there, an empty road with no shoulder and no sidewalk, rarely used except by teenagers for drag racing or making out. At the bottom of the hill is a housing development called Brookside—a tract built in the fifties on the site of an old golf course. Longtime residents never question these names, but visitors almost always ask "Where's the lake? *What* brook?"

17

Before the subdivision, before the golf course, at the bottom of the hill there had been a manmade pond, fed by one of Spring Valley's natural creeks. At the time, most of Spring Valley was ranches and groves. Not engineered by experts, the pond flooded every time there was more than the usual scant rainfall, often displacing residents in the area. So the pond's little dam was dynamited in the late 1920s and the pond was allowed to drain. The golf course was opened in the thirties, right before the depression. It did poorly, and gave way to the postwar housing boom in the early fifties.

But the creek that fed the pond remained through every evolution. Even after the housing development was built, the creek ran down the middle of Fairway Drive, the main street, in a concrete canal. When the creek came out the other end of Brookside, it went back to a natural creek bed, bordered by mud, grass, thick laurel bushes, rocks, and even some of the concrete chunks of the dam destroyed in the twenties. This portion of the creek, no more than 100 yards long, was located directly below our house, perhaps a mile down the hill, via a course of zigzagging paths. From the creek, we filled our parents' old aquariums with mosquito fish, crawdads, bugs that skated on the surface of the water, polliwogs, and dragonfly larva. But the ultimate catch was African clawed frogs—flat, slimy frogs that live underwater. Usually captured only with luck, we fancied ourselves originators of a technique, probing the underside of the creek bank slowly, trying to keep the water clear, waiting to see the sudden jet of cloudy mud that meant we'd flushed a clawed frog out of hiding. The crawdads and polliwogs were native. The county stocked the mosquito fish to help control mosquitoes. Clawed frogs were originally brought into the country for labs, used for pregnancy tests, then had escaped or were thrown out (when the tests proved flawed) and established themselves in the creek. Rumor is they can now can be found (many times bigger than the size they grow to in Africa) in Sweetwater Reservoir where the creek eventually terminates.

Of course we played with dolls, Lincoln Logs, and Monopoly games. Of course we went to the zoo, swam with friends in the above-ground pool, threw balls for our dog. In the summer, we went to the movies—to the Quonset hut turned movie house called Helix Theater in La Mesa—to see *Tammy and the Bachelor, A Hard Day's Night,* and *The Love Bug.* We also caught snakes and lizards, black widow spiders, horned toads, and tarantulas. We caught big green fig beetles and fed them to the chickens. We (accidentally) stepped on wasps' nests and ran screaming, sometimes collecting a dozen stings. We tapped the webs of funnel-web spiders with sticks until the spiders came rushing out to get the fly they assumed was struggling there. We excavated trap-door spider burrows. We even played with ant lions in the backyard.

Ant lions are insect larva that bury themselves in fine dirt then make a funnel about the size of a thimble right over their bodies. When an ant comes along and tumbles into a funnel, it can't climb back out because the ant lion has made the dirt fine enough, and the angles of the funnel's sides are exactly what is necessary to stymie an ant's attempts to scramble out. The ant lion then bursts out of the dirt to grab and eat the ant. We would find a batch of ant lions and either bring ants to drop into the funnels and watch the ensuing drama, or dig up the ant lions and make them build their funnels in boxes or pails. Eventually ant lions dwindled around Dad's property—probably due to Dad's vigorous spraying to control ants. But when my brother bought a house in Lakeside and found ant lions there, he dug some up and brought them to Dad, repopulating the yard.

There are other native animals that are increasingly difficult to find. Although not as prevalent as fence lizards, horned toads were once occasionally encountered. We never caught and kept one as a "pet," so their disappearance probably has to do with much bigger issues—loss of habitat and/or pollution—than kids who want to hold every crawly thing they see. Tarantulas and tarantula hawks, trap-door spiders, foxes, and road runners have joined horned toads on the list of creatures we used to watch living out their lives but are not easily found today. The road runners nested in the bougainvillea, foxes fed their kits earthworms from the compost piles. When houses increased along both sides of Lakeview, with their yards and fences pressed up against Dad's property line, these animals left to seek habitation elsewhere. Those that didn't—coyote, opossums, and skunks—faced the death penalty.

HUNTING SEASON STARTED in late summer, lasting the entire autumn and into early winter. Dove, quail, and cottontail rabbit were all legal to hunt in San Diego County, even in parts of the city.

When Mom started hunting with Dad in 1963, my oldest sister was old enough to baby-sit the four younger siblings. But our parents usually brought at least two of us along on a day's hunt. Partly it was to expose us to the techniques and philosophy. Shooting was something you did with concern for safety as well as preservation of the terrain, including mindfulness of game limits and recognition of which birds were strictly *off*-limits. It was an activity you did as calmly and quietly as possible (except for the report of the shotguns).

But the main reason for including us on hunting trips was that we were the bird dogs. Dogs specially trained not only to find the downed game, but find the spent shells (which could be refilled at home), and decapitate the bird then drain the blood before completing the retrieve. Soft, feathery body in one hand, thumb and forefinger of the other hand in a ring around the bird's neck: in one brisk movement, jerk hands apart—the head pops off.

You learn to stop cringing. Maybe it was the sweat, the dust in our throats, the bleeding scratches from thorny bushes, the constant keening of eyes and prick of ears for the rustle of rabbit or whistle of wings—we'd resumed our place in the natural violence of the food chain.

But a meal of wild game was a Sunday dinner with china and silver. Slow-cooked in a wine-based tomato sauce, the little bodies stayed whole but melted apart when touched. The engorged dark meat could be caressed from the fragile bones, drumsticks smaller than a toothpick, wings the size of bobbypins. We ate with our hands, licked our fingers, dirtied cloth napkins, sucked the tiny skeletons dry. Quail—the same size as dove but all white meat— was fried with oregano. Cottontail rabbit was stewed with tomatoes. Sometimes our teeth hit shattered bone and we would stop chewing, feel with lips and tongue, or use a finger to locate the tiny shot pellet embedded in the muscle.

A hunt started when we were pulled from sleep at three in the morning. The tranquil, liquid chill before sunrise was followed by a swell of dusty heat as soon as the September sun rose. We traipsed softly in our parents' footsteps, taught to stay behind them and squat down when we heard the whistle of dove wings or saw a cottontail dart out of the brush. The retrieve, the decapitation. Defeathering, dressing, cooking, dining. None of it was experienced without a twinge of . . . not guilt, exactly. Maybe some sort of contrite sigh. As we hunted (and thoroughly enjoyed the subsequent meal), as we bred rabbits for similar purposes, as we gave up pet roosters to the burlap bag and hatchet . . . none of these lacked trepidation during the volatile flash of death.

WHEN HE USED to hunt alone, Dad had scouted the county, looking for the right kind of terrain for dove, rabbit, quail, and maybe duck. He often found caches just as valuable. Somewhere in San Diego's North County, where the original El Camino Real was two parallel ruts through the weeds, he came across huge beaver tail cactus, bearing fruits called *nopales,* or cactus apples. This species of thornless cacti, imported to plant on cattle ranches, can still be found everywhere, including the "Native Landscaping Projects" around the lagoons in North County. The old specimens Dad located had been eaten bald up to head level by cattle that free-ranged in the area. He harvested as many cactus apples as he could bring home. Once the thick cactus skin is cut away, cactus apples are extremely juicy, about the size of a small fist. They are a little like watermelon but with pleasant differences: the flesh is not as mealy, the seeds are mere chewy bumps, the taste has a deeper, brighter flavor. Dad also cut several lobes from the cacti he'd found and planted them on his property. They are now as huge, woody, and knotted as the gnarled old ones he'd found.

Another time Dad found an abandoned grove of walnut trees (in what are now endless tracts of housing). So a family outing had us knee-deep in wild oats and grasses, picking up the walnuts Dad shook from the trees, bringing home bulging burlap bags. We then helped to shell the nutmeats, which were frozen in plastic bags for year-round use in brownies, cookies, Waldorf salads (made with persimmon instead of apple), and holiday candy.

In the South Bay, on the present site of a nature conservancy, there was a farm packing house where truck farmers brought harvested produce to be shipped to grocery stores. Behind the loading docks they dumped the rejects. We showed up with the back of the station wagon heaped with empty boxes, and from green-scented piles over eight feet high, we salvaged a stockpile of celery. We took only the hearts from the culls the farmers had cast out. There were also loose tomatoes scattered all over the ground—fully ripe, not squashed but unable to travel to a store without bruising. In a cauldron on a Coleman stove outside, Dad and Mom turned boxes of tomatoes into jars of tomato sauce.

In the same area, we discovered a trash dump. Perhaps an unofficial "landfill" used by the local residents, perhaps a site where migrant farmworkers had been encamped. We started picking up soda bottles. By the time we finished excavating the old trash, we had filled several boxes. Some of the bottles needed to be scrubbed inside and out with brushes at home, but at a nickel each, we had anywhere from $3 to $5 of spending money.

Some of Dad's other early hunting grounds are now a twenty-year-old housing development, two different community colleges, and an Olympic training center for volleyball, race-walking, and other minor sports. He hunted on the site of a mud puddle called Lake San Marcos before houses, condos, a golf course, and retirement village lined the banks with grass and small boat docks. A very early site was off Dairy Mart Road in the Tijuana River valley, part of San Diego adjacent to the U.S. border, where there are now large parcels of park, some houses, and flood-threatened equestrian ranches. In the mid-1960s there was nothing but waist-high grasses, sandy dry washes, native barrel cactus, fragrant sage and anise, coyote and foxes, rabbits, snakes, hawks, owls, meadowlark, roadrunners, horned toads, wasps, and tarantulas. Here Dad came across an abandoned farm. There was rusted equipment—an old well-pump, a wheelbarrow. A dead tree stood sentinel near a house foundation. And beside it, one lone *live* fig tree.

While we played below, Dad climbed the low, thick branches and filled a bucket with ripe figs. Figs can't be picked green to ripen later, and once ripe only stay perfect for a few days. That's why grocery stores so rarely carry fresh figs. Dad eventually established three fig trees on his property—three different types that ripened different months—and we had as many ripe figs as we could devour (and enough to share the squishy ones with green fig beetles and a flock of chickens). But in the mid-sixties, when any trees in our yard were mere sticks, this abandoned tree was like an island paradise for Dad and Mom. Paradise for us too—an easy tree to climb with thick, strong branches close to the ground. Plus bugs and lizards to catch, old tools to pretend to use, and a house foundation to pretend to excavate. Up close, under rocks, a world of ants, stinkbugs, earwigs, and crickets. Stand up and you're wading waist-deep in what could be a sixtieth-generation descendent of a failed grain crop, blended now with fennel, sage, and wild cucumber. Now an island in memory too: We were the only people in a pristine prairie of brown, waving grasses, interrupted only by the dusty dark green dome of the old fig tree, no sound but the mournful cry of dove, intricate piping of meadowlark, rustle of mice, wind chime of rattling leaves or creaking branches. Kids don't notice—and nobody remembers—stickers in our socks, bug bites, or wind-tangled hair. That's what happens when things disappear, leaving us only with phantom recollection.

But Dad's best hunting place—the one he used the longest before having to abandon hunting in San Diego County—was near the coast: a perfect (but not pristine) mixed ecosystem of tidal lagoon and arid coastal scrub. Surrounded by the (now) burgeoning suburbs of Encinitas, Solona Beach, and, inland, the upscale village of Rancho Santa Fe, an old man owned 10,000 acres and ran cattle on his land. Cattle need water, so the small creek making its way toward the ocean had been blocked in several places with dirt dams, creating square watering holes no more than thirty feet across. In an arid coastal region, water attracts birds—especially dove, who feed in stubble fields and on the grain left behind after cattle forage.

Our father asked the landowner for permission to hunt on his land. The man said yes, provided Dad stopped by the house to make known our arrival and departure. The man wanted to be aware that the sound of shots was nothing to worry about. Dad remembers being the only one who had permission to hunt on the old man's land, but we did occasionally find other shot shells there. (We picked them up too—usually Dad could reload more shells than he'd spent). Was the rancher concerned about poachers hunting his land? Maybe cattle rustlers?

This was lowland but not flat. Sandstone bluffs and gullies, slightly higher plateaus, and clusters of huge eucalyptus trees planted fifty to seventy-five years before we hunted there. Dry, arid bushes, sandy washes, bristly weeds where grasshoppers flew in front of each footstep. We found snakeskins and weathered, bleached seashells. The whole tract was crisscrossed by cattle trails, dotted with parched, weathered cattle droppings.

One day in 1969, Dad returned to the car after hunting and found a note on the windshield, "No Shooting West of Hwy 395," so that was the end of hunting in San Diego County. By then houses with ocean views were being built in the exclusive town of Rancho Santa Fe, on the hills surrounding the cattle ranch. Like the cry of suburbanites today, they didn't want to hear guns.

My parents and I drove by there in the late nineties, taking Manchester Road off I-5, then going east past a small vegetable and strawberry farm. Of course the tidal wetland, San Elijo Lagoon, is still excellent natural bird-watching terrain. Dad used to hunt beginning at the edge of the marsh, looking for ducks, then work his way inland. Just east of the lagoon we found the lowest section of our old hunting site is still indigenous and uninhabited. It's within the boundaries of the San Elijo Lagoon Ecological Reserve, therefore is protected. This parcel features a few big stands of eucalyptus trees and a conspicuous lone pine tree. Remnants of barbed-wire fences are visible in the chaparral, and the creek or string of pools is buried in thicker brush. Orange dirt paths suddenly become miniature grand canyon gullies carved in sandstone.

Change was apparent as soon as we looked slightly east where the land rises into small knolls. We used to trudge up the sandy paths on those bluffs, always behind our parents, trained to stay in the half circle behind the axis of their parallel shoulders. Now these low swells are dotted with houses, already ten to twenty years old. Their lawns, shrubs, and groundcovers are established, trees are pruned, the landscaping is modern.

The wooden farmhouse, which had been just off Manchester Road, is no longer there, nor is the dirt driveway that went past the house and across the land to the hills on the other side. Dad spotted a few likely sites where the house might've been—a flat place where several eucalyptus trees grow in a half circle, or beside that on the site of what is now a landscaping company. Along the south side of Manchester, *none* of the houses, horse ranches, landscaping companies, or Christmas tree farms were there when we hunted. The eastern end of the ranch is now a cluster of restaurants, an upscale grocery store, and small boutiques.

Extending due north from the wetlands and lowland hunting area, Father Serra's original El Camino Real has grown to be as big as a six-lane highway, with thousands and thousands of houses no farther apart than twenty-five feet. Thirty years ago, this stretch of El Camino Real had nothing on it, just two lanes through native terrain, as serenely rural as the days when we hunted. Wild mustard still grew thickly in undeveloped lots, descendants of seeds Father Serra dropped to mark his mission trail. Now, I admit, I've shopped at the big Home Depot on El Camino. Directly across the avenue, a flower farm was cleared for an even vaster conglomeration of warehouse-sized retail businesses. Petsmart and Target Greatland, a gigantic electronics store, one of those immense bookstores, and a vast grocery store with sushi, gourmet deli, and produce isles like a farmer's market. There are places to get a lube job and places to get checked by a doctor. There are places to climb a stairmaster and places to shop for a car via computer, there are banks and restaurants and bakeries and linen shops. Anything you could possibly need or want to buy or have done to your car or your house or body is available in that four-mile stretch of El Camino Real, "the king's highway."

One day in the late nineties a San Diego talk radio host chose for his show's topic the "ridiculous" things the government makes us do for endangered species. An employee from the El Camino Home Depot came on the air and reported that he was working in this state-of-the-art hardware warehouse, but when it was built they were required to maintain an adjacent chunk of native landscape, install sprinklers, and keep it wet, "and I've never yet seen one of the stupid little birds we're supposed to be doing this for."

And yet, for all our hunting, at least the dove are still plentiful, in backyards, in the remaining open spaces, in the preserved wetlands. Sadly, it seems that dove, like their disreputable relatives the pigeons, are one of the few species able to adapt to development and rapidly changing habitat. Mourning dove come to my feeders in snowstorms during Illinois winters.

A DAY AT the beach was exactly that—*a day*. We might depart from home at 8 A.M. and not leave the beach until 9 P.M., sometimes later. First, however, Dad checked a tide schedule. There were no spontaneous trips to the beach. We only went on days when the tide would be low in the morning and then start coming *in* in the afternoon and evening. This is because fish feed during a flowing tide, and a day at the beach was a day fishing for perch and corbina.

There were closer beaches—Silver Strand, Mission Bay, Ocean Beach—but we only went to the ocean at Torrey Pines, twelve miles north of San Diego. Morning was always overcast and chilly. We kept sweatshirts on over our swimsuits and sneakers on our bare feet, especially while we unloaded and carried our gear precariously over the huge pieces of concrete, with rusty rebar jutting out, salvaged from demolition of a bridge and piled just off the road to protect the state highway from high water. We had our choice of sand space and fire rings, spread out seven towels, and planted the old brown beach umbrella whose most useful function was to help us spot our campsite when we came out of the waves that dragged us south down the beach. Then we set about making things in the sand, like bathtubs, drip castles, moats, and volcanoes, while we waited to feel warm enough to take our air mattresses into the waves.

Meanwhile Dad began gathering bait. He never used store-bought bait (we had that for dinner). For surf fishing he used what the fish might naturally be eating—sandcrabs, the ones that were freshly molted so their shells were soft. The wet sand at water's edge was etched with the inverted V's of thousands of sand crab tentacles. Sandcrabs are shaped like a beetle. They burrow backward into wet sand at the waterline and leave their two antennae on the surface of the sand, gathering microscopic pieces of food as the waves lick their feathery tentacles.

Dad had made a sieve from carpenter's cloth, shaped like a mini-bulldozer with the "shovel" curved inward instead of outward. Standing up to his ankles in the surf, he pulled the crab net against the movement of the waves, digging it down into the sand, first when the wave came in, and then again as the water drew back. Under the water, he twisted his heels into the sand to keep his balance against the force of the wave, filling the net with swirling, muddy water. Then he stood with his back to the ocean, waves crashing against his calves, held the net up against his waist, and picked through the crabs, discarding all but those with soft shells. A crab might only have a soft shell for a day or two after molting. The crabs he discarded might've been soft the day before or would be soft tomorrow.

We also dug for crabs, with our hands. Torrey Pines wasn't a beach with a lot of shells to collect, no rock crabs or tide pools, but there were always thousands of sandcrabs. We searched for the huge ones, then kept them as "pets" in pails or in the moats around our castles, digging them up and watching them burrow down out of sight over and over. We found the females and carefully lifted the protective flap under their bellies to see the glop of bright orange eggs. All were granted freedom when we left.

After a picnic lunch (sandwiches, peaches, cookies, and the requisite sandy potato chips), when the tide turned in the afternoon, Dad would begin to fish. He always maintained a distance between himself and the nearest swimmers, but it wasn't difficult to maintain a gap because the beach was never crowded. Along the coast road going south from Torrey Pines to La Jolla, the well-known seacliff golf course was there, but none of the high tech labs and biomedical research companies that came later. And no housing, no condos. It was just scrub bushes, eucalyptus groves, and a very young University of California at San Diego. Few people lived where Torrey Pines would be their closest beach.

Surf fishing requires a long pole, a strong reel, two leaders (two hooks attached to the main fishing line), and a good sized weight. Dad waded into the surf up to his waist, twisted so his shoulders were facing the sand, likewise cocked the pole that direction, then he used legs, body, arms, and the leverage of the long pole to cast the weight and the two baited hooks as far out into the surf as possible. With the reel still open, he backed up into shallower water, closed the reel, kept the line taut, and waited. When he felt a hit, he jerked the tip of the pole back to set the hook, then began reeling in. Unlike fishing in lakes or rivers, when fishing in surf you can't feel the fish fighting while you reel in, so you don't know if

29

you've felt a fish bite or if your hook hit seaweed. Probably less than half the times Dad set the hook then reeled in, there *was* a fish (or two) on the hook. When we got tired of catching waves or covering ourselves with sand, we would stand beside Dad, waiting for him to jerk the rod and set the hook, anticipating what he might reel in. He let us hold the pole ourselves, helping us reel in when we hooked a choice hunk of kelp.

Through the afternoon, twilight, and evening, Dad continued fishing as long as the fishing was good—sometimes as long as the tide continued to come in. We repeatedly moved our towels and beach bags, our books and radios farther and farther east, toward that scrap-concrete breakwater just below the road. Mom would hold a beach towel around us while we squirmed out of damp, sandy swimsuits and put old sweatsuits (from Chadwick School) over our bare salty skin. As the sun went down and the coastal layer moved back in, we made a fire, roasted marshmallows, ate more cookies, and even cooked some of the fish wrapped in foil and placed on the embers. Sometimes Dad would fish until an especially high tide would start swamping up over the dry sand right to the edge of the fire rings. We would scramble to rescue our belongings and Mom would call, "*Honey, yoo hoo!*"

But most of the time we sat contentedly around the fire. There were other fires in each of the rings up and down the beach, but over the thunder of the surf, we couldn't hear so much as a giggle from other parties, no radios thumping, no shouts or dogs barking. The roar of water was rhythmic and constant. Gulls continued to call in twilight. The snap of the fire and the pop of dried kelp "floats" we threw into the embers were the only nearby sounds, under the surging of waves.

CLAMMING, ANOTHER BEACH activity, was not done in the summer. For health reasons, fresh shellfish can only be eaten in winter months. Besides that, the extreme low tides of winter are advantageous for clam digging. In the early sixties Dad dug clams on the very south end of Silver Strand, just north of a Navy Communications facility. He would climb a chain-link fence from the navy facility. One day Dad was caught by a military guard as he came back over the fence. Today he might've been arrested and searched for explosives or weapons, but the amicable guard just told Dad he couldn't allow him to climb over *from* the navy facility, but he could go east a few yards and climb the barbed-wire fence there.

Clamming is basically digging in muddy sand. There were no licenses required, but there were mandated limits in quantity (fifty per person) and size of the clams you could take (1.5 inch minimum). Each member of the family dug his or her limit, and Dad filled jugs with seawater, then at home the clams were leached: In a metal tub he put them in the clean seawater with cornmeal, changing the water several times. The clams feed by filtering water, so as they ate cornmeal in clean water, they extracted any sand they'd gathered from previous meals in muddy water. Most of the time, we ate clams raw on the half shell, sometimes in clam chowder. Our parents took turns having Manhattan-style chowder (Dad's favorite, in tomato-based soup) and New England style (the cream style, for Mom).

In the seventies we clammed on the Marine Corps' Camp Pendleton. No fence-jumping was required—all tidal lands, up to the high tide mark, are still public. For several years, however, the clam beds there have been dead, or hopefully just dormant. People like us are blamed for the death of the clam beds, and it's true that if no one had dug clams, they'd still be there. But a variety of things marred these clam fields. One was an influx of other gleaning cultures, for example, when Vietnamese refugees were housed at Pendleton, and like us they brought children to raise their limits. But this alone would not have ruined the area as quickly, and maybe wouldn't've spoiled it at all. People have been clamming in Asia for generations without killing their clam beds. But some time in the seventies, the *L.A. Times* ran an article blabbing about the rich clam fields between Orange County and San Diego County on Camp Pendleton, *come and get them*. People did come, in what seemed like hoards. The most harmful aspect of the deluge was not that they came, but that they didn't know how to take care of the clam beds. Whether or not they respected the limits is speculation, but after digging, they left their holes open, exposing the next generations of baby clams to be consumed by sea gulls.

OUR FATHER DIDN'T fish with purchased bait. But that doesn't mean he didn't *purchase* bait. From the People's Fish Co., near the Coronado Ferry landing (before the bridge was built) Dad bought bait. Squid was twenty-five cents a pound. But he didn't use it to fish. He helped Mom clean out the cuttlebones and cut the bodies into macaroni-size pieces, but left the bite-size tentacles as they were. Then the squid was prepared with Nana's unwritten recipe, in a slightly spicy tomato sauce, served with spaghetti. Recently, in a Chicago restaurant, Dad ordered an appetizer that was the exact same recipe, probably around $8.95. But squid are no longer called squid—they're calamari (even, curiously, in some Asian restaurants), they're no longer sold as bait, and they're no longer twenty-five cents a pound.

Once, driving up I-5 on one of our frequent trips to Anaheim to visit Nana and Grandpa, Dad stopped on the side of the freeway on Camp Pendleton to pick up a pheasant that had recently been hit by a car. An experienced hunter, he could tell how long the bird had been dead. He put it into a bag and brought it to Nana and Grandpa's house where it was defeathered and dressed then roasted to go along with the huge Italian meal Grandpa and Nana always prepared for us.

Through the sixties, Dad and Mom were raising five preteen children on Dad's paltry community college professor salary. As soon as her youngest was in school, Mom went to San Diego State to get her elementary teaching credential. She didn't begin working until the seventies—by that time her oldest children were in college, still living at home. So while he was the sole financial support of the family, Dad taught an overload for an extra paycheck, taught summer school for another extra check, and for three weeks a year he worked the late shift as a gateman at the Del Mar Fair.

For a while they called it the Southern California Exposition—a pompous attempt to boost the county's image—but it is one of the biggest fairs in the country, bigger than many state fairs. And one of the biggest livestock exhibitors was the Golden Arrow Dairy. They delivered milk to your doorstep in glass bottles. Johnny Downs, a former "Little Rascal" who hosted a local cartoon program (featuring Popeye), was a TV spokesman for Golden Arrow. In a stunning special effect of the times, he tap-danced on top of a huge Golden Arrow bottle. At the fair, Golden Arrow exhibited its famous Golden Guernsey dairy cows. The nature of a dairy cow includes the need to be milked at least once a day. Although Golden Arrow didn't sell the milk they took from cows at the fair, they did ladle out free samples of whole milk, straight from the cow, to anyone coming to the exhibit. At the end of his shift (midnight), Dad would leave his post and go to the Golden Arrow stalls where they had saved jugs of whole, unhomogenized, unpasteurized milk for him to take home. This would probably be illegal now. No longer do any exhibitors of dairy cattle give samples of milk to anyone—it's thrown away.

DAD MAY HAVE been a teacher, but that didn't mean he had the whole summer "off." Summer school, the county fair, and the flourishing yard—always in need of weeding, spraying, harvesting, a new sprinkling system, usually a rock wall in progress—filled the months of June and July. When August came, he gave himself two weeks' furlough.

Up in the eastern Sierra, above a desert town called Big Pine, there was a series of rustic campsites—no toilets, just outhouses. A glacier creek thunders out of the mountains, flowing into and back out of seven man-made lakes. Formed in the early twentieth century to provide water for a developing town called Los Angeles, the lakes and the natural Big Pine Creek are part of L.A.'s controversial Owens River Valley Project.

Although Mom brought boxes of canned and dried provisions, most of our dinners and half our breakfasts at camp were fried trout. A Coleman stove and a cast-iron skillet were necessary equipment, as were metal washtubs for bathing toddlers who daily masked faces with dirt and woodsmoke; a baby table or playpen (the old kind, made of wood); big blackened buckets for heating water over the fire and jugs to hold fresh spring water; several sizes of saws and two axes for firewood; seven fishing poles and enough tackle for five kids to lose plenty of hooks; enough socks, underwear, sweatshirts, jeans, flannel shirts, tennis shoes and boots so we could fall into the river every day; a canvas tent with wooden poles from army surplus; a sheet of stainless steel for making pancakes; seven sleeping bags; Coleman lanterns and five cheap aluminum flashlights; a first-aid kit, a dog, and two or three worn-out decks of playing cards.

Packing boxes, dufflebags, ice chests, and tackleboxes, then loading the handmade trailer were day-before preparations that took long into the night. Departure was before dawn. But after eight hours of driving, upon arrival at camp, no one was free to immediately dip a baited hook into the river. Tents had to be pitched and rain trenches dug around each, gear stowed, empty campsites scouted for firewood. Mom unloaded equipment, and Dad packed his saw and ax into the woods to cut logs he lugged or dragged back to our site. It wasn't advisable to drink the river water, not due to pollution but micro-organisms, so he hiked with empty jugs up the side of the mountain where a spring of drinkable water bubbled to the surface. He returned with three gallons on his back, one in each arm. While he chopped wood without a shirt, a muted shout was pushed from his chest, followed by the ring of the ax, but few words. His beard grew.

Our mother was, especially in early years, kept busy with us, as babies, toddlers, and children. She also fished, gutted fish, cooked fish, washed dishes, bathed us, changed our wet clothes, taught us to make campfires, sang us to sleep, and documented everything with her camera.

On a big rock between two trees, we wore out the knees of our jeans and got sap in our hair. It smelled thick and piney, turned black and tacky, and later Dad would have to use gasoline to scrub it off. He walked back and forth, past the rock, gathering dry greasewood for kindling, a red bandanna around his forehead. We played with kids from other campsites, glanced up at him as he passed, but never shouted, "Hey Dad!" nor waved, and one little girl said, "I'm afraid of that Indian."

Our father spent more than one camping trip working with the creek itself. He moved rocks, some nearly boulders, into the cold, quick river, slowing the water just enough to make trout pools and places for fishermen to stand or cross to an opposite bank. He fished early mornings then again at dusk, working both sides of the river.

The stock truck arrived every other week to dump huge hatchery-raised trout into the river. Dad was enhancing the river strictly from a fisherman's point of view, to make better fishing, but from another perspective he was creating hiding places and a more variable environment for the stunned trout suddenly plunged into what was, during the summer, an overpopulated, beleaguered habitat. The habitat began to be stressed even further when more and more people discovered this (at the time) inexpensive, pristine, and lovely place to camp. We'd been taught not to clean fish and dump the guts into the river, not to throw our empty bait jars or soda cans into the water (we were never even *given* soda cans), and not to break the branches of brush hanging over the water—that's where fish hide. We picked up other people's junk when we found it on the riverbank or could reach it in the water. And we completely stocked our own tackle boxes with the hooks, weights, leaders, lures, bobbers, flies, and tools left behind by more reckless fishermen.

Between the ages of five and seven, each in our turn, Dad took us out alone to learn the finer arts of river fishing. Invariably, in the first lesson he hooked a trout and thrust the pole into our hands to land the fish. He exhaled sharply, a nearly inaudible grunt, when we flung the fish out of the water backward over our heads, tangling fish, line, and pole in heavy brush.

But we all did learn to flick our bait into a riffle—not the dark pools but in moving water where the fish feed—one finger hooked on the taut line to feel the traces of activity invisible underwater. We were junkies for the anticipation, legs weak like soft wax, extremities humming, awaiting the jolt of adrenaline in our guts at the moment of the bang-bang-bang of the strike.

At night when we sang with Mom around the fire, when we played card games by firelight, when we roasted marshmallows that burned the roofs of our mouths with liquid charcoaled sugar, when we scalded our lips and tongues on hot chocolate in tin cups, Dad sat quietly across the fire from us. Not singing, not slapping down a winning card. His shoulders seemed to be somewhat hunched, sitting on one of the logs he'd cut so there would be seven seats around the fire, cupping a plastic mug of thin hot chocolate and staring into the flames, resting for the first time since he'd risen at four to go fishing. He slept outside the tent, his sleeping bag perpendicular across the tent's doorway, to (we thought) save us from bears.

Occasionally Dad came back to the campsite late, long after sunset, having been fishing miles from camp when it had finally became too dark to even see the river, let alone be able to flick his bait accurately into the riffle. He came in with fish to be cleaned while we were completing our campfire songs, while Mom washed gooey marshmallow and gritty cinders from our mouths. While we stumbled by flashlight to the outhouse and back, he'd be gutting fish in the glaring white light of the buzzing Coleman lantern, shadows of moths darting in and out of his illuminated circle. In the morning we would eat those fish for breakfast.

But a few times each camping trip, Dad made pancakes on the sheet of shiny metal over a fire pit built with rocks, like the walls at home, so everything was exactly level. He poured big, perfectly round pancakes, nothing fancy, none shaped like Mickey Mouse. Standing in the firelight in a blue Chadwick sweat suit, the bowl of batter in one hand, spatula in the other, the blood of a fish still on his arm from the morning's catch, he made pancakes without smiling.

Another rite of passage was when we were considered old enough to hike with him to fish in the lakes. This meant hiking 2,000 or 3,000 feet further up in altitude, three to five miles on the sandy John Muir Trail, carrying long fishing poles and rucksacks packed with our lunches, with tin cups hanging from our belts so we could sample every spring we crossed. For my sisters and I, the earliest of these hikes was without Mom, who had to stay in camp with the little boys. From behind, Dad urged us to keep our pace up. When in front he quickly was out of sight up the trail. There was no resting and no complaining, no singing and no stopping to yodel back down the mountainside (hiking activities we did with Mom). When the mule pack train passed, using the same trail, we stepped aside, sometimes pressing our shoulders against rock outcroppings that lined the path, grateful for the forced respite, admiring the pack master for his snorting buckskin and creaking saddle and even for the heady equine smell of his animals. Dad always said good morning to the pack master, and also to each set of hikers we passed, either those coming down the mountain or those we overtook. He carried on brief but amicable exchanges with strangers. We spoke and giggled only with each other. Between Dad and us very little conversation passed, and it didn't seem unusual or terrible.

Once we had traversed the alpine meadows and arrived at the lakes, once we baited our hooks and began fishing at a lake's inlet, he might make the familiar chest grunt, or even an audible "oh!" if we lost a fish we'd hooked, or if we had to go to him to extract a hook we'd oafishly allowed a fish to swallow instead of setting the hook in the lip. He would nod his approval for those we landed, or concisely notify us that the trout we'd just caught was a brookie or a cut throat—no hatchery-raised rainbow trout lived in the lakes. Or he would inform us of his whereabouts: "I'll be over there," a point with the tip of his rod, and our one-word answer, "okay," was sufficient. Twelve hours after setting off before dawn, without shouts of *hello* or *we're back!* our boots would come crunching softly back into camp.

Eventually my older sisters learned to play bridge and made an evening foursome with Dad and Mom at a card table under a Coleman lantern hung in a tree. Eventually my brothers could hike farther and faster and catch as many fish. By this time Dad often fished with barbless hooks, throwing back any fish that wasn't injured, because we took care of supplying more than enough trout for every meal at camp. The boys could tie their own flies or catch natural insect bait from the surrounding flora, and we were the ones staying out until long after dark, returning with trout to clean, finding the card game in full swing, water simmering over the fire, packets of powdered hot chocolate waiting for us.

In times to come, Dad would be going to our houses to pick oranges and tangerines, collect eggs, and gather walnuts. He would someday hunt duck around flat lakes on the Texas plains near a son's house and fish the Atlantic coast at a son's beach cottage. He would inspect the banana trees and asparagus patches in his daughter's backyard, and send visiting adult children home to Idaho and Illinois with bags of bulbs, jars of preserves, avocados, persimmons, and fresh vegetables. He would help grandchildren gather pecans in an abandoned grove in North Carolina, take children and grand-children in his boat to fish for albacore and bonita off the coast of San Diego, and return every year with one or two of us, plus in-laws and grandchildren, to Big Pine.

Our parents now stay in a cabin. They haven't been up to the lakes in several years. The trout limit is five instead of ten, which makes fishing with barbless hooks even more necessary unless Dad wants to reach his limit before 9 A.M. That leaves plenty of time for playing cards, reading, and—finally—relaxing in the shade of the pines beside the effervescent glacier creek that still plunges, bois-terous and cold, down the eastern Sierra slopes.

As A KID, it was an interminable two-hour drive up I-5 to Nana and Grandpa's house. Jammed in a station wagon with four siblings, a panting, drooling dog, and two parents unamused by our bickering and whining.

"Mom, he's breathing on me."

"When will we be there?"

"Shep's dripping on me."

But a general lull eventually fell over us, and in my choice seat beside a window (to prevent my habitual carsickness) I hummed *America the Beautiful,* and in my mind filmed a documentary from the passing scenery to illustrate the lines. My sensibility was corn-ball at best, but I had most of the lyrics covered. The *sea to shining sea* part was simple, as it is all too easy for every non–Californian to think of only the beach when imagining California. But I had the *purple mountains* when we hit San Juan Capistrano and the Santa Ana Mountains were visible in the east. And I could always close my eyes and picture ice-capped Mount Whitney and its associates in the Sierra rising out of the high desert. Prairie-flat Orange County's strawberry and orange groves were still the *fruited plain* above which those mountains were *majesty*. The *spacious skies* varied from rich turquoise in the mountains to pale sky-blue to bleached-shell haze to the coastal June-gloom. My documentary wouldn't have true *amber waves of grain* until I moved to the Midwest, but I substituted the rippling wild oats in ditches off the side of the road. California covered the entire libretto.

But the song didn't even bother to mention other things needed for my documentary: The vast otherworldly dunes of sand (used for filming otherworldly movies) in California's low deserts, nor the hard-packed high desert dotted with the eccentric Joshua trees and three-armed cacti. The rippling green aspen forests on the John Muir Trail where spring arrives in June. And it needed lyrics for the in-between: the coastal scrub of sage and sand shrubs that hold water in succulent leaves—painted in the yellow haze of Father Serra's wild mustard. The semi-arid inland hills with no tree higher than twelve feet, and the fire-scarred canyons where fresh green envelopes the black within days of a rainfall.

Yet all of the real lyrics, and all the ones I had yet to add, could be found not only driving California's highways; it was all in a microcosm on three-quarters of an acre in Spring Valley. Instead of a new syrupy patriotic song, I wrote fiction, enriched by what my formal education could not give me: a relationship with the "real" California. A relationship I perhaps didn't value enough until I had to leave it. And now struck with melancholy over the loss and corruption of so much of it. But my childhood angst over not having a new bicycle or fashionable clothing has long dissipated, and what I obtained instead has lasted longer than a Stingray bike or desert boots. An affinity, a sense of coming from and belonging to this landscape — outwardly tough yet in its own way so fragile.

WATERBABY

It's an eight-hour drive from the western suburbs of Chicago to eastern Ohio. It would have been difficult to fly—the airport in Cleveland is a two-hour drive from the college where I was scheduled to read from my new novel. But I'll use any excuse not to fly. Any time I *have* to fly, it's a toss-up as to what kind of experience it'll be: from doped up on prescription antinausea medication; to bouncing through turbulence, clinging to the arm of a stranger seated beside me; to spending the entire trip puking into my precious little bag.

So, happy to drive, I set out on a sunny day in Elmhurst, Illinois. But cold. Early April and hovering below forty degrees. The radio reported there was lake-effect snow in northwestern Indiana, only an hour from home, a region I would be passing through on I-80 as I went around the bottom of Lake Michigan. An unenlightened driver from California. It's *April*, after all, the snow can't be sticking.

Lake-effect snow: Cold air, usually moving southeasterly, passes over a warmer lake and picks up the evaporating water. Then as it hits land, the air rises and reaches the condensation point, dumping large quantities of snow on the eastern and southern sides of the lake. No storm blowing in across the western plain, no system moving down from Canada. It's a homegrown, local-only piece of work.

So while it's glaringly sunny on the west coast of the lake, there's a blizzard on the southern and eastern coasts of the same lake.

Blithely, I drove on, certain that at any moment I would drive out the other end of this bizarre pocket of winter. The flow of traffic was going about 55 mph, not because we adhered strictly to the law, but for safety. Vision was slightly impaired. The snow was blowing around on the asphalt like sand, but it was not sticking to windshields—the wipers weren't necessary, nor was the washer fluid. No salt had been applied to the road surface, therefore there was no slush being slung from other tires. But grass and bushes on the sides of the freeway were rapidly becoming outlined in white fuzz.

A twenty-year-old pickup with an empty truck bed gradually passed me on the right. Then I moved over to the center lane behind him. He was five or six car lengths ahead of me when, in a scene like failing eyesight, like I was going dizzy, cars began to shimmer back and forth in their lanes. Then suddenly the pickup truck was sideways, perpendicular and stopped dead across my lane. *Both* feet jumped onto the brake. *Both* arms jerked the steering wheel to the left. My entirely reliable sport-utility vehicle ignored both demands. I thought the brakes and steering had chosen a fine time to malfunction. But it's called black ice, you can't see it on the asphalt. I was on the same patch that had caused some vehicles to shimmer but had completely twirled the old pickup truck. I'd've been lucky to lose control and likewise spin—the left lane was, at that point, empty. But my sharply turned front tires and locked brakes made my vehicle into a bobsled on an icy run, and I continued forward in my lane at approximately the same speed until I was eventually halted by smashing into the pickup truck's front fender.

The collision finally convinced my vehicle to turn, a forty-five-degree bounce, and I careened across the fast lane until I blasted head-on into the cement barriers separating the eastbound freeway from the westbound. The shoulder was barely wide enough for a car to pull over, but I was perpendicular, so my rear jutted into traffic, and the cars in the fast lane—likewise out of control on the ice—couldn't stop. I watched them approach and received a third impact.

Before I-80 was closed due to a semi jack-knifing a quarter mile behind me, I had several minutes to remain in the car. At some point, I realized I was yelling.

I had been yelling since before my first impact with the pickup truck. *NO*. I was screaming *No No No No No* while momentum from the first collision sent me across the fast lane and headfirst into the cement barrier; and continued *No No No No No* as I watched the oncoming vehicles in the fast lane, which included several large tractor-trailers, speeding toward the side of my now immobile, vulnerable truck, sitting sideways with my back half still in the fast lane. Another booming impact—I was still yelling—and the dog crate behind my seat bounced around like a square basketball.

After that, traffic was able to slow. Cars crept past my still defenseless tail end, merging and crowding over into the fast lane to get past the smashed pickup truck still in the middle of the freeway. Could they see me, still sitting there yelling? Could they hear what I was yelling? At that point, *I* heard myself, and I realized I had added a word to what I was repeating in an anguished voice I never hope to hear coming from my mouth again: I was calling for my mother. I was crying *Mommy!*

But this is mere instinct, and probably universal. Isn't the combined need, yearning for, influence from, and expectations of our mothers one of the most overpowering drives we continue to live with most of our lives? Whether we admit it or not. Don't many adopted children begin, as adults, to search for their "real" mother? And adults with less-than-perfect mothers mourn that unlucky draw, dwell on it, obsess over it, some even blame *her* shortcomings for their own. My college writing students have illustrated this condition year after year, writing "mother stories" where a bossy, igno-

rant, shrewish, religious-fanatic, hypocritical, selfish, abusive, aban-
doning, addicted, immature mother figure is supposed to reveal
herself as the root of all the character's neurotic self-absorption and
self-destructive choices. I've seen so many variations on the disap-
pointing/damaging-mother story, I have begun to wonder how this
most influential figure in everyone's life has impacted *mine* in a way
that's more invisible, subtle, and valuable.

In exploring this question, flooded with specific yet diverse memories, I find myself searching most of all for two connections: First,
what brought my mother from Boston and my father from Brooklyn
to meet at a small private boarding school 3,000 miles away in Palos
Verdes, California? And second: How this woman born in 1925 in
conservative New England—who was a teenager during World War
II, then was nearing middle age with five children of her own at the
height of the feminist movement—was still able to (inadvertently?)
raise her daughters (and sons) in an atmosphere where guidelines,
qualifications, limitations, and prerequisites were determined only by
one's own talents and abilities, not by any societal standards and
boundaries based on gender or class or tradition (and these kinds of
confines *did* still exist in the sixties and seventies).

My mother was not your traditional image of parental or maternal courage—cancer survivor, war survivor, abuse survivor, poverty
survivor, etc. Not a pioneer who overcame tremendous odds and
discrimination. So there has to be a better word than *courage*—a
word suggesting that life doesn't necessarily *need* courage, but does
request a healthy appetite, curiosity, and an unhampered attitude.
Seen in the mundane, as well as slightly unusual details, her adult
life in California brought: Washing away skunk smell and removing
bee stingers from her husband's constantly susceptible body; killing
snakes that had invaded a rabbit's nesting box; leading Girl Scout
troops from cookie sale drives to roller-skating lessons to extended
primitive camp-outs; learning official baseball scorekeeping for

Little League; every other year renewing her Water Safety Instructor certificate then teaching neighborhood children and scouts to swim; hiking twenty miles to view this continent's southern-most glacier. And through it all she took pictures, recording everything. She was also finishing a second college major and earning her California Teaching Credential as soon as her youngest child was in kindergarten; overseeing music lessons involving five different instruments; practicing archery in the backyard; maintaining tropical aquariums; and numerous other activities that being the parent of five native Californian children and the wife of a hunter-gatherer can invent.

Archaeology and prehistory tell us that man hunted and woman gathered. But my father hunted with my mother beside him—she took twice as many shots and hit only a fraction of her targets, although she recalls with delight my youngest brother's beaming six-year-old face the time she felled two doves with one shot. My father fished and my mother fished the next hole downstream. She matched his speed cleaning a trout and defeathering a dove. My father raised rabbits and quail and vegetables and fruits, and my mother weeded, dressed meat, canned, and preserved anything from jam to wine to syrup to tomato sauce to yellowtail tuna. She'd never learned the bland, boiled New England cooking of her youth, but in addition to mastering Italian cuisine, she learned to prepare game—trout on a grill, stuffed or fried, duck l'orange, stewed rabbit, roasted goose, fried quail, and tiny Asian quail eggs. My father sculpted natural rock walls and my mother learned to mix concrete, then satisfied her artistic impulse drawing pictures in wet cement to make a pool deck of commemorative stepping stones, depicting important events in our lives.

That pool is indicative of one of the only things my parents really didn't share: swimming. Sailing and swimming had been a mainstay of my mother's childhood, and swimming remained a consistent motif stretching through all phases and eras of her life. But in water, my father sinks. So at the California coast, my father collected bait then fished in the riptide and waves while my mother—merging her Maine lighthouse-keeper pedigree with her new life as a Californian—body-surfed to shore, over and over.

JARUEL MARR, MY great-great grandfather, a Civil War veteran and survivor of a POW camp, began his career as lighthouse keeper in 1866 at Hendricks Head, on Southport Island. The island is roughly the shape of an arrowhead pointing down, part of the fissured coastline near Boothbay Harbor where the Atlantic seaboard of the United States actually faces south.

Coastal islands should be surrounded by ocean, but on the west side of this island, where the lobster-fishing town of West Southport is located on a tiny bay called Cozy Harbor, the locals say the water there is a *river*. It's a subtle distinction: brackish water, generally moving south into the ocean, but dramatically rising and flowing with the tides. The tidal Sheepscot River also influences smaller channels, called "guts," along Southport's western coast. Some guts are reduced to mud on extreme low tide, exposing all manner of shells, driftwood, even antique cork-stopper medicine bottles and fishing equipment. On schedule, the tide brings the sea back into the gut, with legendary—even mythical—silent swiftness, professedly trapping treasure-hunters on the mud flats, sweeping them out to sea before they can disturb the unmarked boggy mausoleum they dared to visit.

So Cozy Harbor is, technically, on Sheepscot River, or Sheepscot Bay. But sail a skiff outside the harbor, hang a left, and even before you get to the end of Southport, to the curiously named rocks called The Cuckolds, the so-called river becomes open ocean: vigorous incoming rollers crash and roar against a jagged, rocky coastline. Sheepscot River is one of many inlets from the Atlantic to seaports in and around Boothbay Harbor. So, on Dogfish Head, the westernmost point of Southport Island, Hendricks Head Lighthouse was established in 1829 to warn incoming vessels away from the rocks it's built upon. My great-great grandfather as well as his son were keepers of the light for over fifty years. In 1933, three years after the death of my great-grandfather, the lighthouse was decommissioned and became a private residence. The Coast Guard recommissioned (and mechanized) Hendricks light in the fifties.

Local legend says that in the mid-1870s, a keeper at Hendricks Head saw a vessel going to pieces off the rocky coast nearby. An article in the 1955 *Navy Times* recounted the 1875 shipwreck:

> . . . a blinding blizzard was sweeping into Sheepscot Bay. Early in the afternoon, Keeper Marr lighted the tower lantern to guide mariners who might be seeking refuge from the storm. Marr and his wife, wrapped in heavy woolens, stamped their feet and slapped their arms to keep warm in the captain's walk of the lighthouse. As they shivered with cold, they suddenly saw through the dense snowstorm the faint outline of a ship coming up Sheepscot Bay. Before [the ships' captain] could prevent a disaster, his ship crashed on rocks about half a mile from the lighthouse.

Passengers were seen clinging to rigging, so—according to another version of the story—the keeper lit a bonfire to let the passengers know their plight had been noted, and to "guide them" (although the legend doesn't explain how people clinging to the rigging of a sinking ship were supposed to be "guided"). One version of the legend has Keeper Marr seeing a bundle put overboard as the ship went down; another says that after the vessel went under, two mattresses washed near shore, and Marr, despondent that he couldn't save the shipload of people, risked his life going into the storm-level surf, caught hold of the bundle, and was tossed to shore by a giant wave.

The bundle was, in various versions of the story, referred to as two mattresses or two featherbeds. They were sandwiched together, and when the keeper untied them, he discovered a baby girl in a box had been wrapped inside, and she had survived. The legend explains that the keeper's wife had recently lost an infant, so they kept the shipwrecked baby as their own.

My mother's Aunt Libby, who still lives in Maine, found the shipwreck story retold again in her regional newspaper, *The Boothbay Register*. The article's author, a member of the Boothbay Region Historical Society, had decided to investigate the legend with the purpose of debunking it. After her research, this historian reported that Jaruel Marr and his wife Catherine had five "living children" between 1852 and 1871, two of them females. But a family tree, researched and compiled by one of my mother's cousins, claims Jaruel and Catherine Marr had *six* children between 1852 and 1871, *three* of them female. The family tree identifies this third girl child as Mary Catherine, and that she died at age thirty-three in 1899. She apparently is not listed in whatever birth records the local historian researched for her article. But both lists of children only report "living children," and neither record explains why the legend says the keeper's wife had just lost a child.

The local historian had no knowledge of the family tree completed by my mother's cousin, so she had no enigmatic name, Mary Catherine, to vivify the legend of the shipwrecked baby. She assumed she had proven the story to be foundless myth, but *not* due to her failure to discover the female child who lacked a birth record, *nor* due to the absence of a reported dead Marr infant prior to the 1875 shipwreck. Yet if she'd gone to the graveyard on Southport, she would've found a marker for a *seventh* child, a four-year-old boy, son of Jaruel and Catherine, who died in 1871. In fact he died on March 30, 1871, at four years, ten months and twenty-one days old. This would make his birthday May 9, 1866. The exact same birthdate as the one beside Mary Catherine's name in our family tree. Twins. And for whatever mysterious reason, neither of the twins' births, nor the little boy's death, were available in records for the Boothbay historian. If the family lost a child four years before the shipwreck, is that close enough to keep the legend alive?

The historian's chief reason for discounting the legend was, she said, that none of the descendants of Jaruel Marr had ever heard of this rescued baby. She says, "It is simply unbelievable that such an event could have happened without their knowledge and comment." She made this conclusion after interviewing longtime residents of Southport who had known or grown up with the Marrs.

Too bad the researcher didn't actually ask the descendants themselves. When Aunt Libby sent the article to my mother, she wrote in the margin: "I've known about an infant girl from a shipwreck, as your grandmother told of the incident. Also Capt. Bob Marr remembers hearing about it from your grandfather." The way Libby (and others) have expressed this, "hearing of an infant girl," suggests to me that after rescuing the child, Jaruel Marr might have found another family to adopt the girl. The researcher did not consider this option.

As exciting as it might have been to discover I descend from a shipwrecked orphan who sailed to safety wedged between two mattresses—and it might've explained my mother's obsession with water sports—this legend is only something to be intrigued by, since *my* direct ancestor in this lighthouse-keeping family was one of Jaruel Marr's sons, Wolcott Marr.

Wolcott, first child born to Jaruel after the Civil War, was named for the Union army doctor who nursed Jaruel while both were prisoners in a confederate POW camp. As a young man, Wolcott was assistant keeper at Cape Elizabeth's Two Lights until his father retired. Then he moved back to the house in Southport at Hendricks Head where he was born and became the lighthouse keeper there until 1930. A few years before Wolcott moved back to Hendricks Head, my maternal grandmother, Mabel Gilberta Marr, was born at Two Lights, the oldest of ten children.

Always known by her middle name (even then girls didn't like *Mabel*), Gilberta was second-mother to many of her younger siblings, and in the late 1800s and early 1900s, tradition might've asked her to leave school early to help her (probably stressed, always-pregnant) mother, just as my paternal grandmother had to quit school after sixth grade to help the family by making lace and working in a shoe factory. But Gilberta finished high school, taught school in Southport for a year, then went on to attend and graduate from Gorham State Normal School (now University of Southern Maine) where her education also included playing basketball in a long, dark dress and high-topped leather shoes.

The equivalent of "college educated" for a girl in 1910, Gilberta taught in a one-room schoolhouse in the Rangely Lakes region. The schoolteacher, in those days, was not expected to live alone (living alone might've been so frowned upon, she wouldn't've been hired). Instead, she boarded with a railroad man and his wife. To get to the schoolhouse, the railroad man had to take Gilberta on a railroad handcart. The man pumped one side of the teeter-totter–style lever that powered the car, and Gilberta, in her long dress, manned the other side—fall, spring, *and* through the long Maine winter.

Married women were not allowed to teach school, so after working from 1911 to 1914, Gilberta quit when she married Walter Young, my maternal grandfather. Walter's father was a lobster importer from Boston who owned a "lobster pound" in Southport. (A pound is an artificial pond used to keep harvested lobsters alive until they can be shipped.) The Young family lived in Boston but had a summer house in Southport, thus the two children met, perhaps as teenagers. They didn't marry until after Walter received his DMD from Harvard Dental School in 1914.

Gilberta and Walter had four children; the youngest, my mother, born in 1925. Her paternal lobster-importer grandfather had left his estate in trust for his grandchildren to go to college. No gender specified. So even during the depression, my mother's older siblings began attending Harvard and Boston University. When she was in junior high, my mother's eldest brother left Harvard to finish at BU Theological School in order to become a Swedenborgian minister. This may have pleased her father on some level, but as his second son had quit college to join the army, Walter was getting anxious about his successful dental practice: who would he leave it to after building it from nothing and surviving the depression?

When she married, Gilberta had converted from her Lutheran upbringing and took on Walter's family's faction of Christianity, a rare denomination called Swedenborgian or Church of the New Jerusalem. Founded in England in 1887, the church is based on the writings of Emanuel Swedenborg, a Swedish scientist in the Age of Enlightenment. More widespread in Europe, there are only thirty-three Swedenborgian churches in the United States, just nine west of the Mississippi. Hardly sizable enough to sway history. Yet my uncle's decision to become a Swedenborgian minister will prove not only to be the significant factor in how my parents met, but points to the vital influence that (without her realizing) helped mold my mother's outlook on the world she was about to enter.

My uncle's career choice prompted my grandfather to have a conversation with my mother that she still recalls with near perfect clarity. I guessed it was because of how unusual, in 1937, the content of the conversation was. But my mother says she doesn't remember it as remarkable, nor did her father indicate that what he was saying might be considered extraordinary.

In junior high my mother was involved with after-school sports. Always a tomboy who played with her brothers, she wore school dresses with matching bloomers so that after school she could tuck the dress into the bloomers and immediately be ready to play sports or climb trees without first going home. When it became too dark to play, she went to her father's dental office and the two drove home together. One day, during the drive home, my grandfather posed an idea for my mother: since her brothers had gone their own ways, perhaps my mother would be interested in going to dental school and someday taking over his practice. At the time he said this, women were not admitted to the majority of dental schools. Were either of them aware of this? It seems not, because the idea of being a *pioneer* was not presented to my mother, simply the idea of a career in dentistry.

Was it simple worry that his life's work would have no successor that caused my grandfather to have this apparent moment of progressive thought? Or had Gilberta and Walter, because both had postsecondary educations and both had experience as "professionals," somehow inadvertently fabricated in their own minds an atmosphere of assumed opportunity for their daughters? Yes and no.

In 1887, when "The New Church" was founded based on Swedenborg's writings, it was a form of the 1960s "Age of Aquarius." Committed to individualism and social involvement, Swedenborgianism "emphasizes the responsibility of each person to develop his own beliefs and live his life accordingly. In stressing freedom, diversity, and individualism, [Swedenborg] issued a challenge to individuals, churches, and other organizations to be committed to the human growth process and to express their personal commitment in ways as diverse as their numbers." The Swedenborgs also believed science was meshed with the "spiritual life" and endorsed coeducation. Their university, established in Ohio in 1850, claims to be the second coeducational college in the United States. No wonder, then, that the lobster-importer grandfather left education money for *all* his grandchildren. It wasn't a radical thought, it was as routine as the certainty shared by my siblings and myself from the time we entered nursery school: that after high school we would go to college, no different than leaving grade school for junior high. My grandparent's religious beliefs, not preached but put to practical use, certainly affected not only my mother's underlying attitude toward life but how she raised her own children.

So when presented this revolutionary idea by her father, my mother wasn't astonished, she just told her father that she was more interested in sports, and she planned on a physical education major at a private girl's college in Boston.

ISN'T ADOLESCENCE A *physiological* condition that manifests its side-effects in self-absorption, self-consciousness, rebellion, a concentration on personal social life without worrying about national or global or political or civil issues, the seeking of immediate or personal pleasure without being distracted by either one's own mortality or the seemingly distant future of the world? Well, I'm not really *that* cynical. Each generation's group of adolescents *has* to be formed not only by their own hormones, but by both the period of time and beliefs that formed their parents, as well as the immediate era gripping the country as *they* come of age. Thus each generation not only gets named, but subcategorized. The baby boomers include hippies as well as yuppies—all shaped by peacetime prosperity, cold war anxiety, then Vietnam. The U.S. involvement in Vietnam ended when I was a freshman in high school. The Vietnam War had a subtle effect on my adolescent years, but not the direct effect it had on people ten years older. People my age were partially shaped by the fact that *none* of us were asked to go to Vietnam. Likewise, my mother's generation, or subgeneration— those people whose young adult years were tucked between the depression and the war, too young to have much comprehension about the depression, then too young to be drafted—was not as *directly* influenced by World War II as men and women just five years older. For my mother's age group, there were still those other symptoms of adolescence to be distracted by: social life, new independence, the heady feeling of having the future lying before you. My mother's age-group was also inspired in varying degrees by the way women were suddenly empowered—they were all at once not only needed but thriving in the workforce.

The war years were my mother's high school and college years. When my mother characterizes this time in her life, she remembers sailing one- or two-person crafts in Southport's coves, playing field hockey and lacrosse, competing on swim teams. She recalls summer jobs as a life guard and as the sailing counselor at Girl Scout camp where she took two to six *un*-life-jacketed girls out into Cape Cod Bay in skiffs. She worked as a pin-setter in bowling alleys, and she hitchhiked all over New England with her snow skis. She doesn't describe boyfriends or dating. She calls it "a world of women." She attended an all-girls college, but after high school there weren't many boys around anyway. Those that were—attending Harvard for a few months on their way to being commissioned officers then shipping off to Europe—were called "90-day wonders" and weren't worth getting serious about. A few times she served as a USO hostess, but she was more interested in sports than dancing with boys. Her mother saved tin foil. Gas and meat were rationed. Her father tended his Victory garden. Women had no silk stockings so my mother and her friends painted their legs with pancake makeup and had a special pencil to draw the seam up the back of the calf. On V-J day, she went into Boston to wave a commemorative flag in the mob scene.

Sargent College offered only one major: physical education. When my mother's sister, older by seven years, attended Sargent College, the girls played sports wearing dark opaque cotton stockings under bloomers with elastic leg holes, topped by thigh-length tunics over white blouses. When my mother entered college in 1942, the stockings were gone and girls engaged in athletics with bare legs. To differentiate between teams, one team removed their tunic and played in white blouse and bloomers.

When I entered high school in 1971, the P.E. uniform was an article of clothing I'd never in my life encountered: red *bloomers*. Bloomers seem to have enjoyed a long life as accepted custom. Even though my high school had recently abandoned a dress code, and we wore jeans or corduroys and men's workshirts or army fatigues to class, the elastic-legged bloomers remained our P.E. uniform, obviously some last relic of "modesty." We usually pushed the elastic up to our underwear line or rolled the elastic up and created a garment resembling a bulky bathing suit bottom (or diapers). Like the long dresses and high-top shoes of my grandmother's normal school basketball games, the bloomer uniform at my high school eventually disappeared, some time after I graduated.

I was looking through an older friend's yearbooks from 1960 to 1962 and noticed the traditional *Most Popular* and *Most Likely to Succeed* designations in both genders, but there was only one *Most Athletic* (a boy) and one *Best Personality* (a girl). In pre–Title IX years, I would expect to discover this kind of gender division. But twenty years earlier, in 1942 when my mother graduated from high school, *she* was voted *Most Athletic Girl*. One of many subtle hints that my mother did grow up in a somewhat more gender-equalized world than those who came of age in the fifties, sixties, and even seventies. At least by the time I graduated in the mid-seventies, we didn't have a *Best* or *Most Likely any*thing, girl *or* boy.

THE OTHER DAY I asked my mother if she was aware there was now a professional basketball league for women. "Oh yes," she replied, "your father and I have watched some of the games on television."

"Doesn't it make you think?" I inquire, not leading her toward what I suppose it might make her think *about*. I'm imagining jealousy, the same sort I felt when Little League baseball was opened up to girls—*after* I was too old to participate. "I mean," I add, "didn't you think about your mother playing basketball in a long black dress?"

"Actually, no," she answers, without the slightest hint of envy. "I remembered how we had different rules. The forward had to stay in her half of the court, couldn't cross the line, like half-court basketball, and the guards had to stay in the other half, and we could only dribble once before having to pass the ball to someone else."

"Dribble *once?* You mean one bounce? How could you go anywhere at that rate?"

"They must've thought it was too strenuous for girls to run more than that." At last, her tone contains something—but it's mockery, not spite. "But we played lacrosse and field hockey. Those rules weren't *much* different than for boys."

At Sargent College this peculiar form of women's basketball was played in the gym in court shoes made of kangaroo leather. These were $30 shoes—a pricetag that would make them the equivalent of AirJordans in the nineties.

Besides basketball, the curriculum called for other court sports: volleyball, badminton, and tennis; plus classes in dance, including ballet, tap, modern, ballroom, folk, international, and a strange activity called "marching." [This sounds like a precursor to the all-girl units which, starting in the fifties or sixties, began to march behind high school marching bands. The Corps did synchronized routines with white-gloved hands or twirley flags.] Sargent's courses in dance culminated with a show at Boston Garden every spring in which the girls demonstrated all their dance routines, taking both male and female roles. Yearbook photos show my mother wearing shin-length troubadour pants dancing with a girl in flounced multilayered dress, in a performance of a folk dance from Spain.

Sargent curriculum also required gymnastics which included— and note the contradiction, considering the bizarre rules for women's basketball—tumbling and mat work, parallel bars, "buck- and-run," the pummel horse, rope climbing, and "flying rings," which any fan of the Summer Olympics will recognize as forms of men's gymnastics. Thinking back, my mother calmly realizes that the women's gymnastic apparatus had not yet been separated from men's in the forties.

Earning a Bachelor of Science degree in physical education was a four-year full-time commitment: five days per week, 9 A.M. to 4 P.M., filled with academic classes and the required phys. ed. courses. But Sargent College was in the middle of the city of Boston and didn't have its own outdoor playing fields, nor was there an indoor swimming pool. Because of that—and because the winter made outdoor sports difficult—the girls were required to attend two sessions of camp every summer in June and September. Camp sessions included swimming and diving, water ballet (now called synchronized swimming), equestrian events, golf, track-and-field, and archery. There was boating instruction in craft from row boats and canoes to racing sculls and two-sail dories. Plus, of course, all the required field sports: softball, soccer, lacrosse, and field hockey. Looking through her college photo album—with disintegrating black pages, stale photo corners that no longer stick, but dense, wonderfully preserved black-and-white photos—my mother points out one of the visiting coaches during camp sessions. Mrs. Appleby was easily in her eighties. "She had been the one who brought girls' field hockey over from England," my mother says. "She would stand there yelling, *Run, you fool, run!*"

Besides images of favorite horses, a row of archers with arrows poised, a water ballet routine (no one was wearing a nose plug), and lacrosse teams seated on the grass receiving instruction from a coach, other photos contain girls with their jeans rolled to midcalf or lying on the grass with their shirts rolled to expose their stomachs to the sun, posing leaning on each other in front of their kiosk dwellings.

As the final sessions of camp approached before her senior year, my mother and her friends were a little worried. The girls slept in these open-sided shelters that held a dozen beds. My mother's group of friends numbered twelve, so there should've been no cause for anxiety about housing, but two girls in my mother's circle were black, and in 1945 at Sargent College the black girls — girls who attended the same classes as their classmates, swam in the same pool, played on the same teams — were housed separately. My mother's group wanted to stay together, so she and a friend went to the dean to request permission for the black girls to bunk in their kiosk, the "senior bung," short for bungalow. The dean, my mother remembers, gave the (now) familiar and bogus rationale for the school's policy, always couched in terms of what was best for *"them"* — that *"they"* would be much more comfortable if housed separately. No, my mother explained to the dean, they want to be with us. No strikes, no sit-ins or protests were needed, some advancements in civil rights seem to have been won more easily than others. The dean relented, and Sargent's segregated housing policy was suspended that year. Since my mother graduated the following May, she doesn't know if her actions helped end the policy forever. She thinks the administrators and faculty probably monitored the "experiment" carefully, and she doesn't remember any incident that would've prevented the summer of 1945's "provisional" end of segregated housing from being a success.

PERHAPS SOME GIRLS who majored in physical education at Sargent College in the thirties and forties did it as a less stifling finishing school, without expectation that a career would come of it. They got married and began to raise their families. Because of the war and the scarcity of men, my mother had no such option to ponder. For her, seeking work after college was not elective but the necessary next step, and the only career for phys. ed. majors, in an era before professional trainers and exercise gurus, was teaching P.E.

So here's the other Swedenborgian connection: The older brother who'd become a Swedenborgian minister had gotten a position as pastor of a small Swedenborgian church 3,000 miles away in a quickly growing town called San Diego. He'd married a Swedenborgian girl from Palos Verdes. The pastor's mother-in-law was one of hundreds of unheralded woman doing "men's" professional work in the thirties and forties—an architect and former postmistress of Palos Verdes. This woman was a friend of the Vanderlips of Palos Verdes, Swedenborgians who owned most of Rolling Hills, including much of the peninsula. The Vanderlips donated land along the coast in Palos Verdes for the Wayfarer's Chapel, a Swedenborgian church made entirely of glass, designed by Frank Lloyd Wright's son. They also donated another large parcel of land on the peninsula to a new nonreligious private boarding school called Chadwick School. So in the summer of 1946 when her brother heard of a job at Chadwick for a women's P.E. teacher, Mom left Boston and joined her brother in Southern California.

Chadwick School never disputed that it was a school for children of the privileged, but one of its missions was to provide something Mrs. Chadwick felt was lacking in privileged childhoods: a "stable home life." This quality was manifested via responsibility (that is, chores) around the "house." The students did eat in a dining hall and send their clothes to a laundry, but they were required to clean their dorm rooms and the bathrooms—there was no maid service—and they took turns busing at meals, where they ate at "family style" tables with a faculty member presiding like a parent at the end of each. Younger, or single, faculty members also lodged with the students, so my mother became an assistant house-mother in a ramshackle overflow dorm for eight junior-high-age girls, including Jack Benny's stepdaughter. The building had a hallway so narrow that these preadolescent girls *literally* climbed the walls by pressing their backs against one wall and "walking" up the opposite wall with their feet. Their assistant house mother didn't scold; she took pictures.

Chadwick's goal to provide a "stable home life" at boarding school might have been revolutionary. And it's interesting to juxtapose that intent with some of the "privileged" who attended: Christina Crawford, who wrote of her traumatic childhood in *Mommy Dearest*, boarded at Chadwick for part of her high school education, so my mother was her physical education teacher. And Maureen Reagan was a student at Chadwick. My mother recalls a faculty-student-parent softball game and she remembers spotting the handsome actor among the spectators—he had a broken leg and couldn't play. "I didn't think he was much," she muses ironically now with a laugh. And although she doesn't remember Edward G. Robinson's son, she recalls Mr. Robinson's rage over his son's punishment for drinking. Part of my mother's duties included filling in for the receptionist during her lunch hour. One day Mr. Robinson stormed into the office, cursing and roaring. It's my father who remembers the suitcase full of booze the young Robinson had smuggled (unsuccessfully) onto campus. This didn't conform with the "stable home life" provision, so he was expelled.

Chadwick School had moved to its present site around 1938. The campus consisted of a classroom building, dining hall, the headmistress's home, a dorm, a few other miscellaneous buildings (like the overflow dorm), a few small cottages that had already been on the property, and a gym. There was no gymnastics apparatus in the gym except a large trampoline and a "medicine ball" (what Balley's Total Fitness can claim one of *those*?). Construction continued after the school opened, new additions mostly consisting of additional phys. ed. facilities, a locker room, and an outdoor pool surrounded by cinderblock walls. The reason for this design is unknown to my parents, perhaps to keep the tumbleweeds and dirt out of the pool but allow the swimmers a view of the sky. Or to protect them from coyotes and rattlesnakes seeking water?

After my mother was added to the faculty in 1946 and the girls joined interschool leagues for team sports, they were granted a new girls' basketball court. It was made of asphalt and was located outside, wedged in between the gym and the edge of a small canyon in the hills. Whenever the ball went out of bounds on that side of the court, someone had to chase it into the canyon, returning with foxtails in her socks, scratched legs, and, if it had rained, mud to her ankles.

After her first year in California, my mother bought a used 1940 Plymouth convertible with a rumble seat—ostensibly to allow her to pack up and drive home for the summer (perhaps never to return). But she did come back, and in her convertible could become the "real California girl" her daughters never were, her hair lashing as she drove the palm-lined streets of Long Beach, or over the brown hills of Palos Verdes. It was a few years later that my father completed his war-interrupted college degree and returned to teach chemistry at the school he'd graduated from. When they began dating my mother accepted a patriarchal routine—they always went out in Dad's DeSoto.

The gate to the Chadwick grounds was locked at 10 P.M. My parents rarely made it home from their dates by that hour, so my father would have to wake up a faculty member who lived just outside the campus and served as "gate keeper" as well as art teacher. This colleague therefore found it whimsical to announce in the dining hall exactly what time Mr. Mazza and Miss Young returned from dinner and a movie the night before. It was appropriate, then, that my parents' engagement was announced over a cafeteria microphone as they sat at separate tables eating Jell-O and sandwiches, each with a troupe of kids to supervise.

MY PARENTS WERE married in the Swedenborgian church in San Diego, not realizing they would someday return to live in San Diego. After marrying, they left Chadwick for San Francisco where my father would complete his masters' degree. My mother's father took one more stab at finding a family dentist to take over his practice. He offered his Boston-based practice to my father if he would become a dentist. Grandpa was probably disappointed when my father declined, but all four of Grandpa Young's children had freely chosen what they wanted to do, and so had my father and his siblings.

While in San Francisco, my mother found work teaching swimming at the YMCA in a pool so heavily chlorinated she came home each night with red-rimmed eyes. Her reason for quitting was not worry that the chorine would be bad for her unborn child—she left when she was too pregnant to fit into her swimsuit. My eldest sister was not only a natural and accomplished swimmer, she has always had very sensitive eyes.

For a while this budding family was unusually (for the postwar middle class) restless, moving once a year, auditioning new locations and teaching jobs, adding a second baby sixteen months after the first. San Francisco to Wheatland to Bell Gardens to my father's parents' house in Anaheim for a few months. Finally they returned to Chadwick and stayed for five more years.

Already having two daughters, when the next pregnancy occurred, my parents were hoping for a boy. Of course, there were no prenatal gender tests and fathers did not go into delivery rooms in the fifties, so, according to the Chadwick School newspaper, the doctor came out, clapped a hand on my father's shoulder, and said, "Girls are nice . . ." The ellipses left a large unspoken "*but*" hovering in the air, obviously to fool my father into thinking the doctor's announcement would be the joyfully anticipated news that the baby was a boy. Then the punch line, the practical joke, would be that it was "just" a girl after all. This floating "*but*" also insinuates "girls are nice . . . *but* . . . boys are better." I doubt the doctor actually said this because I doubt the student reporter would have been present at the hospital. It was a high school student's asinine joke (and/or a faculty adviser, so-called friend of my father's)—but for years I wondered if the first news of my birth brought a stab of disappointment.

A small stucco cottage on the campus of Chadwick School was given rent-free to my parents, and we were given complimentary admission to the school. My parents surrounded their cottage with vegetable gardens, fruit trees, rabbit hutches, swingset and sandbox, geraniums, amaryllis, and pets—two dogs, rabbits, and an egg-laying duck named Ducky. In the grassy backyard under the clothesline, as well as in the weedy fields surrounding the house, we hung handmade doll clothes to dry, finger-painted on easels borrowed from the art teacher, had backyard birthday parties with games and homemade party hats, and guests who were often children of movie stars. We played "Indian" in a tattered old teepee someone had given us, and "Engineer Bill" (a local cartoon guru) in a train fabricated from wooden crates and cardboard cut-out wheels, and were watched over by our German shepherd, Tracy. One time my mother heard my sister crying and went to investigate. My sister, age three or four, was angry that Tracy wouldn't let her play. He was standing in front of her, barking in her face. She had her eye on a piece of old hose, and since we were becoming skillful scavengers, any found object could become a toy. But Tracy wouldn't let her pick up the hose. The hose, my mother saw, was a rattlesnake.

My father taught full-time at Chadwick, and my mother returned as a part-time coach. Their house was down the hill from the classrooms and dorms. The gym and swimming pool were then still further down the hill from the house. While my mother coached girls' basketball and volleyball teams, those girls who were having their periods—excused from dressing-out for P.E. for five days—walked up the hill and baby-sat with us during their P.E. class. We played with their "pocketbooks" and thought they were grown-ups. During this period of time, one of the girls in junior high phys. ed. was Liza Minelli (when her name was still Lisa), learning the rules of volleyball and field hockey from my mother, but too young to baby-sit the coach's children. By the time she was Liza-with-a-Z, Miss Minelli was known to have some slick moves on a cabaret stage, but my mother can't take any credit for any dancing ability of her privileged, future-celebrity students. When she had first interviewed for her job, my mother informed Mrs. Chadwick, in no uncertain terms, "I don't teach dance." This agreed upon, my mother settled into her position as *coach*—also filling in as jack-of-all-trades, substituting for the receptionist, painting recess games like hopscotch and four-square onto the playground black-top, and designing the logo for the school's mascot dolphin. But year by year, the requests for teaching dance increased. So my mother relented and taught folk dancing to the grade-school children. Every year they presented a Folk Dance Festival for an audience of celebrities like George and Gracie Burns, whose children were participating in the performance on the school's front lawn.

One of my mother's encounters with the "privileged" was more a clandestine plot than the crossing paths of faculty and parent, and in fact didn't involve a student at all. One day Mrs. Chadwick told my parents that Sterling Hayden, chiseled male icon of the fifties, would come to their house that evening. My mother served him coffee and homemade applesauce cake. Mr. Hayden asked my parents if they could take care of his two small children for a few weeks. My mother knew that he was in the process of being divorced, but she doesn't remember if that information came from Mrs. Chadwick or directly from Mr. Hayden. The actor brought his children the next day, a boy around four and a girl who was younger. He also brought a crib, their clothes, and some toys. Mrs. Chadwick asked my parents not to say anything about the arrangement to anyone (a promise my mother kept for several decades). Two or three weeks later, Hayden returned for his children but left the crib and many of the toys. An accomplished yachtsman before he'd ever become an actor, Hayden said he was going to take the two children on a sailing trip around the world. My parents' next three children were raised in the crib Hayden left behind, and slept with the Raggedy Ann his daughter had to forsake. And yet Sterling Hayden had no children attending Chadwick School— how did this secreting-away of his children by two Chadwick faculty members come about? In an interview with Gerald Peary in the late eighties, Hayden says that during the filming of *Johnny Guitar*, which costarred Joan Crawford and was released in 1953, he was "at war with my then-wife in the evenings and with Joan Crawford in the days." My mother thinks she kept his children around 1954 or 1955. Crawford's daughter had attended Chadwick School around this time. Perhaps Crawford, hearing of his impending custody dispute, sent Hayden to Mrs. Chadwick to help hide his children at the school while he wrapped up personal business before he leaving the country with his children on his yacht. My parents never heard from him again.

There's another possible explanation for why Hayden hid his children then left the country. After the war, he had joined the Communist Party. In the interview with Gerald Peary, Hayden said he didn't feel committed and eventually went to ask his lawyer's advice. Hayden's lawyer contacted J. Edgar Hoover, who recommended that Hayden "Make a clean breast of the whole thing." Hayden eventually went to the FBI as a friendly witness "after a great deal of travail. . . . [T]he FBI made it clear to me that if I became an 'Unfriendly Witness' I could damn well forget the custody of my children. I didn't want to go to jail, that was the other thing." So in pre-1952, Hayden was already worried about the custody of his children; perhaps was already engaged in his divorce battle. He said, "The FBI office promised that my testimony was confidential. So I spilled my guts out, and the months went by, and I was on some shit-ass picture, and I got a subpoena. The next thing I knew I was flying to Washington to testify. The worst day of my life. They knew it already, and there is the savage irony. [Ronald Reagan] sent me a cable congratulating me on being a good American when my testimony hit the fan." Hayden eventually recanted his testimony, but in the meantime, after his testimony, in 1952 Hayden "began to work on a very low level of B pictures as often as I felt like it. I sank down into a morass." *Johnny Guitar* came along in 1953. Was it this "morass," and a continuing custody battle, that precipitated my parents' involvement in Hayden's possible abduction of his children? Or had he finally won the custody battle and merely wanted to flee post-McCarthyism America?

McCarthyism did affect Chadwick School, not only in terms of blacklisted actors whose children were students. Instead of a homecoming queen, the campus had always celebrated the crowning of the May Queen every spring. May Day is known worldwide with various deviation in traditions, likely originating from both ancient Druid ritual and Roman festivals. Chadwick, which housed a Scotch reverend in the school chapel, celebrated the British version of May Day, complete with the royal trumpeters in Renaissance costume, a throne made of flowers, a crown bearer and flower girl chosen from the elementary school, a dozen attendants to the queen, and the Maypole Dances. Every year May Day turned the Chadwick campus into an idyllic British country village.

Even though it was seventy years earlier that the Socialist movement chose May 1 as a day for working people to show socialist unity, it was during the 1950s cold war—when the Soviet Union splashed May Day with parades, speeches, and rallies—that the celebration of the spring festival May Day was frowned upon (or banned?) in the United States. Chadwick School likewise ceased May Day celebrations around this time. The large population of children from Hollywood might have encouraged Mrs. Chadwick to be wary of anything that would cause suspicion during the uneasy era.

My brother's birth three years after mine wasn't the only thing that necessitated my family's move from Palos Verdes to San Diego. It was those same movie stars' children at our birthday parties and sitting next to us in school. My parents' apprehension was that if we grew up accustomed to what they perceived in their pupils' attitudes about money and possessions, we might not only become spoiled brats but *frustrated* brats. Although the same education at Chadwick was available to us, teachers' salaries—approximately $250 per month, no medical benefits—would not provide the same *stuff*. My parents valued the education but feared *we* would value the stuff.

TO ME, LIKE to a five-year-old, a mother is someone who has always existed exactly the way she is. I look at a photo of her when she was seventeen and say, "You look exactly the same!"

"*Thanks!*" exclaims my seventy-two-year-old mother, "I need you around more often."

But it is strange to realize that she was an adult, working on the fringes of Hollywood during the McCarthy Era. Likewise, it's bizarre to realize that some of my own trivial childhood experiences now can denote a time, an era, and even an individual parental philosophy.

At the time my parents opened my very first bank savings account—I was four or five—I was told I was "saving for college." So going to college was taken for granted, it was not a question, merely the next step after high school. I have heard stories to the contrary from my peers, and even from girls younger than me: girls who were told outright they may as well not go to college because they would get married, while the same parents would send a son off to whatever university the boy chose. Later, when I was a student at a university, my education subtly suggested I needed to be male to succeed: There were no female professors in my field until my second graduate program—and then only one. No women authors were included on reading lists until graduate school, and then the percentage was not even close to half.

But my sisters and I were oppressed females in the sixties and seventies who didn't know how to act it. We neither wilted in submission to biased attitudes and gender restrictions nor did we openly protest or work for change. Instead, at times, while we hunted and fished and played street football, we seemed blissfully unaware of the lingering differences in opportunity and expectations. Other times, when we were forced to be conscious of what we were not supposed to do, we just did it anyway. Even when the first straightforward statement that there was a gender barrier came, appallingly, from my own mother. I was in second grade watching a jazz combo play for a Girl Scout assembly. I informed my mother I would choose the "slide trombone" for my instrument when my turn for music lessons arrived in a few months. My mother remarked that trombones were for boys. An alarming comment from a woman whose father asked her in 1937 to consider becoming a dentist. But this declaration of a gender barrier is a lonely recollection in my memory because there are few, if any, others like it. So, although I admit to remaining incensed about her careless comment, I have to consider it an uncharacteristic fluke, based, perhaps, on my mother protecting herself from the noise of a beginning trombonist in the house. Besides, something in me must have perceived she didn't—couldn't—mean it. I waited until I was in high school, then did begin to play the trombone, even bought my own instrument with $20 of paper route money.

In 1969, when I was in junior high, a friend offered to share a *San Diego Tribune* paper route with me. I would deliver Monday, Wednesday, Friday, she would do the route Tuesday, Thursday, and

Saturday, then we would alternate Sundays. It was an afternoon route six days a week, and mornings on Sundays. Sometime in the eighties or nineties, delivering papers became an adult job—they leave self-addressed envelopes in their Christmas cards, reminding customers to send tips. When it was a kid's job, we were self-employed retail sales*men*. We bought the papers (wholesale) from the district manager out of the money we collected, personally door-to-door, from customers, who paid retail. Our profit—after paying for not only the papers, but the rubber bands and the plastic bags for rainy days—came from tips. But we never *asked* for tips. Instead, we memorized each customer's preference for where they wanted the paper: "on the porch but don't hit the door," "in the mailbox," "between the screen and the door, but don't let the screen bang shut." When customers cheated us or didn't pay, *we* ate the loss.

There were perks and prizes for delivery boys. Yes, they were called delivery *boys,* and that's why I couldn't go to the Padres game on *Union/Tribune* delivery boys night, nor the circus, nor any of the other trips. Girls were not allowed to have paper routes, but our district manager had not been able to find a boy who was willing to keep this particular route: In La Mesa, near Spring Valley, it was a long circuit that went up and down hills, covering miles, containing houses with large lots and long driveways, which meant fewer houses per mile, therefore less profit for the physical exertion. Our district manager was a woman. It was her idea for us to use boys' names when we took over the route. My friend used her brother's name, but I already had an ungendered name. I don't know if my mother knew that girls were not allowed to deliver papers, but she went with me and advanced me the $30 when I bought my first bike to use on the route—a used boy's three-speed with chrome fenders.

On my weekdays to deliver, I rode my bike eight miles to junior high, went directly from school to do the route, then rode my bike home—we lived four or five miles from where the route was.

Every other Sunday I was up at 4 A.M. I biked the five miles to my friend's house. The weird amber streetlights changed red cars to purple, my blue jacket to violet; the streets—major thoroughfares for Spring Valley—were ghostly. My bike's headlight was powered by a generator gizmo—a gear that pressed against the rear tire, using the motion of the tire to create enough power to throw a frail yellow beam onto the pavement. No helmet, no kneepads, no reflectors on my jacket.

At my friend's dark, spooky-silent house, the double stack of papers already sat at the end of the driveway. I slipped each comics-supplement into the paper, folded the thick bundle and stretched the rubber band around. Sunday papers were so much bigger than weekdays, I had to return to the house after doing half the route to pick up the rest of the papers. Before sunrise in winter and spring, I wore a jacket and gloves. I carried a thermos of hot chocolate that I would stop and sip from at the halfway point, accompanied by an orange from a row of trees bordering the halfway-point customer's long driveway. After sunrise, the jacket was peeled, stuffed into the now-emptying canvas paper bag. Some Sundays I brought my brother. He could carry the other half of the papers so we could do the route in the usual linear circuit. Sweat-soaked, we wouldn't get home until after 8, finding Mom and siblings already engaged in preparing breakfast.

Somehow, someone found out we were girls and the paper route was taken away. I wrote to my congressman to complain—not based on current law (I don't know if there *were* any laws) but on my ingenuous view of pure justice. What my congressman said in his response was that it was "probably" unfair to not allow paper routes for girls, but since we had lied, the newspaper did have grounds to take away the route.

It was, appropriately, after the paper route that I quit the cello and started, finally, to play trombone. Music lessons had been something, like college, that were inevitable for us: like losing teeth or getting a drivers' license, something that started at a certain age and changed your life thereafter. I had watched with jealousy as my older sisters started tooting reeds and scraping strings, dreaming of my turn to hold wood or brass and make sounds come out of it. Both of my sisters wanted to play clarinet. After Phyllis's turn squawking and squeaking on the reed, her teacher pointed and said, "You'll play violin." Lee, the older sister, was awarded the clarinet. Eight years later Phyllis began a music major in college, then became a professional violinist—playing with symphonies in San Diego and Nashville, and in recording studios and musical theater in Nashville and Cleveland—but she still remembers one elementary "orchestra" rehearsal when the director turned to her and said, "Well at least you play *loud*."

There was a similar program at Spring Valley Elementary. We were instructed for three weeks on trumpet, clarinet, and violin. Then the instructor decided which type of instrument each child was best suited for. He seemed to find more girls appropriate for flute and more boys suited for trumpet. For the time being, I let myself be steered toward the cello.

While it was just the two other children playing violin and clarinet, my mother required my sisters to practice their instruments a half hour every morning before they got breakfast. One morning Phyllis's practicing broke off, and she came fuming out to the kitchen where my mother was feeding not only me (probably four years old) but also a two-year-old. Perhaps my mother was pregnant with my youngest brother. Phyllis knew better than to throw the violin, but she did stomp and was adamant when she reported, "I *can't* and I *won't*." My mother left the younger children, immediately took Phyllis by the arm, and led her back to the bedroom, answering firmly, "You can and you *will*."

When we moved to Spring Valley, when I was seven, all three of us shared a room. Both my sisters still practiced—but without the breakfast initiative and at separate times. I lay on my bed reading or rhapsodizing in my journal in the midst of long-and-slow then faster-and-faster drills, major scales and minor ones, fingering exercises, bowing exercises, *endless* and persistent tuning of strings, finally pieces of violin parts from symphonies and fragments of concertos done over and over and over. Phyllis would mutter "no" or "wait," breaking off at the same place every time. I rarely heard a piece of music played all the way through, she was a tape-loop of Beethoven and Tchaikovsky

Playing an instrument, like scouting, was deemed essential by our parents—they calculated music lessons into the stretched budget. But music has never been something traditionally withheld from girls (except certain instruments). In fact, music was one of the fundamentals of girls' finishing schools, although I can guarantee that's not even close to my parents' reason for making music imperative. But I don't know how much my parents *were* aware of the kinds of opportunities that may have been denied to or difficult for their daughters. When Phyllis was around ten and wanted to be a doctor, it was not so very long after a time when most medical schools had a rule that no *more* than 10 percent of the freshman class could be female. I met a woman approximately fifteen years older than me who wanted to be a veterinarian but could not find a vet school that accepted women. A woman ten years older than me was told during career counseling that girls should not plan on becoming vets. Girls ten years older than me had curfews when they were in their college dorms, but boys the same age did not. I heard of a particular college's 1960s-era rule stating that no girl was allowed to wear shorts, except during gym class, without covering herself with a raincoat. My oldest sister, Lee, came home from eleventh grade one day in the late sixties and reported that her counselor had told her that no further science classes were necessary, she could take typing in her senior year. My father must've raised his eyebrows to his hairline. My mother was at the school the following day with their parental response: *enroll her in chemistry*. I'm not sure if any of us ever visited a high school counselor again.

We should've been used to this division in school classes. In junior high, girls had to take homemaking and boys took shop—these were not *ever* coed classes. I just happened to never learn to cook or sew because music classes took the place of homemaking and shop. (Boys who played instruments were considered nerds by their peers—they couldn't saw or nail or use a Phillips screwdriver.) My mother, busy with sports as a child and teenager, had also never learned to cook until after she was married. We were required to help in the kitchen, but it was easier for her to whip up a meal for seven by herself than to worry about instructing a child on browning the quail, seasoning the garden green beans, frying the squash blossoms, removing the cuttlebone from the squid, or leaching the eggplant in salt water. But we did learn to make a fire and cook "pigs-in-a-blanket" and "campfire stew." And she made sure we knew how to hike—carrying her youngest child in an army-surplus rucksack turned into a child-carrier. A major rite of passage was when our growth had slowed enough to get real leather hiking boots—but there was never a rite of passage involving being old enough to use makeup. She taught us how to bank the campfire, how to bait a hook and clean a fish, how to shoot arrows at hay bale targets in the backyard. And as essential as music and scouting: we had to swim.

WE GOT WET wherever we went. The water was frigid in Southport, Maine; milky and warm on the Carolina coast, brown with a steady one-way tow in southeastern rivers; turbulent and rip-tided in the Pacific; quick, rough, and cold in the eastern Sierra; and a fetid, nearly stagnant, algae-infested trickle in the creek down the hill from the house. Of course it was aquamarine and chem-treated in public pools, scout camp, neighbor's yards, and—finally—in our own above-ground five-foot-deep plastic-and-aluminum "Doughboy" planted on a backyard hillside that had required dynamite in order to create a level place. It was in water that our mother was, to us, most clearly magnificent.

If my mother's job as a swimming instructor while pregnant with my oldest sister has anything to do with Lee being the most natural swimmer in our family, then my mother's attempt to hasten my birth by riding in an old station wagon on bumpy dirt roads—then completely *off* the road through tumbleweeds, gopher holes, and rain-washed ruts on the undeveloped Palos Verdes peninsula—would mark me a baby born on dry land. I'm not only prone to severe motion sickness, but also had an exasperating (to my mother) lack of mettle hounding my passage through many forms of swimming.

Not that I didn't *want* to be the kind of swimmer a Mazza kid was supposed to be. My penchant for earning degrees, titles, or designations for my hobbies—from Girl Scout badges to marching in a championship high school band to putting titles on registered purebred dogs—probably started with swimming. In fact, practicing a musical instrument just to improve at making music was never satisfying until I was in that competition marching band, drilling and rehearsing then being judged and scored in Saturday parades, accepting a placement but striving toward the sweepstakes trophy. In swimming, the designations earned were the Red Cross levels of swimming skills: Beginner Swimmer, Advanced Beginner, Intermediate Swimmer, Swimmer, Junior Life Saver, Senior Life Saver, and Water Safety Instructor. Each level had a corresponding class then a test that had to be passed before the title was bestowed, the tangible proof being a coveted pin and patch. I (miraculously) made it as far as Junior Life Saver, and probably only made it that far due to the enticement of titles and badges.

To become a Water Safety Instructor (WSI)—a designation that must be re-earned every four years—a swimmer must learn and successfully demonstrate, under simulated drowning situations, all of the lifesaving carries, breaks, and holds. A "break" is a technique used to remove the deathgrip a drowning person is apt to put on the approaching lifesaver; a "hold" is a method for restraining the panicked swimmer; a "carry" is the means used to bring the rescued in to shore. Besides the lifesaving techniques, a prospective WSI must show endurance in the water with nonstop swimming 100 yards for each of the strokes—crawl, sidestroke, breaststroke, backstroke, butterfly—with no break between strokes. Then there was a timed water-treading test for five to ten minutes.

Renewing her WSI for the last time in 1966, my mother joined my oldest sister (who was earning her first WSI) in the arduous preparation class. My sister was the youngest and our mother was the oldest member of the class at over forty. The others were between the ages of seventeen and thirty, and most were male. My mother and sister had to get in shape in our above-ground pool that wasn't more than five feet deep and only eighteen feet across—enough room for three strokes and a turn. They practiced the breaks and holds with my brothers and me playing the desperate drowning victims.

We started swimming in the Red Cross "Backyard Swim" program as soon as we were old enough—probably around six. In Backyard Swim, cosponsored by the PTA and Red Cross, neighborhood children were given swimming lessons by a qualified Red Cross swimming instructor. Lessons took place in a backyard built-in pool loaned to the program by a homeowner in the community for several hours in the morning five days a week, during the months of June and July. As a WSI, my mother was obviously equipped to teach in the Backyard Swim program, but she was also one of the few qualified to give the Red Cross swimming tests for all the Backyard Swim classes in our area.

It wouldn't take an expert to guess why the Backyard Swim program no longer exists. First the insurance liability of having up to a dozen six-year-olds being instructed by a volunteer—even a qualified one—in someone's backyard pool would by now be astronomical. Even if the Red Cross were fully insured, the pool's owner would still be vulnerable; in such a litigious society, what homeowner would want to take that kind of risk? Second, newer backyard pools rarely come in a shape that easily accommodates swimming lessons. Kidney bean–shaped, with raised Jacuzzis attached, sometimes bordered by natural stone instead of the traditional smooth lip of concrete—all not only make swimming instructing more difficult but are hazards.

I can't remember if my mother was my Backyard Swim instructor. But Backyard Swim only taught the Beginner Swimmer class, so we had to go on to higher levels in Girl or Boy Scouts, and it was my mother who was the swimming counselor at Girl Scout Camp Davidson, San Diego County's Girl Scout property in the Cuyamaca Mountains. It was so cool to have a mother with the designation of coach, who wore a red "racing" suit all day with a whistle around her neck and a white safari hat.

Despite the privilege at having this cool image for a mother, there was no favoritism when one of her own children was in a group she was coaching at the pool, except that she was probably more comfortable (therefore less cautious) in physically handling her own children. For example: diving lessons. First we sat on the pool deck, feet in the water, bent at the waist, faces tucked between extended arms, hands flat one atop the other, fingertips aimed toward the water. We would then "roll" forward and slip headfirst into the pool. The next step was to squat on the deck, bend forward from the waist and roll forward. After that, stand with knees slightly bent and arms extended, bend from the waist and point toward the water, face tucked; then lean, fall, or even hop forward and down into the water. Eventually everyone would do the same from the springboard. But while my fellow troop members moved on, I was still disinclined to graduate from step one to step two. While the others were standing, happily plopping headfirst into the pool, I was teetering on the brink of step two: squatting, preparing for a "dive" but not going anywhere, unwilling to lean far enough forward. Finally my frustrated mother picked me up by my hips then grabbed my flailing legs. I don't know how or *if* she managed to avoid being kicked in the head. She lifted me by my ankles until my whole body extended toward the water, then she let go and I cascaded headfirst into the pool. I surfaced sputtering and furious. But I went ahead and started diving from a standing position.

In Girl Scout camp we were given our first taste of competitive swimming. In fact, in addition to my furor over my mother's "diving lesson," it was the incentive of competition that helped me master most of my fear of diving. So I was all set to do the racer's entry into the water then stroke my way down a lane and back to claim a coveted blue ribbon. Of course I would win; my mother was the swimming counselor, my sister on the high school swim team.

We were grouped for freestyle races by age, not by size, so I stood with my peers on the edge of the pool, not facing the length of the pool but the width. No lane markers, no starting boxes, just a gaggle of girls with lumpy rubber bathing caps holding our pony-tailed hair, tugging at the elastic legs of our one-piece suits, ranging in height from four feet to nearly six, from 70 pounds to 130. On the whistle, we belly-flopped into the water and started churning our way for the other side. My arms were beating, my legs thrashing, my lungs burning—working so hard I had to be winning! But the force of my much bigger and taller peers hitting the water and flailing their way across had created such turbulence, such waves, such an incredible wake, I was practically swimming in place. I didn't get the blue. I didn't even get a red, yellow, or white ribbon.

So I wasn't the natural waterbaby my eldest sister was. And I also didn't seem to inherent an ample enough dose of my mother's vivacity. I *wasn't* afraid to tramp through waist-high weeds (until I stomped on a wasp's nest and was punished with stingers up and down my legs as I ran home shrieking). I wasn't afraid to be out alone on my bicycle delivering papers before dawn, even *after* I was bitten by a Great Dane. I wasn't scared to cross a white-water Sierra creek one foot in front of the other on a slippery log carrying a creel and ungainly fishing rod. I wasn't afraid to put my bare hands into the entrails of a trout or the steaming body cavity of a white rabbit. But I did have an irritating streak of chickenheartedness. Of all my siblings, I was the one who wouldn't go on what we called the "dark rides" at Disneyland—Peter Pan, Alice in Wonderland, Mr. Toad's Wild Ride. One of the gentlest rides at Disneyland in the sixties was Storybook Land where, on a little flat-bottomed boat, you rode through a whale's mouth into the world of *The Wind in the Willows*. I wouldn't do it. I ran away screaming. But it seemed to be my fears around water that galvanized my mother. The waves of the Pacific were another crossroad.

Before I was a teenager, every time the family prepared to go to the beach, I begged my mother to take us to "the beach with no waves." That would be Mission Bay. Once or twice that's where we went, although I have no idea why. My father couldn't fish there, my sisters and mother couldn't ride waves there, my brothers couldn't dig for sandcrabs there. What self-respecting beach has a *lawn*? But I wanted to go there because there was no cold foamy pea-green water that stood upright then came crashing down, churning everything in its path into the sand beneath it. My mother tried to explain: you just duck your head under the surface and the wave passes overhead; when you come back up, the wave is past. My fear was stubborn. So, once every beach trip, my mother would catch me off guard—lying on a towel, playing in a personal pool dug in the warm sand at the tide line, making drip-castles, training my captured bucket of sandcrabs to dig. She would sweep me up and charge into the water. And of course I screamed as any abducted child should. Today it probably would look like child abuse. I was forced, in my mother's arms, into the ruthless violence of the hostile never-ending army of waves. She would duck me under as each swell neared, then we would bob back to the surface, the breaking wave safely on our other side and on its way to shore—but me still screaming. Plus coughing out water I sucked in through sheer obstinate anger. The fun it might have become to splash through waves in my mother's arms couldn't conquer the furious tears I continued to shed as we came out of the surf. She would drop me back into my tepid bath of sun-warmed seawater, or onto my threadbare towel, and the family's day at the beach would continue. My consolation was, at least, that the ordeal was over and the rest of this beach day could be consumed without trepidation.

I did eventually go into the Pacific waves on my own and learned to enjoy riding the surf on a canvas air mattress. But there was no danger of my ever becoming an addicted or even intermittent surfer. Nor, thankfully, did my mother become one of those grey-ponytailed, rhino-skinned surfing relics. But she did get a boogie board.

When my brother's wife's son came from Michigan for his first visit to California, the beach topped his itinerary. June-gloom clung to the San Diego coast. Silver Strand beach was chilly. My father remained in jeans and a sweater, the boy's mother wrapped herself in towels. It was my mother who took the teenager into the ocean with her boogie board, taught him to catch the white-lipped waves at the moment they broke, then ride the tumbling, tumultuous surf toward the beach. She was in her seventies.

Water was part of almost every recreational activity, from fishing in the Sierras, where we waded across and routinely fell into the icy torrent of the glacier creek, to the cross-country drive we did in a camper in 1971. During that sojourn we swam in every nightly campground's slightly cloudy pool. We swam in the bathwater-warm coastal waterway on the southeastern coast, wearing tennis shoes because so many sharp oysters had clustered on the bottom. We swam in the cove on Cape Cod where my mother had first learned to swim, and we collected the shells of prehistoric horseshoe crabs that still live there. And everyone but me swam in the frigid water of Cozy Harbor on Southport Maine. The blue sky and pop-corn clouds and single-sail boats in the bay didn't divulge the below-fifty-degree water temperature. I stood beside my mother on the rocks as she took pictures. My brothers' and sisters' shouts and screeches seemed solitary in a silent landscape portrait. Then my mother handed me the camera, shed her shorts and sweatshirt, and joined her other children in the water, near where the legendary shipwrecked child had floated to shore bundled in mattresses.

IN 1993, ALMOST ten years after they retired, my parents went on a cruise in the Mediterranean. Not your typical banquet-eating, ball-room-dancing cruise ship; my parents were on an Elderhostel trip, the only way my father could see going on a vacation without fish-ing gear. Elderhostels are educational tours planned around topics from nature to geography to geology to history to art or literature. The trips always include some classroom lectures, plus hands-on activities and on-site expeditions. On this Mediterranean excursion in 1993, the topic was ancient Greek myth and literature as displayed in Greek art and architecture. Departing on Easter Sunday, the seven-day cruise among the Greek Islands was only part of this Elderhostel trip; the passengers included twenty Americans and nine crew members on a thirty-two-meter wooden vessel named *Zeus V*.

One morning in the dining room, during a lecture on the Greek deities, the Elderhostelers noticed an odor of smoke. The lecture was interrupted and the group was instructed to go to the sun deck. There crew members issued life jackets and assisted the Americans in putting them on. The *Zeus V*'s engines were dead. The absence of the familiar constant churn produced a new sort of stillness that magnified the slap of water against the hull, clarified the crisp Greek dialogue exchanged between the busy crew, then called attention to the drone of a car ferry, the *Apollo Express*, approaching the bow.

The Americans covered their faces with handkerchiefs and, outfitted in bulky lifejackets, filed through the smoke to the lower starboard deck. The car ferry, which had been on its usual route between islands when it spotted the smoke, had veered from its course and was already drawn up alongside the *Zeus V*. With a Greek crew member on each side, the Americans were one by one assisted in making the small leap from their cruise vessel to the ferry's deck.

Most of the crew stayed behind on the *Zeus V*, attempting to save the vessel, which had also been attached to the ferry with a tow line. As the Elderhostelers watched from the deck of the ferry, the *Zeus V* continued to smolder. Twinkles of flame flickered in the smoke, the flames grew, remained visible longer, finally stood upright and lashed in the wind like flags. Fishing vessels that had stayed nearby since the smoke had first been spotted, now drew up alongside the burning boat to take on the remainder of the *Zeus V* crew. Shortly afterward the tow line was cut, and the cruise vessel burned itself out as it sank into the Mediterranean.

Without any of their personal possessions, the twenty Elderhostelers were carried to a mainland port on the car ferry, a trip that took until 8 P.M. The cars being ferried between islands that day were brought a great deal out of their way. Both individual and official reports on the potentially disastrous incident, which the Greek newspaper *Eleftheros Typos* called an *adventure,* concurred on the relative calm displayed by the rescued Americans. Unanimously they voted to continue their tour of Greek antiquity on the mainland, and they did so, after a day spent shopping to replace clothes and toiletries, faxing doctors in the States to replace medications and corrective lenses, and (for my mother) searching for postcards or gift books that carried the sights and scenes that were still on the film in her camera that now lay somewhere under the Mediterranean. When the cruise vessel owner offered the Americans a free cruise the following spring to make up for the abrupt end of their excursion among the islands, my mother was the first to sign up. As she watched the cruise vessel burn and sink, I sincerely doubt my mother cried or called for her own mother. But she might've exclaimed, "Oh, honey, I forgot my camera."

A GIRL AMONG TROMBONISTS

I n my adolescent mind, I could've starred in a popular type of advertisement where a hard-hatted construction worker or jet pilot displays resplendent macho prowess. Welding a girder twenty stories up, supported only by a leather harness and mountain-climber line, boots braced against the steel frame, silhouetted in a spray of red sparks. Or in formations of fighter jets, turning in precision movements and landing against a flawless peaceful twilight; then four leather-jacketed, still-helmeted pilots in slow-motion walking from the parked jets, showing in every step the fluid comfort of their trained bodies, and the fluid ease of their camaraderie. Then in each image, the welder or one of the pilots, still in romantic slow motion, removes the helmet—the eyes are shut in dumb animal comfort as the head shakes off the feeling of shackled confinement, and the beautiful, tresses of silky long hair reveal that the macho figure is a stunning, gorgeous woman.

In *my* ad, this astonishing and magnificent creature would wear a red-and-black wool military-style uniform, white gloves, white military dress shoes, carry a trombone, and, following a breathtaking performance of precision and endurance, would make her startling emergence—shaking free her long hair—from underneath a busby hat. (Gorgeous? Well, I had the long hair.)

It was often the allure of contests, of winning something, that pushed me to overcome timidity. Before marching band, the only forms of competition available to me were the junior high science fair — my projects involved spiders and bees — and swimming races at Girl Scout camp. Both involved facing down things that scared me. Joining the all-male world of trombonists also put me face-to-face with a thing that scared me. A thing harder to name than black widow spiders or jumping from the high dive. Was it *boys*? *Sex*? My own gender's "place" in the world of the seventies? Or my gender's new "place" in the decades to come, and the complications it would bring that hadn't even, at the time, been named yet: sexual harassment and date rape?

So, before the questions had even been asked, I was a pioneer: first girl trombonist in my high school. And in Southern California, where trends and trailblazing are often experiments before moving east, it does seem a little late for this barrier to first be crossed in the 1970s. *Crossing* the barrier took nothing — I picked up a trombone and said *I want to play this*. But life as a trombonist took a subtle kind of nerve, a courage I didn't have: to join the boys without acquiescing in various ways, without *needing* them so anxiously.

THE FALL OF the year has had many designations for my family: dove hunting season, the start of the academic year, fire season, the time for Southern California's Santa Ana winds, and — in the late sixties and seventies, when my sisters and I began one by one to enter high school — September announced the start of marching season.

What teenager *doesn't* want to get up on Saturday at four in the morning, get on a bus at six to get to a parade route at eight, spend four or five hours on a hot September day in a decidedly unsexy wool uniform and hat, soaking undergarments with sweat and causing the gnarly-est case of hat-hair ever seen. Easy sacrifices in

the honorable pursuit of excellence, improvement, accomplishment . . . the pursuit of *winning*.

Marching band was and still is a competitive sport in California.
When the 1970s Title IX ensured equal funding for boys' and girls'
athletics, it didn't include marching band—it didn't need to as
marching band had always been a co-ed activity where boys and girls
received equal funding, when the band was funded at all. Around the
same time as Title IX, homeowners screamed that their property
taxes were too high, and Proposition 13 was passed as the taxpayers'
reassertion of their rights. School districts reeled. I don't recall a single football program limping away with severe wounds, but many
music programs were decimated to the point that it took a decade or
more to bring them back. Many students couldn't play in the band
when it meant as many hours in candy and T-shirt sales as in
rehearsal, when instruments couldn't be repaired, when each band
member's individual uniform allowance soared, when music classes
were no longer offered *during* the school day so all participation
(including that of the band director) was extracurricular. We thought
of Proposition 13 as the voters' revenge on the band that thundered
in rehearsal through their quiet tract neighborhoods every fall day
from 11 to 12:30 and again after school from 3 to 5.

In competitive marching, the first requirement is precision.
Bands were judged on a military standard, so precision dance-steps
didn't, at the time, count. Precision was sought first of all in the
obvious: straightness of ranks (individuals marching in shoulder-to-
shoulder rows), straightness of files (the front-to-back lines), and
even the visibility of accurate diagonals as the band passed down
the street. This meant that each individual in the block band had to
remain the same exact distance from all four individuals around
him or her, side to side and front to back.

Precision was also desired in the less obvious: Each step had to
be the proper length so that six steps fit equally in five yards.

Instruments had to be carried in exact horizontal or vertical positions—each like instrument carried in a uniform way—and had to remain as stone-still as humanly possible, whether being played or not. Obviously the musician's fingers, hands, or arms could move if that was how sound came out of the horn—pushing of valves or moving of the trombone's slide—but the rest of the instrument had to stay motionless, no jazzy body language with the horn. Instruments needed to be raised into play position and lowered into carry position with identical simultaneous movements by each individual. While playing the march, all the instruments, except those played vertically like clarinet, saxophone, and baritone, had to be carried parallel to the ground, no dipping trombone slides, no trumpet bells tipping skyward, no sagging flutes. Feet had to hit pavement at precisely the same time, nothing even slightly out-of-phase in the way people clapping to music in a large auditorium can't seem to stay with the beat. And the tempo of that beat had to remain precise: 120 beats per minute. Accuracy existed in the position of each individual's torso, shoulders, arms, and rhythm of the arm-swing, in focus of the eyes and slight upward tilt of the head. Obviously there was no head-turning side to side.

And then there was the precision required by military-type inspection. Not something that could be accomplished in daily rehearsal, this entailed a clean, pristine, and spotless objective for everything from white gloves and shoes to brass instruments and surfaces of drums, to no facial hair nor hair showing on the neck or back of the head, no jewelry, no makeup. Pant cuffs had to be exactly long enough to touch the top of the shoe and cause a slight break of the pant crease, jacket cuffs exactly long enough to touch the top thumb knuckle when the arm hangs at the side.

We were trained military-style to obey the drum major's whistled commands. One whistled order meant form-up, another was for attention, another for at-ease. There were whistles for turns and countermarches, and a specific whistle calling for the "roll-off," the percussion introduction cadence that included our cue for the precise maneuver of instruments snapping into playing position just before playing the music. From afar, and to some of our nonband classmates, we may have seemed more like Nazis than kids in the seventies. But we were actually a paradox, little flower-children rehearsing marching in straight lines wearing bell-bottoms, fringed leather vests, long and loose hair on boy and girl alike, peace signs on our notebooks, distrust of "the establishment" on our lips (but no boy from this band would have to go involuntarily to Vietnam).

In fact, a microfilm of my adolescence-to-young-adulthood would show that the August before I began the eighth grade, Sharon Tate and six other people were murdered. The spring before I started high school, protests against the war in Vietnam escalated on college campuses until students were killed by National Guard troops at Kent State. From the summer before my freshman year through the following spring, Charles Manson was on trial. The summer after my sophomore year, Republican burglars broke into the Democratic Party headquarters in the Watergate Hotel. Sometime in my freshman year, the draft ended before any of the boys my age had registered or received lottery numbers. In August before my junior year, the last American ground troops were withdrawn from Vietnam; by January all military operations against North Vietnam were halted. When I was a freshman in college, Nixon resigned, Saigon fell, and an influx of Vietnamese refugees poured into this country, a large percentage coming into Southern California. My first year of graduate school, Iranian students took sixty Americans hostage. The only mob scene I recall on my campus (which doesn't mean there weren't others) was between American and Iranian students. Women were not admitted to the U.S. military academies until I was in college, but the ERA would not finish its slow death until 1982.

Meanwhile, back in the seventies, we marched and drilled and pursued military precision . . . and the victories it would bring at weekend competitions.

Most competitions were in the Los Angeles area, so this meant bands in San Diego County and counties north of Los Angeles put in the extra hours of travel. We met at our dark, cold school at around 4 or 5 A.M., boarded buses and tried not to waste too much energy on silly adolescent diversions during the two-hour trip. As we likely didn't really have the maturity to make this determination ourselves, often we were required to travel at least the last thirty minutes to the parade site in silence. For competitions in our own area we traveled the entire distance from our school to the site in complete silence, then proceeded to change into our uniforms and form up in our pre-parade location also in absolute wordless quiet.

Upon arrival at the parade site, we debarked with our cumbersome busby hat boxes, our shoes and other equipment stowed in airline carry-on bags, and immediately went to the uniform trailer where "band parents" were handing out the freshly cleaned uniforms. We each always had the same uniform assigned to us—tried on at the beginning of the season and tailored if necessary, or else a new uniform assigned. The boys must've presented quite a challenge as their cuffs continually crept up their growing legs and arms and their jackets tightened across the shoulders.

We came from our assigned locker room fully transformed into identical cogs in the band. To complete the elimination of individuality, we each had stuffed our identical, drippy long hair up into the busby hat. The use of an eight-inch segment of nylon stocking allowed us to look as though we'd shaved our heads for each important competition: we drew the segment down over our heads and pulled our long hair through so the nylon loop was around our necks like a discmbodied turtleneck. Then we slowly pulled the nylon up over our faces, allowing it to gather hair as it went, continuing to stretch it until our faces were free again and the nylon tube was being worn on the top of the head like a stocking hat, and it was filled with all of our hair. The busby hat fit neatly on top, successfully androgynizing, or android-izing boy and girl alike. As we came out of the locker room, a band parent handed us a pair of baggies to slip over our white shoes. Another parent handed out the plumes—like small, straight red feather-dusters—which attached to a slot on the sides of the black busby hats.

So, trouser cuffs turned up to protect the black wool from white shoe polish, baggies covering our shoes, our gloves on our left shoulder under the epaulet, we usually had to get back on the buses at this point and be taken to the pre-parade area where a crew of band parents began to unload the instrument cases and line them up beside the buses. As soon as each gleaming instrument was taken from its case by its owner, now with gloves on, the case was loaded back on the bus because the buses would be moving to meet us at the other end of the parade route.

The whistle sounded to form up. To make it easy for 126 people to quickly form a block band the drum major blew the whistle long and steady while lifting his or her baton vertically above his or her head. The trombone rank then quickly formed, nine across, arm's length apart, the center guide directly facing the drum major. We raised our trombones over our heads, holding them by the bottom-most loop of the slide, arms fully extended, so the long instrument was extended upright over our heads. The remaining thirteen ranks could then quickly fall into position, each individual locating his or her file behind the trombonist who was at the head.

During warm-up, while the director led the band through long tones, scales, and soft tonguing exercises to limber our lip, tongue, and diaphragm muscles, a small swarm of band parents made their way through the ranks, armed with shoe polish, lint removers, hair-spray, masking tape, and needle and thread. Those with the shoe polish crouched at the feet of each band member, removed the plastic baggies and touched up the white shoes as necessary. The hair sprayers went head-to-head to plaster any loose wisps up into the hat (also liberally using the long weapon on the opposite end of hairdresser's combs). The others removed specks of lint from uniforms, taped or sewed cuffs that looked too long, tightened buttons, turned trouser cuffs back down, straightened and hooked the high collars under each chin, wiped the last fingerprints off the plastic brim of the busby hat, straightened the angle of the plume as well as the hat's chin strap, and threaded the strap's end through the catch-loop. The angle of the tall busby hats all had to be the same, so several parents would go through the ranks setting hats, jamming them down so the visor came right down over our eyes.

One at a time, on a parade official's cue, like big tractor-trailers the bands pulled out of their warm-up positions and joined the parade. At first more like a traffic jam than a parade, it would be stop-and-go, each stop another opportunity for the director to continue warming us up, rehearsing troublesome sections in the music, or tuning: he would take a tuning fork with him down the center of the band, adjusting the pitch of each instrument to the fork. And every time we stopped, the parents swarmed in again, checking, fixing, polishing, adjusting, jamming hats forward and down.

Each competition *was* a real parade through the streets of a city, including spectators lining the sidewalks. Usually it was exclusively bands—no floats or (god forbid) horses. The competition part of the parade consisted of three zones: first a warm-up zone where the band halted on a line, then stepped off with its full competition fanfare and roll-off and began playing the march exactly as it would later in competition. About halfway through the warm-up area, the band would hit the silent zone—marked with a portable sign—

and had to at that point immediately cut all music and drumbeat and march silently with only the tap of one drumstick on the rim of one drum to set the beat. The purpose of this was to allow whatever band was already being judged in competition, further up the street, optimum conditions for its performance.

The beginning of the competition zone was a solid line painted across the street, also marked with a portable sign. Here, with the front rank of trombonists' toes on the line, the silent band was halted and put into military "at ease," with feet apart, the left hand flat against the small of the back, and instruments in a uniform down position, with just as much precision and unwavering focus of eyes. The band waited, motionless, in this situation until another parade official gave the cue to begin the competition performance. During this last-minute delay, the band parents had their final chance to filter through the ranks, checking for smudges on shoes or untied shoe laces, water spots on the instruments, hair loosened from under hats, or lint on uniforms. Once again problematic hats were jammed down over our brows.

Judging was in four areas: music, marching precision, military inspection, and showmanship. The music and showmanship judges sat at a rostrum midway through the competition zone, the other judges stayed on the street with the band. The podium also held the drum major judges, the twirler judges, and even a judge for identification-unit competition — the girls (never boys) who carried the school's name in front of the band.

On the drum major's signal the performance began: a fanfare followed by percussion roll-off (which usually included cues for the band to come to attention) with a flashy method of popping the instruments into carry position. Then the band stepped off and snapped instruments into play position during an opening flourish by the accessory units — drum major, twirler, and "banderettes" carrying the school's name. This opening was the majority of what the showmanship judge was concerned with. He also noted the overall picture of the band and accessory units, the "entertainment value."

Our step-off was redesigned each year, usually with a trumpet fanfare during which the block band would snap to attention—raising instruments and shouting out the school's name. One particularly effective step-off had two trumpet players set up ahead of the band, ahead of the drum major, standing in place after playing the fanfare until the advancing band engulfed them and they fell into step in their positions. Meanwhile, after the percussion cadence had given cues for popping instruments up to our mouths, the band continued advancing, marching for four steps in sudden absolute silence—not even a drum tap—before the first vibrant note of music came in unison from our horns. An astonishing and potent overture, risking, of course, a nervous or overeager musician miscounting and shattering the four beats of silence with some sort of chicken squawk.

So, after all the fanfare, the band began playing its competition march. The music judge scored the band without watching, often seated with his back to the parade so as to not be swayed by the appearance of the band's performance. Musicality was judged in terms of tempo, intonation, accuracy of instruments playing together, accuracy of technique (playing all the right notes), as well as musical interpretation (not much leeway in a military band playing a march), which included use of dynamics, tone, and phrasing.

To judge marching precision, the marching judge began by falling in step beside the right guide of the front rank. For two years, that was my position. As long as the front rank—the trombonists—stayed in a straight line, that judge would stay beside the right guide. If the front rank stayed straight the whole way through the competition zone, the judge would not even look at the other ranks and the score would be perfect. As soon as the front rank bent or an individual stuck out as slightly in front or slightly behind, the judge dropped back to the second rank and stayed there until that rank was no longer straight. He continued this process until he'd finished all the ranks, then, from the back of the band, checked each file one at a time. Only after finishing with the files would the judge check diagonals. Keeping straight files and diagonals was directly dependent on the front rank—the trombonists—because, instead of following someone, we had to be sure we stayed on an invisible line stretching out directly ahead of us, maintaining the same distance between each individual in the front rank. Without precision in the front rank, files might snake, and there would be no diagonals. So the front rank bore extra responsibility in the marching score. Not only were we crucial for straight files and diagonals, the longer we kept the judge beside the right guide (me), the less time he would have to judge other ranks, files, or diagonals. He could only judge while the band was in the competition zone. I usually had an impression of what kind of marching score we might have, depending on how long I felt that judge lingering beside me through the competition zone.

The awards ceremony was usually held in a high school football stadium. For the granddaddy event at the end of the season, the Long Beach All Western Band Review, the awards ceremony took place in the evening and was held in the sports arena. Each band sat together, some in uniform, some already changed to street clothes but wearing identical jackets or windbreakers. The stadium would rock with spirit contests: one block of kids screaming in unison "*We've got spirit, yes we do, we've got spirit, how about YOU!*" then point as one to another section, a rival band. That band would then be forced to answer with the same chant, trying to make it louder. By the time I was a junior and senior, an arrogant attitude of superiority had taken over our band—we won a lot—and we felt such displays of adolescent giddiness were below us. A rival school would lay down the spirit gauntlet, and we'd stare back mutely, flexing our dignity.

One by one, placements for the classes would be announced. For each class (based on school size) there were placements for drum major, for twirler, for identification units, for the corps (behind the band), and the most important award, for the band itself. After each announcement, the drum major, who would've under most circumstances been a gawky teenager, would majestically march to the podium, do an elaborate salute—involving twirling of the baton or mace—then step forward to receive the trophy.

The two final awards of the ceremony would be sweepstakes trophies, one for a grouping of the three or four smallest classes, the other for a grouping of the three or four largest. Placements were okay, but sweepstakes was the only trophy we truly coveted. We often responded with more of a groan of disappointment than a wild vocal exclamation when our school's name was read for a placement in our class, because a placement meant there would be no sweepstakes trophy. *Not* having our name read for placement could only mean we were either swept out of the placements altogether, or we'd won the big one.

Despite the smugness, the attitude of superiority we'd both earned and allowed to mutate, the next weekend, the same swirl of hot adrenalin would overwhelm me, as I stood on the competition line at attention in dress uniform with my glossy trombone, as my band's front-rank right-guide. The director, who marched beside the right-guide up until the competition zone, would tap my shoulder and disappear from my peripheral vision, and we were on our own to carry out what we'd trained so ardently to do.

WHEN INSTRUMENTAL MUSIC entered my life in fourth grade, I didn't play the trombone. In an effort to create harmony with a violin and clarinet currently being practiced in the bedroom I shared with my sisters, I was guided toward the cello. But long before I entered high school, from my first sight of a marching band coming toward me down a street, my second-grade aspiration to play the "slide trombone" came back to me: I wanted to march in my band's front rank. No girl ever had before me. The second time I marched in the Rose Parade, my senior year, I was right guide of the front rank. Every inch of the seven-mile route was either lined with high overflowing bleachers—like marching down the middle of a narrow football stadium—or, when there were no bleachers, the streets on both sides were packed ten-deep with standing spectators. My trombone slide sometimes barely skimmed past the front row of spectators. I saw them pull their feet back toward the curb and grab their children. They could've reached out and touched me as I floated past on the balls of my feet in spotless white shoes.

PEER GROUPS WERE my parents' focus when directing us into extracurricular activities: chiefly Scouts and music, with only a smattering of sports. While scouting and sports may have been gender quarantining activities, music was not. I don't think, however, my parents realized the whole learning situation that music would provide for us, beyond the noise that came out of our instruments. Marching band, it turns out, was as character-building as my parents would've wanted . . . and less.

Most of us, in adolescence, caused ourselves extra pain due to the kind of social attention we valued and thought would make us important. "You're Nobody 'Till Somebody Loves You"—like us, girls in the fifties and early sixties viewed "love" as the greatest ego-boosting attention they could earn. But in one generation, just what that thing called "love" *was* had shifted to lust. By the mid-seventies, after the Summer of Love, and the images of Woodstock, communes, and flower children, many girls' notions of what would prove their value had been modified. Protecting or preserving one's virtue was no longer part of the game. *Protecting one's virtue.* It *still* sounds like a narrow-minded morality adage from an unenlightened century, especially since "virtue" meant *only* virginity. *Virginity* wasn't what we should've been protecting; it was our dignity that some of us left open for assault, and we were both perpetrator and victim.

In California in the 1970s, although the ERA was floundering, public school dress regulations were dismantled and Title IX mandated equal funding for girls' and boys' athletics. Everywhere there were more doors opening for girls. We were free to do things and try things, but at the same time the sexual attention by which we measured our significance would likely be out of our grasp if we went ahead and did those new things. Even though the social battlefield of the era had (in addition to "free love") stressed "do your own thing," the revision of the traditional adolescent measurement of self-value—from being loved to being sexually desired—seems linked to the steady tearing down of the "no girls allowed" signs. But let me not be misunderstood: The equalization of opportunity was *unspeakably* valuable, requiring no defense. That it caused some confusion in how my breasts fit into the picture when I entered the all-male world of trombone players was an unfortunate side effect. Yes, some of us wanted to do the things boys did, things that girls hadn't been allowed to do, but we still wanted the boys to think of us as special. This created a catch-22. I *was* special to them, but was it in the way I hoped for?

The band didn't need Title IX to ensure equal funding for girls and boys, but Title IX was part of the atmosphere, along with the abrupt abolishing of all dress codes and grooming regulations the year I entered high school. No longer were girls required to only wear skirts or dresses. When a girl did wear a skirt, no longer would the length of her hem be mandated. No longer were boys required to have their hair cut short enough to be off the collar. No longer were there rules banning facial hair. Naturally, we took the freedom as far we could. Levis and corduroys were the daily uniform; with denim workshirts, army fatigues, sweatshirts, flannel shirts, or T-shirts. Shoes were desert boots or wallabies, tennis shoes, sandals made in Mexico from used tires, mountain boots, or Vietnam jungle boots. Dress code freedom that became androgyny was, in part, I think, either a symbol or result of the budding changes in attitude about gender, which even included an experiment in co-ed home economics. Still, it was only the beginning: No longer were girls directed toward typing courses and boys toward science, though I do remember a discussion in my tenth grade social science class where the topic given to us was "Should women work?" In this confused, even unprepared social atmosphere—just on the brink of what became a turbulent gender-equalization struggle—I began playing the trombone.

When I became a trombonist in tenth grade, there was no display of rejection, no dirty tricks to try to chase me away, no ugly harassment for the purpose of warning me that I had entered a domain where I didn't belong. In years since, I've heard accounts of the brutal treatment experienced by women entering certain male fields, intended to make these women give up, quit, and leave the field to its "rightful owners." Yet I was welcomed without guile into the inner sanctum of trombonehood. But not received in the way just any new male recruit was admitted. The difference was subtle. It was almost as though I'd broken up doldrums that had settled there.

Beyond the subtleties of adjusting to a girl in the trombone rank—an adjustment even we were not cognizant was occurring—gender separation in the marching band sometimes seemed to be: band members were "men," auxiliary units were "girls." September is the hottest month in Southern California, and October can offer up some equally warm days. One Saturday we were warming up for a parade with ashes from a nearby backcountry wildfire raining on us like a snow squall. The temperature was close to 100 degrees. "Band parents" buzzed around the all-girl unit of "banderettes," fearing they would faint, squirting water into their mouths from special bottles with crooked-necked spouts, holding umbrellas over them, even patting their necks with damp towels. Their uniforms were little skirts and Spanish-style frilled blouses. Meanwhile *we* were out in the same sun in wool uniforms in the hottest part of the day. I think some girls in the French horn or saxophone section pretended to wilt from heat exhaustion, just to draw attention back to themselves *as* girls. I had no respect for that gesture — if the boys could survive the heavy instruments and wool uniforms, we girls certainly had the same kind of stamina. And my position as a trombonist was one step farther into the "band-equals-men, auxiliary-unit-equals-girls" rearrangement of genders, because trombonists were *always* "men." But I was one of the boys who also had girl parts.

Yet when they accepted me as a trombone player, suddenly they could *not* think of me in the same way they viewed the girls who played clarinet and flute, the saxophonists and cymbal players, the girls who carried the glockenspiel, the baton twirler and "banderettes." What does "one of the boys" really mean? And who was more confused, me or them? They knew I had girl parts, could be teased, could be shown-off to as they did with other girls. But with me in the ranks, they could still spit and swear and grab each other's crotches and make innuendoes about the "banderbutts" who marched twenty feet in front of the band, in plain view of the first rank of trombone players. They showed me how to blow out the saliva that accumulates inside a trombone slide with as much disgusting noise as possible, the "trombone handshake" (a savage goose, best administered from the rear by surprise), and the entire imaginary clubhouse of trombone brotherhood. It had been the only full section in the band, the only full rank that had remained all male up to this point, so their behavior, whether in the band formation or seated indoors in concert set-up, had always been more like a locker room than co-ed classroom. *"Trombones!"* the director would bellow and we would dive behind our music stands laughing after doing the "trombone sneeze" on the back of a saxophonist's head: you vocalize the sound of a sneeze while spraying the unsuspecting head and neck with the spray bottle a trombonist uses to keep the slide lubricated. The victim believes he has caught a juicy sneeze on his neck and hair.

And it must never be presumed the phallic symbolism of that slide escapes the trombonist. The trombone handshake could also be performed using the trombone's slide. The slide, in its different positions, is what makes different pitches come out of the horn. The slide is also used, although infrequently, for glissando — the sound made when the slide is used to slurp from note to note without breaking. This was the motion needed for the trombone handshake, which was offered to the oblivious recipient from the rear. It worked best during warm-up or outdoor music rehearsals when military rigor was dropped and the block band curled about so everyone could see the director. The trombone section could move in behind another group of instrumentalists; a slide was extended as far as possible, the end noiselessly inserted between the knees of someone standing in front (the victim's legs must be slightly spread). Then quickly, silently, the slide was pulled in while the angle of the whole instrument was raised, so as the slide slipped back into place it also zipped along the victim's crotch. Done within ranks — them to me, me to them, them to each other — just as often as to unwitting trumpet or tuba players who forgot to keep their guard up while in the vicinity of the trombone rank. But I never saw them do this to another girl.

In my junior year — after all the boys who had welcomed me to their world had graduated — I was chosen to be trombone section leader. Who was bothering to be politically correct or exercise affirmative action in the seventies? But again, as leader of an all-male section, my instructions were never ignored or ridiculed, no conspiracy of intimidation or mockery ever disrupted a sectional rehearsal. The power had a different kind of consequence. Apparently no alluring creature came from underneath that busby band hat, shaking out her mane of hair.

All of my beloved trombone buddies—each of whom I carried a special flame for—eventually had girlfriends. Girlfriends who played flute or clarinet, French horn or piccolo, or twirled a baton. Girls they could sit beside on long bus trips to out-of-town competitions, girls they could nestle beside in the dark at Disneyland or invite as dates to the annual band banquet. But they also still had me, a trombone-crony, and the girl they, more or less consciously, realized they knew best.

One day after outdoor band rehearsal—as we streamed back into the band room through a narrow corridor that extended from the parking lot where we practiced, behind the auditorium and directly into the indoor rehearsal room—Danny drew me aside. He ushered me through a side door into the dark areas behind the stage, draped with black curtains, each of us still with a trombone in one hand. Before our eyes had adjusted, he hooked an elbow around my neck, his hand hanging down over my chest, and he cupped one breast, squeezing rhythmically.

"I can't do this to Debbie," he said, seriously, calmly, "so I'll practice on you."

He practiced on me almost daily.

These boys had not yet touched their girlfriends' breasts. I was a pal, so they turned to me to rehearse male-female touching. They were relaxed, comfortable, and familiar with me, could be *themselves* with me. And I was flattered. I was touched, in more ways than one. It made me *special* that they could be themselves with me and do things with me that they were too inhibited to do with their girlfriends. I was *important*, more important than their girlfriends. But

I wasn't going to be getting any other attention from them, no movies, no dances, no basketball games, no days at the beach, no . . . what *did* teenagers do for dates in the seventies? I don't know because I never went. *Because* they were free to be themselves with me, I couldn't be a girlfriend.

Naturally it couldn't go on forever with me playing surrogate girlfriend in sexual situations. When I was one year out of high school and Danny and a few others were still seniors, the girlfriends requested they stop fraternizing with me. This was long after breast-squeezing practice sessions had ceased, and, I imagine, after they'd finally put their rehearsals to use and had begun to touch their girlfriends' breasts without a go-between. The threat of losing this privilege was likely enough for them to comply with their girlfriends' wishes. Their acceptance of me turned to a form of rejection.

It was an era when the feminist movement was making us realize we could do things that had been restricted. But it was still before we knew that crossing barriers meant more than just doing the restricted thing itself. The first girl trombone player required being more than a *girl* to know how to handle it. I wasn't a lily-white victim, and the boys weren't lascivious perpetrators. Girls like me made ourselves available for the side effects of misuse and disappointment because having a boy grab a breast *seemed* like a kind of attention that made us important. Since we had been accepted as equals doing a male-only activity, why wasn't that "important" enough?

On retrospect it seems an evolutional time, both in terms of women's progress and in my generation's development into adulthood. These were just *boys*. I eventually learned that there would be men who *would* accept a woman as an equal in his world and still want her for a life partner. Not all adult males would do this, not even a majority; but *men* would. And I sometimes wonder if my trombone-boys finally turned into men.

It was a small, ironic twist of justice that ten years after I first entered the all-male world of trombonists in my high school, when I married, I married a trombonist in the San Diego Symphony. Then a few years after that, the symphony hired *its* first female trombonist—and she sat in the principal chair. I doubt she ever was a girl among trombonists. She was only a trombonist.

EXEMPLARY LIVES

He came of age in the sixties. He had sex with countless females and sired innumerable children. The consummate playboy, but, with a few notable exceptions, he slept home, alone, at night.

She lived the prime of her life in the eighties and nineties. She had a successful career and made a resolute decision not to have children.

He filled his vast quantity of spare time "doing his own thing," expressing his inner needs, fulfilling himself. If asked to perform a duty he hadn't chosen or didn't "relate to," he might disappear for an hour, couldn't be walled in. Yet, on his own terms, he remained fiercely loyal to his family unit.

She doggedly accomplished the necessary tasks of her profession, and the bond formed with her life and career partner was the foundation of her world. She never rejected any assignment her partner asked of her, except motherhood.

Shep lived his contented life among children, sharing their unencumbered and sanguine world—accompanied them on excursions into the undeveloped fields of Spring Valley, chased sticks thrown into the canyons, sang along as they practiced their instruments, attended birthday parties carrying a small plastic football in his mouth. He had plenty of his own time while they were in school to carry on his own pursuits.

Vixen lived with an adult who was confronting the usual goals, disappointments, difficulties, and measures of triumph that adulthood can offer. When Vixen sang along to an instrument, it was played by a professional struggling for promotion. When she carried something in her mouth, it was a specially made dumbbell used in the performance of her career tasks. When she traversed the back country, an adult's knowledge of the dangers of foxtails necessitated asking her to remain on the trail.

Before the proliferation of sexually transmitted diseases, at the height of the sexual revolution, Shep's progeny populated the hill in Spring Valley where he was unneutered and unfenced, left the child rearing to the bitches and never returned to visit.

At a time of less naive views on sexual relations, Vixen refused to give in to the paid-for stud, was impregnated by artificial insemination, then declined to mother her children, choosing instead to return to her life with her human partner.

A SILLY, MANIPULATED analogy, but on a certain level it's worth more than a snicker. Granted, it's not a new idea to view the ways dogs share our lives as more meaningful than dumb unconditional devotion. Just a glance at bookstore pet shelves, now holding more than training manuals, will exhibit the changed attitude: everything from the history of the dog-human bond to the psychology of how dogs love to an explanation of canine social lives. Not that these new dog manifestos are free of their share of nonsense, but their appearance may represent the era that produced them—a time, for aging Boomers, when what we like to do has to be ultimately "profound." So as I search for meaning in my relationship with dogs, I find Shep and Vixen are exemplary of the periods they lived.

SIDEWALKS WERE PRACTICALLY unknown in Spring Valley, California. The county roads might be sided by dirt areas large enough to be sidewalks if they had been paved, houses might be well above or well below the road, with mailboxes mounted on posts on the narrow dirt strip of road shoulder, at the ends of driveways that slope drastically downhill to the house's burrow or uphill to its perch. Many houses were separated by empty space—lots, canyons, hillsides—which supported only the native vegetation, mostly wild oats, tumbleweeds, sage, buckwheat, anise, and a few large bushes called laurel sumac. Residential property might include dirt-floored horse corrals surrounded by small citrus or avocado groves, and modest stucco houses engulfed within overgrown backyards resembling islands of tropical jungle amid the coastal scrub: tall eugenia hedges, huge snarled bougainvillea vines, honeysuckle, and hibiscus. A naturally semi-arid landscape, Spring Valley's trees are immigrants. From our hillside house, the sunset view of the western skyline above Sweetwater Road was a blend of star pine, eucalyptus, and three varieties of palm tree. Trees on people's property ranged from the old olive trees left over from vast tracts of olive ranches to Italian cyprus, magnolia, Brazilian pepper, eucalyptus and palm (three or four varieties of each), and even some deciduous varieties from the East. Lawns varied from a traditional small patch of green to a scrubby place that *would* be a lawn, if it had ever been watered.

Except for the horse corrals, many, if not most, Spring Valley yards forty years ago were unfenced. Here a dog's territory could include not only the owner's property but any extended canyons or fields adjacent to the property. Even in cases where houses had adjoining neighbors, most lots were anywhere from a half acre to several acres, so a dog could forage pretty far before he was in someone *else's* henhouse.

We knew all the dogs on Hartzel Hill, and if we wanted to play with them, we went to their property and called. Our first summer in Spring Valley, someone up the lane had three puppies, which we named Brownie, Blackie, and Whitie. Brownie lived on the hill his whole life and I never found out if that was actually his name. There was Buster, the old Boston terrier, and Blondie, an old cocker-mix, both of whom might come woofing to the edge of their property, then turn back to resume sleeping on the porch. Heidi the dachshund was a particular favorite, as was Penny, another mixed-terrier. And of course, there was our own Shep, a Shetland sheepdog. All of these, and others, lived and roamed unfenced, unleashed, *unaltered*.

I don't remember ever removing Shep's droppings from our lawn. He was free to go to some secret place to do his business; we didn't know where it was, and we didn't wonder—no one complained. When we came home from school, Shep was always on the cool front porch, lying with his back against the house where he created a patch of brown on the white paint. (My mother twice yearly scrubbed the spot clean.) Even when the whole family went away— shopping or to the beach, for an hour or all day—Shep was left outside, and he was always there on the porch when we returned, racing up the driveway to run barking circles around the approaching station wagon, using his herding instinct to guide the car into the garage. He must have been only twenty-five pounds, but my parents never worried that they might squash him under a tire. Free to come and go, to populate the neighborhood and poop where he pleased, to snack on whatever he found, from garbage he would later vomit in the kitchen to snail poison that almost killed him.

The day my parents had taken all five children to go look at a house for sale in Spring Valley on Hartzel Hill, they found not only the homestead they'd imagined for raising their family, but a litter of pups for us to play with while they appraised the house and largely undeveloped property. Our interest in the fuzzy brown pups was even more keen because the dam and sire, both owned by the current residents, were miniature versions of Lassie, our favorite television star. I can't say which deal came first: investing in the house or the dog. My parents decided they would buy the hillside property, and we were endowed with a puppy. On the way home, five of us jostling in the back of the station wagon, taking turns holding him, we named him Shep. Like a good farm dog, Shep was born at the house where he would live out his life.

The reason Shep became part of the family was simple: Kids should have a dog. Maybe there were parental ideals that caring for a pet would teach us responsibility or help us learn to treat others (even another species) with compassion. I can safely vouch that my parents did *not* entertain a single thought of their children learning about "the miracle of birth" nor gaining "our first experience with death" by having a dog.

Not a week after Shep was buried under a grapefruit tree on one of the rock-walled terraces my father had carved into the sloping acreage on Hartzel Hill, I vowed I would someday own, breed, train, and show Shetland sheepdogs. Just "having" dogs wouldn't be enough, for me *or* for the dogs. Although unaware of accolades or accomplishments, dogs need to feel they have a purpose in the pack, a necessary routine, a job.

EARLY IN MY "dog career," I attended a seminar by a big-name trainer. Techniques and philosophies about training have changed so much since then, I barely remember any details from his methods. What I do remember, though, is his prologue: "Lord, Lord, *Lord*," he intoned like a gospel preacher, "All I ask you, Lord, is *don't* let me come back as anyone's second show dog."

He explained, but it was as though he was a psychic delivering a message from *my* second dog, Vixen. A novice's first dog is acquired without education, picked for color or a lower price, chosen because it's the smallest or biggest, the squirmiest, the calmest, or even chosen out of pity. The new "dog person" has either already entertained fantasies of earning prizes through their beloved puppy; or the bewildered new puppy-parent seeks training for a list of difficulties never foreseen, then a class trainer encourages her to compete with her pet. Either way, the competition bug bites, and she's all set to knock the dog show world on its tail with her canine partner who, by virtue of being *hers*, obviously deserves the title of Exalted World Champion. It is at this point she discovers they're actually champions of a whole new world of pitfalls. The dog turns out to be too shy to display its winning personality outside the sanctuary of the backyard. Or the dog lacks some key natural drive: It won't chase or it isn't motivated by food. Or the dog she chose for its color or size has a flawed head shape or ears that flop when they should prick or a tail sailing gaily over its back when it should be a level rudder. Or, through ignorance, the new trainer has already made so many mistakes, she's inadvertently instilled some measure of unwillingness in the dog. This budding dog show competitor will likely do exactly what I did: get a second dog. The second dog carries the burden of hard-learned lessons and new higher expectations.

An opposite scenario is also possible: the first dog was, by raw luck, a perfect windfall. With natural drives and willingness, the dog learns and achieves despite a new trainer's bumbling. The dog seems to have innate knowledge of what is meant by precision and an inborn desire to perform the judged routines. Now the second dog must live up to possibly unattainable criterion.

The second show dog: All they're asked to do is either make up for the first dog's deficiencies or live up to the first dog's excellence. Simple.

Directly after I finished graduate school, I bought my first show dog. I told people (and myself) that I needed a hobby that could provide me with the satisfaction of accomplishment and success while I continued to write and work toward getting my novels published. But my first Shetland sheepdog, "Tara," chosen unwisely for mostly the wrong reasons, quickly revealed that she had some serious stumbling blocks to overcome. Even though I remained determined that Tara *would* go as far as she was capable, I did, with a small measure of new education, locate and purchase another puppy. "Vixen" was intended to carry my highest goals to fruition.

At first, Vixen's purpose was to be a breed specimen, and my goal was a breed championship. I wanted a *champion*. I got one. But not the way I thought.

A breed championship is earned through how well a dog fulfills the official breed standard: a detailed description of each breed's physical makeup. Every year the AKC awards over 10,000 breed championships. In the same span of time, only approximately 100 dogs earn an AKC Obedience Trial Championship. Obedience trials are a separate form of dog competition, having nothing to do with how a dog looks. In obedience trials the dog and handler are striving to live up to a different "picture of perfection"—one of willingness and precision performing a standard set of exercises.

The reason considerably fewer dogs earn the Obedience Trial Championship is simple: It's more difficult. Obedience trials are judged on the uncanine concept of precision. It's a human idea, and it can take years to master.

Precision while working obedience exercises means: Is the dog consistently in heel position with its shoulder in line with the handler's left leg? Is the dog "straight" beside the handler—is the midline of the dog's spine parallel to the midline of the handler's when they're viewed from the rear? And when the dog is sitting in front facing the handler, does the midline of its back line up with the midline of the handler's body, not off to one side, not cocked at an angle? This precision must be maintained while performing such complex exercises as *Scent Discrimination,* where the dog locates one article touched by its handler from a pile of others touched by someone else; *Directed Jumping,* where a dog is sent out away from the handler—and must run in a straight line—until told with one command to stop, turn, and sit, then is directed to return by jumping one of two hurdles, one on a right angle to the dog's right, the other to the left; *Signal Exercise,* where the dog must obey several hand signals without vocal commands from a distance of about thirty feet.

The dog show world is a self-contained place, one that may be invisible to anyone outside it, but nevertheless a big, complex world with its own publications and politics and scandals; moral leaders, self-absorbed stars and upstarts who challenge the established system; seasons and statistics, methods to measure success and year-end rankings. There's even a parallel to political parties with leaders and followers of each; each with their belief-system(s), each hotly criticizing the other(s). In the dog-show world, the AKC is Washington, D.C., regional clubs are states, the ebb and flow of entries is the economy, the improvement of the recognized breeds is the idealized mission. But the only "real world" parallel to the dog-world's system of competition, point-gathering, and rewarding of titles is the education of children, kindergarten through advanced university degrees. But our show dogs aren't learning and earning titles in preparation for any *future* life's work, like becoming a police K9 unit or seeing-eye dog. Their comparatively meaningless dog show accomplishments *are* their lives' work.

Why does this world attract so many? I can only guess at the obvious: These dogs are an extension of us and a mask for our own fragile egos. In fact, not just an extension, they *are* our identities. Perhaps it seems that when our dog "has it all," when our dog succeeds, no one wonders where else in our lives we've failed, where in our characters we're weak.

SOMETIMES WHEN I marvel at the number of miles Vixen must've logged heeling beside my left foot, I also have to marvel at the number of miles Shep put in, herding his flock of five kids and two adults, mostly on high Sierra trails. He led the pack from the front for a while, dropped back to push from the rear, then passed us again at a run.

When my family left Allied Gardens, one of San Diego's older subdivisions, and moved east, out of the city and into unincorporated Spring Valley, we considered it "moving to the country." It was 1963. My new best friend in second grade got *Meet the Beatles* as soon as it came out. One day in November we were sent home from school because the president had been shot. During the funeral, a whole Saturday of cartoons was wiped out. But since we weren't often allowed to watch Saturday cartoons, the funeral meant a Saturday we weren't asked to do our requisite several hours of yard work around our new house "in the country."

Naturally we assumed "living in the country" would include having animals. Our favorite television show was *Lassie*. Lassie lived on a farm—a strange farm with only a few cows and chickens, but we didn't perceive this strangeness. Our new neighbor had a horse that was bred; a year later we ran next door to see the hours-old colt and were allowed to let him suck our fingers. Soon we had our own "livestock"—rabbits in hutches suspended above the ground. My brother named the first buck "Mister Blister." This was a great name, considering our pet-naming history: Ducky the duck and Birdie the parakeet. Even Shep was an unoriginal choice—my sister had just read a book called *Shep: A Shetland Sheepdog*. Later the chickens would collect a variety of stupid names like Whiteness, Chickie, and Little-Red-Hen. But all these animals, with the exception of the parakeet, were productive. They either gave up their meat and hides (ergo their lives) or their eggs. Shep didn't have any sheep or cows to herd, there was no well on the property for him to save us from, he wasn't suited to retrieve game when we hunted. He barked a lot, so it could be argued that he guarded the house, but he protected it from all manner of innocent invasions, from the milkman to the paperboy to the neighbor's cat. While we all watched *Lassie* together on Sunday evenings, we tried to encourage Shep to pay attention so he could become as much of a dog as Lassie was.

Our first summer in Spring Valley, at ages seven, nine, and eleven, before we'd made new friends, my sisters and I took Shep on a hike a mile down the hill to see our new school. The county road snaked the round humps of Hartzel Hill, flanked by dirt shoulders that served as sidewalks. Much like switchback trails in the mountains, one dirt edge of the road often sloped upward—at places a steep embankment—and the opposite road shoulder fell off into a downward sloping grade. Along the way we found colossal eucalyptus with supple dangling branches, inviting us to climb the roadside's higher embankment to grasp the branch then swing out over the road and back again. There were immense century plants, with arm-long thick rubbery leaves tipped by a big single thorn; mini avocado groves where we could find recently dropped avocados in the mulch leaves; even a loquat tree where we could stand just off the street, pluck and eat the small, sweet-mealy fruit, and stay completely shielded from the tree-owner's view.

We reached the bottom of the hill at Bancroft Road, a two-lane street passing through what may've been one of the busier spots in 1963 Spring Valley, with some light industry, a cash register company, mysterious buildings where some kind of welding went on, truck farms and nurseries, and a tiny family-run grocery store on the corner where school kids crowded in to buy penny and nickel candy and ice cream after school. We actually had to ask the man for what we wanted and he would get the item off the rack behind the counter then punch the penny or two-cents or nickel into the cash register. His wife stood by the door to collect dimes from those who had selected ice cream from the single free-standing top-loading freezer.

But we had no money on this exploratory excursion, just a dog tied to a long piece of clothesline. He, by that time, was panting hard, wearing his thick, bushy coat on a summer day. Perhaps he looked bedraggled as well as tired and thirsty. Later, my oldest sister would cup water in her hands for him, from a fountain at the school we'd almost reached, but before we got there a police car pulled slowly to the curb beside us.

Had we been spotted stealing loquat? Picking up avocados? Breaking tree branches or walking on the wrong side of the road? From inside the green-and-white county sheriff car, he asked us where we'd gotten the dog. Instantaneously we began weeping, thinking he was going to take Shep away from us. The three of us crouched on the sandy sidewalk beside the schoolyard fence, surrounding the dog who sat, mortified and confused, as we clutched him and sobbed.

I don't remember how the sheriff disentangled himself from three crying girls on the side of Bancroft Road. I don't even remember how or when I received the explanation: that he was just checking because there'd been an announcement of a lost Shetland sheepdog. He didn't recognize us, our dog was tied to a rude clothesline instead of a leash; he thought perhaps we'd found the dog that day and had incorporated him into our play. I only remember sobbing, more than once, "he's *ours*," and Shep's distressed expression, ears pressed flat, head dipped, eyes softly bulging.

What I came away with was not shame at my instant response of guilt, fear, and hysterics—I'd seen Lassie taken away from Timmy a few times, a popular plot device to allow Lassie to find her way home. But another childish notion took root. In child logic, the sheriff's interest meant this *kind* of dog, this smaller version of Lassie, was an *important* companion. Combined with my romance over Lassie's fame and heroism, it's a likely moment when the dog-show bug first burrowed into me, to wait, dormant, for over a decade. I can only hope, and try to live up to my hope, that my infantile need for attention and esteem did lead, eventually, to a partnership with dogs that's not only challenging and rewarding, but also enlightening.

WHEN I WAS in elementary school, public education experimented with new math, the "open classroom," teaching reading without phonics, and self-directed learning. At this same time, however, dog training was still an undisputed one-method technique born during World War II when dogs were used in combat. For twenty-five years since the war, and for nearly twenty years to come, trainers were basically forcing dogs to perform the desired behaviors. Corrected with force when their behavior was *not* the desired goal, dogs learned to avoid the penalty by behaving in the only way that didn't result in punishment. For example, applied to heeling, the desired behavior is that the dog ambulate beside the trainer's left leg. The heeling dog will turn when the handler turns and stop and sit when the handler stops. In old-style training, the dog would be "forced" to comply with the desired behavior by being put on a leash with either a choke or pinch collar—now respectively called "slip" and "prong" collars. (The change in vocabulary foreshadows the change in training techniques.) As the handler walked and changed directions, whenever the dog went outside the desired heeling location, it was "popped" back into place with a firm yank of the leash. The dog learned that any location other than right beside the handler's leg would result in discomfort to its neck. So the dog discharged the desired behavior, but was apt to perform with compulsion, not with interest, with resignation, not with zeal, in submission, not in partnership.

Liberal, creative techniques flourished in classrooms in the sixties and seventies, but dog training remained a ball-and-chain subjugation, with vestiges of this technique still remaining in the early eighties, when I began training Vixen. By then the subtle distinctions included that she was not on a metal choke chain but a nylon slip collar, and after the "pop," she was then vocally praised and given a treat for performing correctly. I practiced consistency, never letting the undesired behavior go without correction; and diligence, training at least six days a week from the time she was three or four months old. She performed without appearing browbeaten or cowed, without an air of bondage, but also without the zest with which she chased pigeons or played tug-o-war. She was, basically, amiable and wanted to be with me, and that's why she was able to win, and eventually became an Obedience Trial Champion.

Midway through Vixen's career, the burgeoning new techniques took hold in the world of competitive obedience, and, unlike some of those controversial classroom experiments in my elementary-school years, these dog training ideas were a definite breakthrough. But we faced extensive relearning, and considering the importance of early puppy training, this was far more plausible for me than for Vixen.

Modern dog training techniques are based on teaching the dog to think of the trainer as its favorite *play* companion. From an early age, the prospective competition puppy is not allowed to play with other dogs, but fulfills all its play drives with its human training partner. Training begins, almost as early, *as* play. The dog's natural drives to chase, retrieve, and bond in a pack are encouraged as games and developed into the rudiments of the exercises it will perform in competition. So, for example, introducing heeling is no longer the pop, jerk, and drag method. Now, almost as soon as a puppy is comfortable walking on a leash with a buckle collar, heeling is introduced as a game: With pungent food visible over the puppy's head in the handler's left hand, the handler repeats "ready" in a happy, we're-going-to-play-now voice. The puppy, already accustomed to the handler as a source of fun, eagerly looks at the food. The handler begins walking slowly. The puppy's pack instinct causes it to keep pace with the handler, while it continues looking at the food. After just two or three feet, the handler says "get it!" allowing the pup to leap up and take the food or toy. The *game* the puppy learns is: Keep your eye on that reward, the mounting anticipation will be exciting, and soon you'll get to jump and win it. The behavior being developed will eventually become heeling, without resulting in a bullied dog slinking along (or behind) the trainer.

A dog is always eager for something fun to do, and they begin as puppies developing their individual concepts of what's going to be fun. The successfully raised competition dog is one that has come to believe whatever the *trainer* decides to do will always be entirely enjoyable, interesting, and worthwhile. Training this way through more advanced exercises, the dog is constantly eager for whatever its partner chooses to do, instead of being eager to do whatever it has come up with on its own, whether that be digging, sniffing, chasing birds, herding people, foraging, or chewing something to an unrecognizable pulp. The correctly trained dog performs its exercises as though they are what dogs were born to do.

This change in dog-training philosophy, which finally became the norm in the nineties, seems not only vaguely parallel to education experiments in the sixties but also even more similar to a new conception of career preparation in the seventies. Instead of gearing for the traditional (girls as nurses and teachers, boys as doctors and lawyers) or the lucrative (banking, real estate, corporate business), more college students were being encouraged — either directly from advisers or subtly by a more coddling society — to find the activity they were best at, the one that allowed them to *express themselves*, the activity they *enjoyed* doing, and educate themselves in that area, even if it meant there would be few job opportunities or low pay or both. Although the cynical may see this as the road to disaster, providing the world with too many unemployable literature, sociology, art and music majors, the less cynical see more and more people who embrace their life's work as their identity, as something they relish, something they want to do well. Dogs trained properly view their exercises in this same way.

For the sake of brevity I've simplified, and simplification provokes exaggeration. Vixen was not trained entirely by means of force, and current competition dogs are not trained entirely without force. Now before any kind of "force" (physical pressure) is used, a dog is introduced gradually to what will become a correction, is taught what it means and how to accept it. But while Vixen had been brought along through most phases of training with force used only after she understood what she was being corrected for, an important ingredient of the new philosophy had not been manifest in her training: *play*. Her willingness to work with me was loyalty, pure and simple. But *play* was something different. She played boisterous chase with the other two dogs. She played violent tug-o-war on my pant cuff or with a sock. She went berserk for walks. Her attitude during play, unlike during her work, was fervent, excited, and enthusiastic.

Due to the exceptional durability of Vixen's body, it was apparent that she was going to be capable of a long career. Therefore, I wanted to improve her performances by investing as much of the new play-training philosophy into her work as I could. The difficulty: more than half her *play* experience was with dogs instead of me, and no matter how much we try, once a dog has played with other dogs, it's not easy for a person to be as much fun. I wore myself out being happy, joyful, and entertaining. As a trainer, I remade myself. As a competition dog, she was a little better. She continued to trot, jauntily if not passionately, at my side and through her exercises until past her fourteenth birthday, eight years after finishing her Obedience Trial Championship.

But what a different career she could've had if I'd known

enough to teach her, as a puppy, all the various ways to play with her human partner, and therefore that her obedience work *was* play! If only she'd considered obedience exercises the pinnacle of what she craved to be doing with me! She might've been one of the top-ranked Shetland sheepdogs of all time. *She* had no regrets, these are *my* dreams of glory.

It does seem a paradox—to speak of *teaching* a dog to *play*. The truth, I learned, is that not all dogs are born retrieving tennis balls for fun, but most can be taught, as puppies, to delight in, even thrive on this game. And when I fantasize the career Vixen could've had, what I often, maddeningly, remember is Shep—the most zealous play-retriever I could've hoped for or imagined. And no one had to teach him.

He would've done it for hours; he would've done it any*where*—coarse asphalt, rocky hillside, dense weeds, in the midst of a birthday party full of eight-year-olds; he would've done it with any-*thing*—tennis balls, plastic mini-footballs, real baseballs, sticks, even rocks. What Shep wanted to do was chase anything that could be thrown, bring it back, drop it, and bark continuously—eyes moving from the slimy thing to the hurler, and back—until it was picked up and flung again. While we played other games outdoors, cops-'n'-robbers, mud pies, or camp, Shep would be there with something in his mouth, barking barking barking until someone would throw whatever he had, relieving us of the barking for the few seconds it would take him to find it and bring it back. Tangled with foxtails and burrs, scarlet tongue fluttering from the side of his mouth, his canine teeth actually worn down to square tops from years of abrasive tennis balls and rocks, sometimes his pads cracked and bleeding, he simply would not quit. It was what he loved to do best, it was what he *did* best (besides making puppies).

Baby boomers, coming of age, were already changing attitudes toward work and career, from the compulsory obligation one satisfied to feed a family to achieving higher quality of work through the personal fulfillment of loving what one does. Unarguable, isn't it?—the pursuit of that which one enjoys will impel one to continue striving to improve, rather than turn the activity into rote. Our childhood dogs already exemplified this idea even while our parents' generation may have continued to express misgivings, suspicion, even disgust. If Vixen's career, fifteen years after Shep's death, *finally* represents the transition from the former to the latter in dog training, it is only because old trainers foolishly didn't apply *their* desire to enjoy their work to the careers they expected from their dogs. Growing up with a dog who did what he loved and loved what he did makes it seem as though our dogs led the way into the "me generation." Perhaps people, as people will, took the "me" too far. But didn't dogs have it right to begin with?

EVERY SUMMER OUR family vacation was two weeks camping in the eastern Sierra. Rude campsites that were established along the roaring Big Pine Creek cost something like $3 per night. My father clipped an envelope with a check to a post marking our site number. No reservations necessary, we drove up from Big Pine, past the lodge and cabins, up to around a 7,000-foot altitude where we selected a site beside the glacier creek.

Naturally the campsites were not fenced, but we didn't even tie Shep to a tree. Perhaps we were able to do this because, as a Shetland sheepdog, he couldn't be convinced to go voluntarily into the creek, and more important, he didn't have independent foraging in his makeup (except when it came to bitches), so staying where his family was came naturally to him. Most of the time. Once, without noticing he'd been absent, Shep came back to our campsite with a whole steak. Someone in another site had either put the steak out to thaw or had been keeping the meat fresh in a makeshift icebox kept cool by the icy creek. Still, Shep remained unrestrained at camp—until his perseverance to what he believed he was meant to do was actually detrimental to his physical well-being.

Every year, more than once, we hiked up to where the creek had been dammed into the string of lakes. In fact, it was a major rite of passage when we were considered old enough to make the hike. I still remember my first sight of "First Lake" (its real name) glinting through the trees. Actually it didn't glint, the water was opaque and green, the proper cloudy color for a glacier lake. But while any of us were still too young to hike all the way to the lakes, my parents took turns staying back in camp, or placating (and preparing) us with shorter hikes up the same trail to the falls, later to the meadow, then to a rock cabin (that had been owned by Lon Chaney) halfway to the lakes. When my youngest brother was around two, my mother fashioned a way to carry him in a World War II rucksack that hung off one shoulder—baby backpacks hadn't yet been invented.

Although conflicted about leaving half his pack in the campsite, Shep always accompanied the group hiking all the way up to fish in the lakes. This meant that as my parents took turns staying behind and/or doing shorter hikes with the smaller children, Shep took *several* treks up several thousand feet in altitude, approximately eight to ten miles round-trip on the rocky, sandy John Muir Trail. He might've covered half again the distance that his people hiked because he would double back to the end of the single-file line to make sure the stragglers were keeping up, then quickened his pace to pass each person one by one and take his place at the front again. The hikers wore boots; Shep wore his pads bloody.

So, dressed with children's socks on each foot, Shep bore the indignity of standing on a leash while we watched my dad and my two older sisters set out just before dawn for a family-first-time-ever tour of all seven man-made lakes. After a pancake breakfast in the liquid dawn and licking syrup from each tin plate, the danger that he would attempt to follow the hikers had passed, and Shep was allowed off the leash.

Another year, taking care not to let his feet go raw before the big hike, Shep was allowed to accompany my mother and sisters as they attempted the longest hike in our family history: twenty-two miles round-trip to the Palisade glacier, the southernmost glacier in the Western Hemisphere. This portion of the John Muir Trail—shared with pack mules bringing supplies for cliff climbers or backpackers—switchbacked up hot, dry sides of mountains, looped through aspen meadows, zigzagged back and forth to continuously meet up again with the frigid creek. In places, the creek spread out to flow smooth and quiet among tall stands of trees. Other times it crashed, white and foaming, directly down the rocky side of a mountain. The eastern Sierra is less densely forested than the western side where Yosemite and Kings Canyon are located, but is characterized by its own, more subtle kind of beauty, including abundant sunshine glittering on speckled white granite boulders, dappled light through flickering aspen leaves, the bare sheer Palisade peaks cutting against the blue sky, and the glacier.

They didn't quite make it to the glacier that year, but Shep did the entire twenty-two-mile hike with them. His determination was never diverted to venture off the trail to sniff or chase, he didn't even bother to mark much with urine. He hiked diligently, ever vigilant that everyone stay together, even fell off a narrow board section of the trail into an ice-crusted swamp while attempting his distinctive back-to-front passing of the single-file line of people. My mother groaned, perhaps wanting to share a secret smile with Shep, when one of my sisters said, "Well, next summer we'll be a year *older* and will be able to make it all the way." The following year, I joined the expedition to the glacier, but Shep stayed in camp. He had to be tied.

SHEP'S UNRESTRAINED LIFE did not merely happen at camp, but, as much as he was among us as a family member, it was often best to leave Shep (unrestrained) at home. Hunting, beach trips, the county fair, and Girl Scout camp—these were events and activities Shep did not share with us.

In my adulthood, my dogs have accompanied me on numerous trips across the country, both by car and by plane. On one trip, a December cold front dipped into New Mexico and Texas. It was minus-3 degrees and the mini pickup's heater was woefully inadequate. We stopped at a Wal-Mart and bought blankets, then huddled together as we drove, dogs and people sharing the tiny bench seat, wrapped in blankets and under a sleeping bag. My dogs have chased deer in Tennessee; they've waded in Lakes Michigan, Superior, and Huron, in the Mississippi and Illinois Rivers; they've run through the woods in Wisconsin, a tall-grass prairie in Illinois, and patches of cockleburs in Texas and Arkansas. More important, my first three dogs shared or endured every sidetrack, change of direction, and speed bump my life has come upon. Moving across the city or across the country, picketing during a lockout, changing jobs, ending a marriage, surgery, duress, and grief. Are the dogs compassionate or sorry when I'm sick? No. They may be bored or itchy to go play or they may be content to lie beside the bed all day. Vixen would rub catlike against me, leap up and hit my butt with her front paws, and spend all day no farther away than three feet. She would watch my every move from her seat in the car while I filled the gas tank on our cross-country trips or stand up at the window to oversee the filling of the bird feeders. But if I tried to extract compassion—a hug, a kiss—she did not reciprocate. In fact, she might snarl a warning; she did not want to be held tightly or have her face pressed against mine. These human forms of affection were, instinctively to her, an un-called-for display of dominance, even aggression.

ONE OF THE consequences I experienced after entering an all-male venue in high school and becoming "one of the boys" was when my buddies discovered it was easier (on them) to use me to practice touching intimate female body parts before turning to their girlfriends. I should've, therefore, been well practiced myself, but my skewed introduction to sexual relations continued to go wrong. Around the time I was seventeen, when I finally began "dating," dates consisted of a boy taking me home from school or band events, parking before we arrived at my house, and playing out a weird ritual that could've been dubbed "Can You Get Out of *This* One?" In fact, he actually said that to me, on many occasions, as he would devise ways to pin my arms and immobilize my legs so he could touch, squeeze, and grope parts of my anatomy. He actually did articulate his desires as a competition, turning what he wanted us to be doing into a contest pitting us against each other. I don't know if literalizing his desires into a contest was his way of dealing with my unnatural resistance to normal teenage petting, *or* if his method of declaring a rivalry *was* his way of initiating petting, and my resistance to it was natural because it was more like an attack. In fact, less than a decade later, the same event would be redubbed date rape.

The end result for me was not forced intercourse. It never got that far. And I came away from it, each time and eventually altogether, with the belief that my dislike for this activity meant something was wrong with *me,* and that not being able to relax and enjoy it—let alone reciprocate—indicated that I was frigid. This did, I believe, directly manifest into an unhappy sex life in my marriage. A disaster of my own making, a self-fulfilled prophesy.

Given adolescent experiences with sex, it might seem strange that at nineteen years old, when I vowed to get into dog showing, my plan included breeding. In truth, after having bred rabbits in the backyard for many years, part of me probably viewed nonhuman "breeding" in a different domain than the sweaty struggles I was experiencing in cars with boys, encounters I dreaded and loathed but tried to force myself to continue to endure (so I could "learn to like it"). I supposed (or hoped) my sexual failings would eventually be cured with seasoning and experience. Instead, even when experience eventually became marriage, even when I moved from a boy to a man, my anxiety did not abate, and, stranger still, Vixen seemed to be acting out this troubled part of my life.

What was I thinking when I would quip to dog friends, "Tara is a natural breeder, but Vixen just says *no!*"? Is it significant that I was never present for Tara's natural breedings, but went through every frustrating attempt with Vixen until I gave up and subjected her to the indignity of an artificial insemination? And what was I thinking *then*, making a hand-collection of sperm from a stud dog and transferring the sperm via plastic syringe into my dog, the same summer my husband and I were attending five or six sessions of sex therapy until, helplessly, we abandoned that approach too, and left the therapist pretending to be "cured."

But the complex collaboration between my sex life and my dogs began much earlier, long before being scissor-locked and squeezed in a funky-smelling parked car.

WE HAD A little male puppy. I also had two younger brothers. I knew what male genitalia looked like. When I wanted to know something, like what were those big bandage-looking things in the pink boxes mom bought in the toilet-paper aisle, or what did "circumcised" mean, I asked my mother. The sanitary napkin explanation is part of another story, but her definition of circumcision was that when they're born, boys need to have their "pee-pees fixed."

What, I asked, would they look like without being "fixed"?

"They'd look like Sheppy," she answered mildly.

Sheppy? His penis was glued along his stomach. If he was standing upright, it would point toward his chin. So, my understanding was, that when a baby boy was born, he had a web of skin that connected his penis to his stomachs and the doctor had to cut it so that the penis would dangle down.

What I didn't know, of course, was that Shep's visible organ was his foreskin. Shep never "showed his lipstick" around us, never unsheathed the bright red shaft used for breeding. I actually learned about procreation from breeding the rabbits, although in that instance, one never sees the buck's "gonads" (so-called by my father). But I knew about the rear-mount, the rapid agitation, the "fall," which, in rabbits, is the buck's ejaculation—still mounted over the doe, he would seem to fall to his rear with his hind feet flying up toward his head. But I didn't know why I sometimes heard about, perhaps saw in the distance, two dogs "stuck together," tail-to-tail, the way dragonflies and moths did in elementary classroom projects. Shep hid from us the dark secret of his intense sexual drive.

Gradually, as the unfenced bitches in the neighborhood had litters of puppies, the resemblance to Shep grew more and more apparent. Equally hard to ignore were his forays away from home, sometimes overnight, whenever a bitch was in season in about a mile radius, sometimes farther. Once Shep was gone for five days. No Lassie-Come-Home in him, my mother drove the streets of Spring Valley every evening, calling, searching, and asking every child out playing, every adult watering a lawn. Miraculously (and without the aid of the county sheriff), she found him. She arrived home after I'd gone to bed, but the commotion roused me. There he was, his sheepish self, sitting with lowered head and softly bulging eyes as we surrounded him, welcoming him home. He stunk and was a tangled mess. Another time, trying to get at a fenced bitch in a subdivision at the bottom of the hill, he went into the backyard next door and ran back and forth at the fence, tearing up a flower bed, so animal control was called. Shep wore tags, buried in his heavy coat, but it wasn't animal control who called us. Everyone knew who the "Mazza dog" was, so, after being tipped off that Shep was in custody, Mom went to the shelter to get him. There he was, all twenty-five pounds, alone in a cage with a big sign posted on his bars: DANGEROUS DOG. Naturally, he'd bitten the animal control officer.

Most of the time, Shep's home base, his den, was on the cool pavement of the sheltered porch running along the front of our house. One day as I sat beside him, idly rubbing his belly—which he willingly rolled over and exposed for such pleasures—I couldn't help but notice that he had a large knot, about the size of a walnut, bulging in the middle of his penis. My instantaneous fear was cancer. My concept of cancer must've been a little odd because my first response was to rub the lump to see if it would go away. I still remember the look on Shep's face, that same embarrassed, how-do-I-get-out-of-this-one expression he wore when we dressed him in our shorts and T-shirts or wrapped towels around his head to make him the Queen of Sheba. Overall I learned two things. By *now*, of course, I know that you can't rub cancer away. More immediately, I was able to grasp that this particular lump wasn't cancer.

When Shep was thirteen, deaf but still unfenced and unneutered, slowing down a little but still living as he always had, the dachshund up the street, Heidi, came into season. Hartzel Road swung around a blind corner right below Heidi's house, the very place where Shep would cross and climb the embankment to Heidi's property. It was probably a tremendous thump, yet the car didn't even stop. There was no visible mark on his bushy body, but the internal damage must've been enormous to kill him instantly as it did. A neighbor kid recognized him lying just off the asphalt on Hartzel Road on his way to school. Had we not even noticed Shep was missing when we got up and ate our cereal? It was the first day of my second semester of college. I sat with my brothers sobbing around the dining room table, and caught a glimpse of my father carrying the body down the driveway, holding his front legs in one fist and rear legs in the other, Shep hanging upside down. My mother didn't say he died doing one of the things he loved to do, and I didn't even think of it that way until now.

But it wasn't really an activity that he was able to *love*—it was an inherent drive too strong for him to resist, too powerful for me to conceive.

BUT HOW DOES your body *know* you're married?

I remember pondering this question, although I don't remember asking it. My mother must've told me that girls don't have babies until they're married. There was a childless couple up the street; they weren't old like grandparents but weren't very young either. I wondered what had gone wrong; had the woman's body not gotten the message when the wedding march was sending the signal to her "stomach"? I was four or five.

A few years later—at that moment of panic when we clutched Shep in fear that the sheriff would take him away, an instant my ego first paired itself with a dog—I wonder if that concept of the need for a dog in my life planted itself in an empty place that should've been my maternal drive. Or had it been the hot and sticky high school grapplings inside a car, finally getting home with just shreds of nylons clinging to my legs like spiderweb, that doused my natural drives?

My maternal drive has been as absent as girlish fantasies of a wedding. I've heard of young women dreaming of dress styles, maids of honor, the music, the food, the flowers, their glorious day of undivided attention. But I never thought about it, never imagined it, never planned it. When I married, I was completely content to stand in a minister's office on a Thursday evening wearing a brown corduroy skirt, accompanied by my parents, two witnesses, and my groom. He was the one in white—white jeans, the best pants he owned other than the black tuxedo and tailcoat he wore to work as a musician. No flowers, no self-scripted vows, no music. We had banana bread and tea afterward.

Some might've chastised me, saying I spent too much time in reveries over future dog show victories instead of concentrating my efforts, contemplative or otherwise, on the sexual dysfunction that plagued my marriage. But I'd asked myself all those questions too many times. What's wrong with me? Why do apparently millions of people do it, effortlessly, and even with pleasure, and even when they're not supposed to, with partners they shouldn't have pursued . . . yet I alone am incapable? Why is it so easy for everyone else that they have overpopulated the world, have gotten sick and died because of it, have used it to get ahead in their careers, have made it a pastime, a hobby, a pursuit, a calling? What am I doing wrong? Why does it . . . ?

Hurt. It was painful. Something was defective, something flawed. I'd begin to respond to his bids for intimacy not with out-and-out rejection, but ploys: I laughed when he kissed me—presenting him a mouthful of teeth to kiss instead of lips. I prattled, silly talk, when he attempted cuddling, caressing, or fondling. I talked to and patted the dogs when they wandered over to see what we were doing. And I unromantically treated foreplay as a requisite modus operandi, with specified procedures, and called it "getting me ready." After all, that concrete goal *had* to be recognized or the object, regardless of discomfort, would never be realized. The problem was physical. The muscle, which books (like my tattered copy of *Fear of Flying*) had extolled as limber, flexible, versatile, efficient, resilient, and amenable, was instead stubborn, rigid, and went into fits of resistance. By happenstance, a radio medical spot gave me a diagnosis: vaginismus *n.* A painful contractional spasm of the vagina. But it didn't tell me *why*.

Although eager and ardent, my husband was anything but demanding or selfishly relentless. Considerate, gentle, even channeling his impatience into heightened desire, he was tender and slow, and I was sure that with him it would be the way books had told me it should be. But it wasn't. And even finally achieving "success" (which happened without any enjoyable physical sensation that I remember, just brief satisfaction that I'd finally completed the act) didn't make it begin to be easier, less painful, less confusing, less distressing, or allow me to feel less anxious about it. I just kept saying "it'll get better," patting myself on the back when I "accomplished" coitus once a week. Wasn't your body supposed to understand, once you were married? Avoiding my own sexual anxieties and difficulties, I tackled Vixen's.

One generality about the sixties says that wives and mothers were being told, "You can't *want* to be doing this, you've got to go find yourself, express your inner feelings." The message must have gotten through to Vixen in the eighties: when it came to procreation and domestic responsibilities, Vixen simply didn't want to be a wife and mother.

My rationale, deciding in 1988 that Vixen would have a litter—that she had the kind of temperamental stability needed in the breed; that she was well constructed, sturdy, moved fluidly, and jumped effortlessly—will make no difference for those who view all domestic dog breeding as evil. Likewise, my carefully considered reasons had little impact on convincing Vixen herself.

Girls who live together usually menstruate together, and it's no different for dogs; all three of my bitches were in season, in stages about a week apart. On the eleventh or twelfth day of her season, when ovulation was eminent, Vixen began flirting and flagging with the other two bitches in my backyard. Flagging is when a bitch plants her body for a stud's mount, and lifts her tail high and to one side to expose her vulva for him. My bitches would stand

135

beside each other, head-to-tail, flagging simultaneously, each look-ing over her shoulder at the other. So, laughing at what I assumed was her frustration, I thought Vixen would welcome the introduc-tion of the stud dog. But Vixen's enticing flirtations stopped as soon as the stud dog made any move to mount her. She snarled, she snapped, she whirled to face him. We tried tying her, muzzling her, two people holding her on each side. The strength and will of her twenty-pound body was astonishing, and she thwarted every attempt. The stud dog was exhausted.

Vixen was artificially inseminated. This meant a collection taken from the stud, at which point I witnessed, for the second time in my life, the knot that appears in a canine penis when breeding. A collection is made by manually ejaculating the male—that is, mas-turbating him. Then, while still warm, the sperm—collected via rubber funnel into a test tube—was shot by syringe into a semi-flexible hose that had to be inserted gingerly into Vixen's tiny vulva, then carefully threaded six inches into her body. After inject-ing the seminal fluid, I had to hold her on her back, her rear ele-vated on my lap, for twenty minutes. I gave it an extra ten to give the sperm ample opportunity. Even so, when the semen came gush-ing out of her as soon as she stood up, I was sure we'd failed.

While the equally inexperienced owner of the stud wiped our prospective puppies from her kitchen floor, I called an "old-timer," a member of the local Shetland sheepdog club who'd been breed-ing for decades, to ask her what it meant that all the semen had come out of Vixen after the A-I. The woman laughed and said, "Well, it comes out of *you* after you've had sex, doesn't it?"

What could I say? Well, yes, I guess that did happen, back when we . . . before we stopped . . . well, yes, I *could* remember that far back, a year, maybe year-and-a-half. I laughed a little too, thanked her and hung up. I'd been married seven and a half years when I bred Vixen.

The pregnancy itself was uneventful, and by this time in my dog career I'd already whelped three litters with my other two dogs, so felt no anxiety at the approaching due date for Vixen. She began the process by the book: her temperature dropped suddenly, she paced, she turned abruptly to stare at her sides, contractions began to arch her back. But Vixen assumed the cramps meant she needed to make an emergency trip to the yard. Even after several such ventures, during which she defecated and continued to attempt to defecate, she wasn't any more convinced that the contractions were her body's signal it was time to give birth. Perhaps, finally, something in her hormones did signal the truth to her, and once again Vixen just said *No* to motherhood. She halted her contractions. Forty-five minutes passed without any further development. The lives of the puppies were at stake, so I rushed Vixen to the vet where, after a shot to induce labor—on the floor on a blanket— she popped out four beautifully slimy puppies.

The only part of the birth process she did voluntarily, Vixen immediately ate each placenta. Vets speculate that the placenta provides the bitch with needed nutrients, helps the milk "drop," and aids in continuing to deliver immunities to the pups. The placenta also causes loose, mushy stool, which may be nature's way of making defecation a little easier on a female body that's just given birth. Two placentas would've been sufficient for all these benefits, but Vixen would not be denied her rightful claim on the third and forth. We actually had a little tug-of-war with the last one, but her teeth had a better grip on the slime, and it slipped away from me. In three gulps it was down her throat.

If the placentas were supposed to stimulate her maternal hormones, however, it didn't work. Safely home with four less-than-a- half-pound puppies, I assumed too quickly that Vixen would feel a call to nurse them. As family and friends came by to see the litter, each viewing took place with Vixen "proudly" in place beside her brood and the little things suckling. But I had to *put* Vixen there for each visit. A true woman of the eighties, Vixen would've gladly given her children over to day care, and Tara (who'd loved mothering her pups from the moment her water broke) volunteered for the job. Tara began spontaneously lactating and stood gazing hungrily into the whelping box.

Bizzy, Tara's daughter, had also already had a litter, two puppies that had caused her to scream as they emerged. For several hours she had been completely disconcerted by her supposed relationship with these six-ounce blind slugs. When the hours-old pups accidentally pointed their muzzles toward their mother, she responded in the way an alpha bitch does, growing at the witless, helpless newts. But both the concept of and passion for motherhood suddenly arrived within eight hours after the pups were born. The growling stopped, she cleaned them, and rushed to the whelping box if they squealed in alarm or squalled in hunger. I assumed Vixen would make this same transition.

What I was failing to notice was that Vixen was not choosing on her own to go into the box. Three days later I had two very listless puppies, too weak to nurse even when I put Vixen in the box with them. From that point, for nearly three weeks, around the clock every two hours an alarm would sound and I would rouse myself from wherever I was currently resembling a pile of dirty laundry, put Vixen into the box, hold her on her side, hold one of the weakest pups onto the best nipple for ten minutes, then hold the other weak pup for ten minutes, then let the two hardier pups join the meal. Feeding lasted about a half hour, then I had ninety minutes to doze again. Several times a day I smeared the pups with butter to persuade Vixen to lick them. I probably did something else during those three weeks, but it remains in my memory an extended suspension in sleepless haze, swirling with the squeaks and grunts of nursing pups, and the dense, moist smell of the heated whelping box.

Two months after her pups were weaned, when they were settled in their new homes, beginning the play-training that would fulfill their lives with gratifying work, Vixen was spayed. A year later my ailing marriage finished its slow death, without even the formality of an effort to resuscitate it, a union ultimately containing less life-force than either Vixen's resistance toward reproduction or her fierce drive to be with me.

LAND OF MAKE-BELIEVE

First of all, I would be a boy. Second, I'd try a life without parents, without siblings. I'll live in an orphanage with other boys. And we'll each have a pony.

Not a childhood escapist fantasy due to abuse or neglect or substance-addicted caregivers; there was no divorce tearing the family asunder, no "mom's boyfriend" nor "dad's girlfriend," no stepfather nor stepmother to further divide attention and parcel out affection. None of the now-popular afflictions that damage contemporary childhood and give adults more excuses than they should be allowed for their inevitable transgressions.

And the gender switch? Seems natural for a girl in the late sixties, no matter how my parents (without consciously being counter-culture advocates) tried to ignore the imbalance in opportunity for women. Start with the dresses we were forced to wear to school; factor in the patrol *boys* who had the power to stop traffic, the paper-*boys* who had financial independence; the school electives for boys (wood shop) where they created toys for themselves versus the girls' electives (home ec) where we learned to make dinner for phantom husbands. The bottom line: who *wouldn't* rather be a boy?

All societal, cultural, historical factors aside: Around the time my age entered double digits, I entertained myself with a role-playing life in an alternate universe. Not one with spaceships and tentacled aliens. One with boys—boys doing things even *boys* only dreamed of doing.

The boys and I lived on a large compound, with one main lodge and several outpost cabins separated by rolling wilderness, mostly California coastal scrub. Each orphan boy living in this utopian institution, roughly ages eight to twelve, had his own pony. We may have gone to school (those times when I extended the reverie to my own schoolday) but we also were intensely involved in plotting and engaging in a "war" between the individual cabins. Each cabin's residents would be its own militia, with officers and privates, with spies and infantrymen. Our tools of war included BB guns, also issued to each boy in the orphanage, and the taking of prisoners. There were pacts and alliances made, broken, used as fronts for invasion or intelligence-gathering. What this war was supposed to accomplish, I either never decided or have forgotten. It was more like coup counting, besting the opponent at strategy and tactics, earning honor with each display that outdid the enemy—all for the development of our futures as men in the real world.

The boys had names that I kept in a "log book." Some were names of real people, athletes or musicians or actors I liked, or boys' names I would've liked to have. And I was all of them, at one time or another, sometimes scouting territory as the handsome, elusive Clay; sometimes planning strategy as the elegant, natural-leader David; occasionally scrapping it out as the tough runt Gary. The log book—kept discreetly, though not very originally, between my boxspring and mattress—listed the boys under which outpost they belonged to, and included basics about their appearance, what color their ponies were, and kept track of their demerits and honors. Besides doing chores for a self-sustaining orphanage—feeding and watering rabbits, raking the manure pile smooth, weeding under the orange trees—I galloped around on my black or buckskin or

pinto ponies up and down the dirt paths between my father's vegetable gardens, held strategy meetings in the treehouse in the pepper tree, and put prisoners in the cool, musty basement, careful not
to move any of my father's tools or he'd know I'd been there.

This private surrogate life as a boy literalized itself in my "real
world" once, but without the orphanage and the war, without the
ponies and the BB guns. My Girl Scout troop was at district camp
where troops from all over the county gathered for a week, each
troop occupying a campsite, but all troops coming together for flag
ceremonies, softball games, swimming competitions, campfires,
archery, and other activities. I was in seventh grade, the least developed girl in my troop, likely the grubbiest (two eyes peering out of
a smoke-darkened face, mop of short hair never combed, hands seldom washed). My mother was the troop leader, and among her talents as a Girl Scout counselor was her capacity to not give her own
children preferential treatment. This allowed me the same sense of
unchecked spontaneity as the other kids who were away from their
parents for a week. That year, the first time a girl from another
troop asked the inevitable question, the one I frequently heard from
new peers—"are you a girl or a boy?"—I didn't cogitate at all and
answered, "a boy, I'm the leader's son."

So the ruse was set in motion, aided by comrades in my troop:
Through every activity that week at camp, I was *David*. We even
managed to get through swimming class without detection. Each
troop used the pool by itself at an assigned time, so we simply put a
cap on my head and, without my mother's knowledge, everyone
helped make sure I ducked under water if anyone from another
troop walked past the fenced pool area. As soon as my jeans were
back on, I was David again. Girls from other troops started telling
my friends how lucky they were to be able to go camping with a
"cute boy" accompanying their troop. Girls began to show obvious
signs of flirtation when I was around, waiting for me at places where

they knew I would walk past, embarrassing friends by calling out that so-and-so wanted to ask me something, giggling as I went by. Then there was the junior high intrigue where one girl's friend says to one of my friends that so-and-so liked me and wondered if I liked her. Unabashed at our gall, we forged onward, and at the end of the week of camp, the girl with the biggest crush on me was given my address. Letters exchanged between us for the rest of the summer, her big looping girl-writing expressing feelings she would've never been able to admit in person. Finally when she began to express her feelings more ardently, when she began speaking of coming by bus from her part of the county to visit me, I knew the jig was up, and I confessed. The last letter I got from her was, rightfully so, filled with the venomous anger of one who's been duped and humiliated. Understanding her shame, I retreated back to my private and secret land of boys—where my boys were also starting to catch the attention of girls, trying to escape, but eventually succumbing. I must have, once again, been playing all the roles.

BUT I WASN'T crazy. For most mammals, the playful activities of the young are practice for adult behavior. In this case not war, not courtship, not ambition—what *else* could I have been practicing but the adult behavior of a novelist, imagining other lives to explore, living vicariously in personas I created. And, an incidental symmetry, it's interesting how many of my novels' characters *are* orphans.

My living vicariously is now all exercised in the fiction I write. The changeover was both gradual and inevitable when I entered adolescence—when rescue fantasies (played out entirely in my head) fostered and consoled me. Then I finally left puberty behind. With graduate school and a new already-troubled marriage to sustain, focus on my own "real" life became necessary during those times I wasn't creating fiction. But what if, instead of writing fiction, I'd continued to "play" in imagined worlds, in alternate lives:

would I *then* be crazy? Would any new land-of-make-believe, like my boys' orphanage, be similar to the world that my Aunt Marie — permanently institutionalized as a paranoid schizophrenic in 1937 when she was twelve — inhabited by herself?

SCENE #2: IN my early thirties, sitting in a waiting room with my husband, filling out forms before our first sex therapy session. The forms were standard for any new patient to the mental health facility. One question asked, "Have any members of your family sought help for mental or emotional disorders?" My husband just wrote *no*. His family in the South was devout Methodist. If they needed counseling, they would go to church. I recalled my sister having some counseling sessions after her divorce, so I wrote in the little space, *sister, divorce therapy*. Then recalled a cousin who'd abruptly put all his belongings on the lawn with a for-sale sign. *Cousin, nervous breakdown*. The forms were collected and we continued to wait. Then suddenly I gasped, "Oh my god, I forgot to tell them I have an aunt who's been an institutionalized schizophrenic her whole life!"

"I don't think it'll have anything to do with this, Sibyl," he answered mildly.

SCENE #1: IN my early teens, hanging out in Nana and Grandpa's kitchen, too old to use the roller skates we kept in their garage (there were no sidewalks in Spring Valley, so coming to Anaheim where we could skate around the block was exotic), tired of playing cards with my brothers. Today the kitchen would be considered retro-fifties, chic and kitschy, but then it was just a grandparent's outdated but familiar central room where everyone congregated. Yellow Formica tabletop, silver metal edges and metal legs, matching yellow-seated chairs, the kind of vinyl pad with a raised piping outlining the cushion. A freestanding bulky white refrigerator, biscotti in a cookie jar kept on top. Smelling perpetually of olive oil, garlic, and basil, windows often steamy, water running in the sink, pots bubbling on the stove, something being chopped on a cutting board, something else being unwrapped from greasy butcher paper. At least five adults fussing over five different antipasto dishes, no one sitting, hard for an eavesdropping kid to not be in the way. Not that I anticipated anything earth-shattering. But it comes when we least expect it: Whatever brought about the comment is long forgotten, but Nana's voice in the conversational din said, "I thank God all of my children except one turned out right."

Wow, what a scoop. Which aunt or uncle did Nana think hadn't turned out right? Could she mean my dad's brother who, in his thirties, wasn't married and appeared to still live at home, even though when we visited he always found someplace else to sleep? He'd tried to get into the FBI but was colorblind, but now he was principal of an elementary school and also owned a bookstore, wads of cash from the day's receipts on the floor of his Thunderbird. Or did Nana mean the aunt whose only child's father was gone before the baby had turned a year? The toddler had been left with Nana and Grandpa while his mother, my aunt, went to Las Vegas as a showgirl. A few "uncles" had come and gone when I was five or younger; then—a social rebel in her forties in the sixties—my aunt dared to cohabitate premarriage with the man who would become husband number two. She could look at the latest fashion and reconstruct it on a sewing machine, interior decorate a set of rooms so they looked like a lavish honeymoon suite or posh ski lodge, organize and cater extravagant bridge tournaments with smorgasbord refreshment of fried artichoke, cracked crab, cheeses, and Italian salami. Not possible it could be her, but equally impossible that Nana could mean the other aunt, the one whose marriage was seven days old when the war broke out, so her new husband enlisted in the navy while she completed beautician's school. The model postwar wife in still-agricultural Orange County, she worked from her home as a hairdresser, raised three Catholic children; on New Year's Day she always filled her dining room with a banquet—lasagna, ham, scalloped potatoes, honey cakes, broccoli quiche (an early pioneer in California cuisine). And I knew Nana wouldn't be referring to my father, a physics professor who'd had to quit school after ninth grade to help support the depression-crushed family, wartime army officer, sire of five, including the only two boys with the family name.

I waited until we were driving home, the interminable two hours from Anaheim back to Spring Valley, usually mostly after dark. Leaning over the front bench seat from the back, I could see my father's fingers tapping silently on the steering wheel in rhythm to the easy-listening station. He stared forward into the swath of his headlights on the freeway and didn't turn when I asked my mother (although the question was for him) what Nana had meant. And my mother answered for my still-silent father: I had another aunt who'd been in the hospital since she was a little girl.

AUNT MARIE HAD lived in a land of her own involuntary making, starting as young as seven or eight years old, possibly even earlier. In fact her birth, to my southern Italian grandparents, may have seemed like the delivery of an angel: dropped among a family featuring black curly hair, deep brown eyes, and smooth olive skin, was a blond, blue-eyed cherub. Her peculiar behavior, however, soon grew further and further from angelic. She was highly intelligent and reveled in going to school. Yet this doesn't seem to jibe with her annoying mannerisms. She "collected things," the family euphemized. Meaning she stole things from around the house and hid them in her dresser drawers. Whenever something was missing—jewelry, silverware, sewing notions, books, rosaries, knick-knacks—Nana said, "Look in Marie's drawer." She also spit, wherever she was, in the house or outside, on a sofa or in the kitchen, she spit on the floor, bedding, or upholstery. "Will you stop spitting?" begged her exasperated older sister, while Nana tried to wipe up Marie's spit markings as quickly as they appeared.

Then Marie starting perceiving sounds no one else could hear. "Who's making that noise?" she demanded, perturbed not so much that no one else heard the disquiet, but that someone was making it just for *her* to hear, a subtle assault on her peace. And for Marie there was a constant lack of serenity, perhaps alleviated only by the distraction of her own brain learning—reading, figuring math problems, taking in information—which is why going to school continued to be feasible until she was thirteen years old.

By that time the family had lost everything, including their pre-depression middle-class status; had uprooted from Brooklyn and moved slowly across the continent, via Texas, to California. Marie drew an imaginary line down the bed she shared with her older sister and prohibited her sister from crossing the border. This wouldn't have seemed so unusual for two girls suddenly sharing a smaller space as they grew older. But Marie was now not only hearing noises unavailable to anyone else, but having conversations with "people" only she could perceive. She never made any friends after the move to California; instead she preferred, more and more, speaking to "those people" over her family, which had grown to include five children, with two siblings born after Marie.

When the family moved from San Pedro to Anaheim in 1937, instead of enrolling Marie in school, Nana took her to the doctor. The doctor called Marie's condition an "adolescent snap" which (he said) sometimes happened to girls just before they got their first menstrual period. The "scientific" term for this diagnosis was *hysterical dementia*. At this point, holding out hope that Marie could get over the "hysterics" associated with a maturing female body, his recommendation was that she be sent to the state mental institution in Camarillo, about seventy-five miles north.

FRANK F. MERRIAM
GOVERNOR OF CALIFORNIA
HARRY LUTGENS   THOS. W. HAGERTY, M.D.
DIRECTOR OF INSTITUTIONS   MEDICAL DIRECTOR AND SUPERINTENDENT

STATE OF CALIFORNIA
DEPARTMENT OF INSTITUTIONS
CAMARILLO STATE HOSPITAL
CAMARILLO, CALIFORNIA

IN REPLY REFER TO FILE NO. 1752

April 19, 1938

Mrs. Anna Mazza
1034 W. 13th Street
San Pedro, Calif

                              Re: Marie Mazza
Dear Madam:

Replying to your letter of April 15, we will say
that your daughter, Marie Mazza, is getting along
very nicely here at this time and is showing interest in things here as well as outside the hospital.
We advise you to leave your daughter in the hospital a while longer. It will be impossible for her
to resume her school work at this time and it would
probably be upsetting to her mentally if she found
that this would not work out. Perhaps she could
start in the next school year without very much
difficulty.
     The patient may have embroidery work if it is a
type of work which does not require a long needle.
No doubt she will write to you as soon as she has an
opportunity. We have certain days for letter writing.

                         Yours very truly,
                         F. D. Garrick, M.D.

149

Some sixty years later, the subject of Marie comes up (because I ask) at a family reunion. While filling plates with smoked oysters and pickled herring, fried artichoke hearts and chopped tomatoes marinating in olive oil, provolone and prosciutto, one aunt— Marie's youngest sibling, who would've been six or seven when Marie went to the hospital—at first blurts out, "Oh, is she still alive?" And then: "Didn't it have something to do with sex, with someone getting fresh with her before she was ready?"

From the doctor's diagnosis to family lore: for sixty years a boy cousin's flirtations held up as the provocation for Marie's schizophrenia.

FRANK F. MERRIAM
GOVERNOR OF CALIFORNIA

HARRY LUTGENS   THOS. W. HAGERTY, M.D.
DIRECTOR OF INSTITUTIONS   MEDICAL DIRECTOR AND SUPERINTENDENT

STATE OF CALIFORNIA
DEPARTMENT OF INSTITUTIONS
CAMARILLO STATE HOSPITAL
CAMARILLO, CALIFORNIA

IN REPLY REFER TO FILE NO. 1752

                              May 26, 1938

Mr. Cris Mazza
1034 W. 13th Street
San Pedro, Calif

                         Re: Marie Mazza

Dear Sir:

We are writing you in regard to your daughter, Marie
Mazza, who is a patient in this hospital.

It may be possible for her to go home at some future
time, but meanwhile we advise that she be operated on
for the purpose of sterilization, inasmuch as the
trials of childbirth are often the cause of mental
disorder and the frequent cause of relapse in case of
those who have recovered from insanity. We are of the
opinion that this operation would greatly enhance her
chances of recovery and, in the event of recovery, do
much toward preventing a relapse of her mental state.

There will be no expense to you in connection with
this operation; we only ask that you please sign the
enclosed permit and return it to us at an early date.

                              Yours very truly,
                              F. D. Garrick, M.D.

Before I could see it, even from the outside, let alone prowl
clichéd spooky hallways or peer out tiny barred windows,
Camarillo State Hospital was closed—in June 1997. After an exten
sive renovation, it will become a new campus in the California
State University system. Too late for Marie to appreciate the irony:
the place where a latent genius' life was consumed will transform
into an institution of higher learning.

BUT ANOTHER HOSPITAL did materialize in my life, complete with
patients who were wards of the state, locked doors (albeit glass ones);
funky-smelling corridors; vague lines of gibberish hurled into the
hallways from institutionally furnished rooms; half-eaten plates of
mass-produced pureed food hardening on stacked brown plastic trays
that sat on a cart in the hall through the slow afternoon; bewildered
visitors rapping tentatively on room doors that are never allowed to
be shut; chattering bossy nurses in squeaky shoes administering meds;
and a grunt-staff of minimum-wage, part-time employees who fed,
washed, changed clothes, made beds, and said goodnight.

151

Summer work was an expectation during my college years. The previous summer I'd put in three months with a fast-food chain, and vowed hamburgers and fries would be my last resort. So as soon as my final exams were completed, I rode my bike up and down Broadway in the village of Lemon Grove and filled out applications for part-time work at a pet shop, an ice-cream emporium, a pizza parlor, a doughnut shop, a fabric store, a mom-and-pop motel. Skipped the bank, post office, beauty salon, Chinese restaurant, lawyers' offices, a few bars, the Catholic church, and flew downhill past the Ace Drive-In — now closed and slated for demolition to make way for a condo development. Then I stopped, breathing hard, and contemplated the convalescent hospital. What was I thinking? That I'll go in there and make a difference in some lonely wretch's life; that I'll break through to an unreachable, misunderstood psychotic and discover the road to treatment; that I'll soothe the pain of being abandoned, of bedsores and boredom? Did I think of my Aunt Marie? No. I thought I would work in the kitchen, washing pots and stirring cauldrons.

Although I didn't recall it when applying for this job, and I didn't remember it during the years I worked in this hospital — I did have previous rest-home experience. In seventh grade, my Girl Scout troop leader (my mother), devised a plan by which we could all earn a community service badge. She contacted the Spring Valley Sanitarium and had them make a list of residents who would benefit from correspondence and companionship. In scout meetings we made cards and crafts, paper flower bouquets, seasonal room decorations, even small lap quilts. We visited the hospital as a troop to sing Christmas carols and camp songs and we were free to write or to stop by as often as we wanted or as often as we could. (Spring Valley was still a sweeping rural region of hills, winding roads, with few sidewalks and no public transportation.)

Likely her hair was white and wispy-thin, her cheeks etched by a lifetime of California's long sunny seasons and sunken by tooth loss, her hands gnarled with bulging joints and delineated with blue-black veins. I don't remember my pen pal's name. Perhaps it was Helen or Sarah, names that would conjure a pioneer woman who'd come to Spring Valley in the late 1800s, to her husband's dry, rocky ranch, where, after failing with cattle and wheat, they hand-tended—using water from the wooden flume that extended from the Cuyamaca Mountains—an acre, two acres, then ten acres of orange and lemon seedlings, until grids of mature trees with thick dark green leaves circulating the sharp scent of citrus, spread every-where over the low, round hills and valleys. Except I didn't know enough to be able imagine the pioneers who'd settled Spring Valley. Plus, Helen or Sarah immediately referred to herself as Grandma.

The roughly 100-bed facility I worked at in Lemon Grove was one story, with three wings extending from a central spine; every hall swathed with synthetic industrial carpet; a plastic-furnished lobby where a receptionist hid behind a tall counter topped with plastic flowers stuck into Styrofoam in a plastic planter box. Outside, patches of yellowish Bermuda lawn were bordered by scrubby bushes, and equipped with a never-used shuffleboard square. As pathetic as the facility was, the assistant hospital admin-istrator, who handled personnel, was dressed in a short, tweed power suit and spike heeled pumps as though she administered a high-rise brokerage.

There were no openings in the kitchen, where most of the employees my age were assigned. I never learned how to make pureed liver or creamed-cheese potatoes. Instead, I was hired as a part-time housekeeper.

The full-time housekeepers cleaned the patients' rooms. Each had assigned wings—including bathrooms situated between every two rooms—which, if worked deliberately, could be finished at the end of an eight-hour shift. My daily duties would be to vacuum the halls, scrub the handrails that lined the walls, and wash the big locked glass doors at the ends of each wing. During my training with one of the full-timers, I learned that housekeepers were not responsible for removing or cleaning meal trays (that was a nurse-aide duty); not responsible for sorting or putting away the laundry that arrived on wheeled racks from the basement (again a nurse-aide chore); and especially not responsible for mopping up human waste or bodily fluids—the latter was the nurses' job, hence also consigned to the nurse-aides. We housekeepers were to inform them if we found a code-yellow or code-brown (no color was reserved for vomit).

Unlike the full-time housekeepers, I was never told I had to purchase a uniform of white nurse dress or nurse smock over (preferably) nurse pants. It was summer, and I wore shorts—boy's Bermuda shorts. The vacuum is a hot machine and I stood for hours rocking back and forth behind its exhaust of warm air. After I was informed by the slick-dressing assistant administrator that bare legs were not proper working attire, an elderly man residing on the private (non Medi-Cal) wing asked why I wasn't wearing shorts anymore. When I told him I'd been told not to, he sighed through his oxygen tubes and said it was too bad, it had brightened his day.

That my efforts were confined to the hallways did not keep me from encountering the patients. At any one time easily half were in the halls: on their way to the dining area, lobby, or the nurses' station (a trip that might take hours), or dispatched in their wheel-chairs into the hall as a morning outing or afternoon excursion, a reason to put on a clean dress or show off a new coiffure. With the industrial-strength vacuum cleaner I moved up the hallway from electrical outlet to outlet, sweeping around their immobilized or barely moving chairs. And, as days progressed, I began to recognize some of them.

Their names, if I was ever told, didn't stick. I knew them only by the names I invented: The help-wanted woman, the several get-out-of-my-way women, various runaways, the suspenders man, the smoking club, paint-by-numbers, bedridden bellowers, sleepers, the chess player and the factory worker.

The help-wanted woman truly wanted help. It was her daily pursuit. She was able to power her wheelchair, most often by holding the hand rails and pulling herself along. Her pace slow, perhaps twenty feet in a hour, but steady. And as she proceeded, she advertised her need, "Help me, please, someone help me."

Only during a first week on the job would an employee have stopped, as I did, to offer assistance. Obligingly, I inquired of the help-wanted woman what kind of help she needed. I assumed she needed to go to the bathroom and required facilitation, which I was not qualified to give. I'm sure if I asked, "Do you need to use the bathroom?" that she replied, "Yes, help me, please, help me." If I'd said, "Do you need tutoring with your algebra homework?" the answer might well have been the same. But, fitting the pattern of most first-week employees, I left my vacuum and wheeled her to the nurses' station and declared that this woman needed assistance, could someone please help her?

"What's the matter, Mary?" (or Agnes or Virginia) the brusque, but not unpleasant, nurse asked in a loud voice. "Are you bothering the housekeepers again?"

"Help me, please, help me."

"You don't need any help right now."

"I don't know where my room is."

"Yes you do. Do you want to wait here for cigarettes or go down and wait for dinner in the dining hall?"

"Just help me, please."

"I'm busy here, Mary, I'll be around with your medicine pretty soon." Finally the nurse looked at me, without raising her head from counting out the afternoon meds into a tray holding tiny paper cups and name cards—just raised her eyes over half-glasses, and, again not unkindly but bluntly she said, "You'll learn. She does this all day."

While I learned to ignore the pleas—the requests to help someone catch a bus, go to the store, have a cigarette, find her room—the get-out-of-my-way women presented a distraction I wasn't asked to sidestep. They could in a moment's notice turn from blurry-eyed dreamers into churlish bullies. Wielding rubber-tipped canes or less obvious weapons like plastic hospital-issue vomit bowls or heavy books from the ratty collection in the rec room, they would attack other patients for infractions such as sitting at the wrong place in the dining hall, pausing a wheelchair to rest too near a hallway intersection, or meeting face-to-face coming in and out a door. Traffic jams typically occurred when a number of patients were on their way to play bingo, listen to records, or make crafts in the rec room, and also around cigarette time at three in the afternoon. With wheelchair footrests tangled in another chair's spokes, invariably someone behind the mess would push on the back of the disabled chairs, even whack the back of the immobilized patient's head.

"Move, move, you're in my way."

"Get out of my seat, that's where I eat."

"That's my sweater, she stole my sweater, give it back."

The best way to handle these situations was to transport each, whether victim or perpetrator, to a far end of a wing. By the time they made their ways back to where they were going, the urgency of the moment, and the animosity, would have dissipated.

The suspenders man was a fellow constantly on the move, ambulatory but always in a slow shuffle, one foot pushing six inches forward on the rug, then the other. Never using the handrails, he kept his hands clasped in front of his body, arms loose, so his enjoined hands formed a little basket just below his crotch. He never seemed to arrive at a destination and he never said anything. Identified by suspenders that he wore because his pants would not stay up without them. Unless the suspenders were pinned to his pants—and fastened to the inside of the waistband where he couldn't get access to the pin—he would drop the trousers down around his ankles and continue walking that way. But only if he'd accidentally wet himself, otherwise he had no quarrel with keeping his pants up.

The paint-by-numbers, bedridden bellowers, and sleepers were all residents who never left their rooms, who might never leave their beds, those whose bodies were hanging on to life, stubbornly breathing, processing food, discharging waste, without consideration to the vanquished person who'd already taken leave. Sleepers had it best—they just slept. Like the first three months of life, the last several months were spent asleep unless someone was there, sitting on the edge of the bed, issuing liquid food past their toothless gums. The bellowers were similar to the sleepers except they were more aware of their hunger, and woke to call out for food—in this way I suppose they were more similar to babies as well. Around four in the afternoon, sometimes earlier, they would start to low like cattle, eyes shut and chins tilted up, mouths open. Patients who painted by numbers took protest to a new level. The numbers were just *one* or *two,* the canvas was the wall closest to their bedside, the medium was their own urine or excrement. Usually these residents had their bodily functions monitored so a nurse or aide could be there on schedule to clean them, and their garments fastened in such a way to eliminate all possible entryways by their hands.

The smokers club were the residents who'd come to the facility still addicted to nicotine. Those who were given cigarettes may not have been the most lucid, but they had to at least be out of bed during the day. Cigarettes were not allowed in rooms, and certainly no one was allowed to have matches or a lighter. So they began arriving at the nurses' station a half hour before the scheduled smoking time. Some were brought in their wheelchairs by aides who were making up the room, others propelled their chairs themselves by one means or another, even hanging onto the back of another chair—the front occupant usually complaining, even turning around to swat at the freeloader. One or two ambulatory smokers stood at the station with an ashtray on the counter. The others sat hunched forward, ashtrays on their laps, rhythmically lifting the burning cigarettes to their pursed mouths, perhaps with slightly shaking hands, then slowly lowering them. Those who couldn't manage the fine-motor skill of holding and lifting a cigarette had their chairs parked in a small gathering around a seated nurse who held an ashtray on her lap or on a tray-table in the circle's center. Each in this smaller group had his or her own cigarette perched around the rim of the single ashtray. The nurse made sure each filter pointed to the cigarette's owner. Each in turn had her cigarette brought to her lips by the nurse. Sometimes the nurse had to lightly smack their hands away if they tried to reach for the burning cigarettes, to get them to their mouths faster or out of turn. At their turns, they leaned forward, withered mouths opened eagerly to receive the tobacco, more eagerly than when they were spoon-fed mashed potatoes, creamed corn, or vanilla pudding. For some, the desire (or need) to smoke was all that was left of who they used to be. I could imagine them as housewives in shirtdresses in the forties—perhaps entering the workplace for the first time during the war years—a burning cigarette always either between manicured fingers, or, besmirched with lipstick, perched on ashtrays kept in easy reach on every end table in their heavy-curtained, doilied living rooms, and at their workstations where they were phone company operators or in a typing pool.

The chess players didn't need to actually play chess. It could be checkers or dominos, anything that retired men might play in the park for pennies or beer or pride. These two patients weren't old. One had been in an auto accident and had head injuries that had caused physical disabilities—spasticity and rigidity—making it impossible for him to care for himself. Often I saw him with a chessboard and pieces on his tray table, waiting for a volunteer or aide on her dinner break or even for his doctor to come and engage him in a game. When he had the chance, he could carry on conversation with precision and acumen, the words slow and thick but the essence more intelligent than the chitchat from most of the aides, housekeepers, or kitchen workers.

The other chess player was on the far end of a fight with muscular dystrophy. He was in his forties or fifties, couldn't speak or propel his chair, his body like a knotted fist, but if he could've held a queen or bishop in his twisted fingers, I knew from his eyes that his mind had the capability to make the moves. Similarly, his eyes registered mortification if his need to use the toilet had gone unnoticed and he soiled or wet himself.

These two men had bedside photos of relatives. They had clean, unragged clothes, even crepe-soled loafers and cardigan sweaters. I imagined the car-accident victim as a boy who'd delivered papers on a Schwinn, perhaps ripened into a war-protesting teenager, grew his hair long, and convinced blushing girls that sex was beautiful. The other patient would've been slowly declining, perhaps his wife forced into a career while he stayed home, disciplining his kids or playing catch from a wheelchair, hiring neighborhood teenagers to mow his lawn until his son was eight or nine and took over.

The factory worker was one of the most intriguing patients because she, more than any other resident, incited our imaginations to speculate about her life. Evidently I wasn't the only one to wonder and theorize, since the conjecture (recited as fact) that she'd been a lifelong factory worker was passed to me by another employee who couldn't remember where she'd learned this information. Everybody just seemed to "know." The reason she was commonly known as someone who'd worked for years in factories was that this elderly, wheel-chaired white woman was the first rap artist any of us ever heard. She spoke rhythmically, the same rhythms over and over, repeating final syllables, but especially her favorites, a combination of *rue* or *row* and a double *coo* or *coe*. Like this: "Hey you-coo-coo, It's time for who-coo-coo, can help, can help, can help, Oh row-coe-coe, hello-coe-coe, what's that, tatta-tat, tatta-tat, oh no-coe-coe, I thought you forgot-tot-tot, I need to *go*-coe-coe, rue-coo-coo, rue-coo-coo. Once I had some-de-dum-de-dum, isn't it time to eat, tatta-teet, tatta-teet?" We would stand outside her door and listen, sometimes asking her a question to get her going again, even bring visitors to marvel at this result of a life span of labor around rat-a-tatting machines.

What, I wonder now, did the aides and caregivers invent as the story of Aunt Marie's life when she sat for hours with her fingers so knotted together, her hands so rigid, that for an aide to separate her hands not only would require the strength available of a male athlete, but would cause severe damage to Marie's joints and tendons in the process? Did they imagine she'd "gone crazy" as a child laborer in a lace-making factory (except for the going-crazy part, that was my grandmother's life); that she'd been a young acolyte in a convent and, with perpetually folded hands, had prayed herself into a mental frenzy from which she had never awakened; or did they somehow trace her clasped hands back to the same "sex too soon" theory? Did it matter that, due to employee attrition and Marie's longevity, no one who helped care for her knew her true story?

AN IRREVERENT, SEEMINGLY insensitive attitude is a necessary aptitude in these places. An employee will either develop it or terminate employment. To think otherwise might paralyze one's ability to administer any service at all. But in shoring up one exposed sensibility, other chinks in our armor became vulnerable. Inventing *pasts* for patients on a downhill slide—with no hope for recovery—seemed harmless enough. The nerve we left exposed came about not when we speculated on pasts but when we invented *futures*.

I was laid off from my housekeeping job near the beginning of August. They could ask a geriatric nurse aide to squeeze in the vacuuming between making beds, feeding, sorting laundry, helping patients onto the toilet, and taking them to the big wheelchair-sized shower stalls. "But," the power-suited assistant administrator apprised me, "we will be hiring new part-time aides for the children's wing soon."

The kids' wing. I sometimes lingered there as I vacuumed, not because I'd ever been drawn to kids, but because the aides were my age, many of them college students. Also because the atmosphere there was without the melancholy sense of nebulous, collective past—unknown pasts, but lives that couldn't be denied to have once thrived, prospered, made plans, chased goals, before beginning the process of slowly dwindling. The ambience on the kid's wing was also made synthetic, a world apart, because of the absence of any suggestion that the patients required even the pretense of adult regard and interaction. The patients there were *not* adults, did not come close to adult or even juvenile cognition. And they had no pasts. They were multiply handicapped, meaning both mentally and physically, to such an extent that even home care had proven impossible. Whether spending time as vegetables who never changed position, or acting out endless repetitions of aberrant behaviors, or attempting—despite spasticity—to be playful as crippled kittens, they were born that way and knew no other life. The days they lived stretched out like a string of identical beads that could be threaded onto a shoestring in any order. Although the occasional visitor often recoiled in horror, believing that debilitating pity was the only appropriate response and would prevent them from being able to work there, those who did work there had another way of dealing with this comprehensive collection of misfortune.

After morning classes at San Diego State University, I spent two hours playing a trombone in the WPA-built Aztec Bowl in cutoffs and a halter top, then got on my bicycle and rode eight miles to Lemon Grove, slipped my smock right over the sweat, and put in a four-hour shift providing basic care for my assigned group of eight kids.

With the same layout of two rooms sharing a bathroom, there were three or four kids per room. Almost every room was equipped with a B&W television that used only rabbit ears for reception. Some rooms had radios, most had at least one colorful poster or cartoon cutout on the wall, plus the occasional handmade chart reminding caregivers of an a patient's special needs. The rooms were crowded with wheelchairs or positioning chairs, beanbag chairs and bolsters, tray tables, nightstands, and, of course, beds. For the bigger kids, the familiar metal hospital beds with fold-down rails; high long-legged cribs for the others. Most beds were equipped with some sort of restraint: The diaper restraint had thick material that passed between the patient's legs then, with long straps, tied to either side of the bed or crib. The vest restraint was the same coarse cotton but worn like a vest with straps tied to the bed. Or the crib-net, a large cotton net that draped entirely over the top of the crib and was tied to all four corners. Those patients not restrained were the least mobile, the deadweight or the nearly brain-dead. Some were tucked in with bolsters to hold them in a particular position—a chart by the bedside reminding the aide which position to use on which night. The hope was that this would forestall bedsores.

The variety of seating apparatus also indicated the variety of physical impairments and deformities. The tilting positioning chairs held the patients with little control of their muscles in a semi-upright position so they could be out of their beds. The beanbags held immobilized patients who were too large for positioning chairs or who, due to extreme spasticity, had contorted bodies that were locked in a position not conducive to sitting—some rigidly straight as a plank, others folded in a permanent fetal position. To use a wheelchair, a patient must be able to independently sit up, that special stepping-stone normal babies master sometime before the end of their first year. So those capable enough sat on wheels, and there they stayed. Depending on their mental or physical deficiencies, they either passed time placidly in the same location, or they worked with one unwieldy arm, just one wheel, so the chair traveled in a half circle, thumping from a wall to a bed. Some let their spines drape over one armrest and dangled like a noodle until a passing aide righted the limp body.

The P.M. shift's routine began at three, getting the kids up from afternoon naps, changing their diapers and positioning them in their seating equipment, changing their beds if wet or soiled, then—before the dinner cart arrived from the kitchen at five—carrying out therapy prescribed in their charts by the nomadic state-employed physical and occupational therapists. The second half of the shift was occupied with feeding the eight kids, then washing, changing diapers, putting on pajamas, and positioning or restraining them in their beds for the night.

The kids ranged in age from a year to twenty, with most clustered between six and thirteen. So, simple tasks, like changing diapers, which we conceivably had done while baby-sitting or helping mothers with younger siblings, took on new dimensions. These were adult feces, all too often in the form of diarrhea, and some of the girls menstruated. The hospital-issue diapers weren't anything like boxed disposables, no scientific breakthroughs for absorbency: They were thick, stiff, unbleached cotton squares. We began our shift waiting for the diaper cart like bargain hunters staking out a store's front door before a sale starts. The minimum we needed was sixteen diapers for two changings, but if we could stock up with twenty or twenty-four, it allowed for accidents, and for some kids to have doubled diapers. There were finger-painters among the kids, so their diapers had to be pinned to their garments, front and back, to prevent hands from sneaking inside.

Vomit was not a particular problem. It was getting the food *down* we struggled with. The meals came either pureed (almost liquid), chopped (more like ground beef), or regular (recognizable slices of carrots, actual string beans, cubes of meat or sliced hotdogs). Those with pureed diets usually had difficulty swallowing, had thick immobile tongues that got in the way and pushed food out, had seemingly nonexistent muscles in their throats or esophagus, and/or had jaws so rigid with spasticity that we could barely get any food past their lips. After each spoonful was discharged into the mouth, the spoon had to remain to catch the majority of the liquid that dribbled back out. Each successive spoonful, now mixed with saliva, was more slimy and difficult to swallow. Some of these pureed-diet kids had their weight charted nightly; their bones were sharp under their translucent bluish skin. The chopped diet was assigned to kids with far better swallowing abilities, but who, for one reason or another, couldn't or wouldn't thoroughly chew their food. This was more like spoon-feeding a baby, often a big baby of fourteen or fifteen. Most regular diets had to be spoon-fed too, although some kids could be trusted to pick up the cubed meat and sliced vegetables with their fingers and put them into their mouths.

The nurse, only one per shift for the kid's wing, prepared and administered the considerable number of meds and, during these rounds, informed us which patients required temps taken (always rectally), and which were constipated. Three days with no bowel movement, and we were required to give an enema. We strategically timed this as our final task of the shift, then securely diapered the recipient and said our goodnights.

Through the P.M. shift we laughed and chattered like girls sharing albums and makeup on a hall of dorm rooms instead of food-encrusted nurse aides washing loose bowel movements down the toilet. We tuned our radios to pop music stations and the televisions to cartoons or the afternoon reruns: *Andy Griffith, Gomer Pyle, I Love Lucy,* and *Leave It to Beaver.* Somehow, somewhere, we found a resiliency in the face of not only malodorous human waste, but masturbating eighteen-year-olds with toddler intellects; fifty-pound ten-year-olds whose only voluntary movements were thick, lolling tongues; eight-year-olds whose eccentric habits included swallowing so much air their bellies bulged like pregnancy or who continually manufactured bubble-filled saliva with which they painted their heads and faces; and little boys whose eyes rolled into their sockets and who ritualistically crashed their heads against walls and crib bars so they had to be perpetually helmeted. Their charts were filled with palsies, disorders, birth defects, and the medical term *idiot.*

Besides the natural youthful sense of immortality, with our futures ahead of us, it was the aforementioned therapy that helped both color our attitudes and skew our perceptions. But even that wouldn't have made an impression if part of our coping mechanism hadn't been a form of pet adoption. Each of us, sooner or later, adopted a kid as our own favorite. These chosen children received the benefits of our taking their laundry home instead of sending their personal items through the hospital system, and we supplemented their wardrobes as much as we could afford on our minimum wages. We brought them posters and stuffed animals. We kept their music boxes wound or made sure they could reach their favorite toys, talked or sang to them while we worked, and grew especially indignant if we found them dirty or wet when we arrived for our shift. We religiously maintained their therapy schedules. And through all this, we essentially invented their personalities and their conceivable futures.

My kid was David. In my first short story in high school creative writing, my character was a cryptically attractive little boy named David who dies mysteriously at camp, leaving his camp counselor with a baffling feeling of emptiness. Without my being aware of what I was doing, this dreadful melodrama was a distorted outgrowth of the David I'd impersonated at camp. Now the David of my fantasies had come back again, this time not me masquerading as a boy, but a real boy, seven years old, who could say three words: ball (pronounced *buh*), hi there (pronounced *I-der*), and mama (pronounced *muh-muh*, and conferred upon anyone who paid attention to him). He could sit up in a wheelchair by himself, but more frequently he was allowed to crawl on his belly on the floor, down the hall or from room to room. That's where he played with his "buh," batting it with a not-fully-proficient hand, then following with an arm-over-arm crawl that resembled a slow, fat lizard more than a puppy. He had long, silky blond curls and a natural blush in his cheeks and lips. He also had a malformed mouth, a slightly protruding tongue that didn't work the way tongues should, and teeth that had come in brownish and askew. One arm was stronger than the other—he would grab handfuls of my hair in such a way that I thought I might have to shave the spot to free myself—and one leg longer than the other. Both legs were twisted like crumpled then restraightened pipecleaners, his feet curled inward, his eyes crossed.

David had a few things most of the other kids didn't: he had a custom-made wheelchair instead of hospital-issue, a mother who visited and did his laundry, and he had braces. Leg braces, foot-to-hip, complete with boots. David's therapy included range-of-motion exercises where (after brief instructions from the therapist) I was to extend and stretch each leg and arm muscle, and maneuver each major joint. This could be painful for him, as muscles on weak sides atrophy, causing tendons to further shrink and "pull in."

On his back on the floormats while we did range-of-motion, he would alternately babble his three words to me, shriek a happy parrot sound, or whimper and cry. I distracted him from pain and frustration by tickling and singing during exercises, usually,

"There was a crooked man who walked a crooked mile
He had a crooked face with a very crooked smile."

Following range-of-motion, David was put into his braces for an hour. The braces locked his legs straight, so his crooked feet faced forward, applying a slow stretch to his calves, hamstrings, and tendons. But this meant no crawling on the floor, so he would scream unhappily, lying on his back on the hallway carpet. Thus he was allowed to have a little board with wheels. He was tied prone to this board with a towel, and, using slightly more effort than for his regular crawling, he was able to roll himself down the hall or across a crowded room, often tangling his scooter-board with tray tables or wheelchairs; then he would squeal in protest, and I would come running. Once I heard his call accompanied by another familiar sound: "Help me! Someone please help!" David was down the hall, his back arched, face tilted up, quizzical crossed-eyes trying to focus on the adult in the wheelchair above him, his good hand patting her shin. The help-wanted woman had gotten lost and found her way to the kids' ward, and now David was blocking her path. "I-der," David said, "muh-muh."

In addition to physical therapy, David was prescribed occupational therapy: toilet training and self-feeding. While I diapered the other kids in my group, David was placed naked on a little potty chair with a bucket underneath. He spent twenty minutes to a half hour on the potty, up to the time his physical therapy started. If I found urine (often enough) or feces (rarely) in the bucket, he was to get a sweet treat, usually a little dish of pudding. For the self-feeding therapy we used a special spoon with a Velcro strap: the spoon was fastened to David's palm, so even if he opened his fingers, he couldn't drop the spoon; therefore he also couldn't fling it, a favorite trick. But even though he was "holding" the spoon, every mouthful had to be scooped and brought to his mouth by an additional hand—mine—cupped around his.

Surely, I interpreted, David must be scheduled for these therapies for a *reason*. Furthermore, unlike many of the kids, David's mother took him home every weekend to visit his family. She took wheelchair, laundry bag, braces, and—good hand batting her head, legs straddling her hip like any normal toddler—David. Someday my happy little puppy-boy would be going home for good, obviously still handicapped, but perhaps sitting in a steadily-getting-larger custom wheelchair at the family table for meals, signaling his mother when to put him on a custom-designed toilet, standing in tailor-made braces—altered each year for his growth—using wall-mounted handrails installed throughout the house, enabling him to ambulate, however slowly, wherever the rails lead. And this, or some version of this, would be possible *because* I gave David my best attentions, providing good basic care to all my charges but adopting him for special treatment, for zealous continuance of his therapy, because he had a conceivable future.

> *Camarillo State Hospital*
> *Camarillo, California*
> *April 17, 1938*

Dear Mother,

Please forgive me for not writing to you more often as they only give you a chance to write every two weeks here, which they call "state day." A woman here gave me that card I sent you because she had so many I suppose. I was wondering why she'd give cards free.

Please don't forget to come and take me home some time next week as I have already missed five weeks of school and I can't afford to miss any more school and will have to make up my school work and I am missing the Auditorium entertainment at Dana. I don't like it here. The hospital may look nice on the outside but inside it smells pretty bad. I don't feel any healthier than I was before I came here because I have nothing to do and it makes me dull and restless.

You said in your last letter that Papa bought me the "Charlie McCarthy" dummy. I was very glad to hear it, and please put it away for me, and don't let anyone touch it or any of the things I left on the sofa which I asked you to put back in my drawer for me.

Time doesn't seem to fly here. As a matter of fact the time is very slow and my eyes get sore from waiting for breakfast, dinner and supper here, which is all I do all day long and which doesn't taste half as good as your home cooked food. Don't forget to save me the newspapers and "Family Circles" and any greeting cards you get and save me some of the palm of Palm Sunday. Please try to come to take me home either April 20th, 21st, 22nd, 23rd, 24th 25th or 26th as I can't afford to miss school next Monday and you said you'd come in a couple of weeks to get me, the last time you came to see me. And I don't want to miss any more Mass.

Love and kisses, your loving daughter,
Marie Mazza

May 1, 1938
Dear Mother,
I wrote in my last letter I couldn't afford to miss any more school and I can't. There's only about three weeks more left of this term and I want to be present for the A-9 party, and want to get my report card marked and want to make up all my missed work and want to be present on graduation day. Every once in a while I hope and pray that you'll come take me home before graduation. You know I wouldn't want to miss graduation for nothing in the whole wide world. You said last time you came that you thought it was good for me to stay here because I could get some recreation, but I'm not getting one bit more recreation than I was before I came here and am not getting any recreation by sitting out in the sun doing nothing, as there is nothing to do. I thought I'd save up my money for a

two-wheeler bike. If I had some friends in the neighborhood we're living in, I'd have reason to go out and play, but in California, soon as you get to be fourteen, playing isn't good enough for you anymore.

I asked you to put away all the things I left on the sofa back in my drawer and don't let anyone touch them. I also asked you to put away my "Charlie McCarthy" dummy and don't let anyone spoil it.

You don't have to ask me to be a good girl 'cause you know I already am a good girl. The reason I got cranky once in a while was because I was touchy and everybody picked on me all the time. So please don't forget to take me home either May 5th, 6th, 7th, 8th, 9th, 10th, 11th, 12th, 13th, 14th or 15th, and no later. I am not enjoying my time here, as there are no girls here about my age, and the nurses are strict and cranky and there are a lot of grownup women here with their troubles and you know how some women stink the place up. That's why I think I'm getting sick here instead of better. I don't know what you mean by better because I'm not sick, and the next time I see you, I'm going to ask what you mean by me getting better.

If you possibly can come to see me before next Thursday, and don't have any excuses. The reason I wanted you to come take me home before next Thursday is that we shower on Thursday and I might have some trouble with my clothes.

Some people wondered and asked me what a little girl like me was doing in a place like this, and I didn't know what to answer them, which convinces me more that I don't belong here. Each time a day goes by I get madder and madder, I get burned up every time I think about Lola being present for graduation and me having the worry that I might miss it. So don't bother answering this letter, but on the day you'd probably answer, save the money that you'd spend for stamps, and put it to the fare you'd have to spend to come take me home before it's too late. So don't forget to choose one of the dates I wrote in this letter or I'll never forgive you. Now no excuses. I can't stand it here and if you don't come see me before it's too late I'll lose my patience. Make Up Your Mind to Take Marie Home.

Your loving daughter,
Marie

May 15, 1938

Dear Mother

I was disappointed to receive a letter from you after I asked you not to answer my letter, but come to take me home instead. You said in your letter that you had to write to the doctor. If he answers that I can't come home for some time yet, don't pay any attention to him, because he'll probably write back to you and say that I can come home just as soon as you take me home. In my last letter I said you could come to take me home on the 5th, 6th, 7th, 8th, 9th, 10th, 11th, 12th, 13th, 14th or 15th of May and all those days have gone by and you still haven't come, and don't bother answering this letter if you can't come to take me home instead. I don't care what the doctor says, you come to take me home. You have a right to take me home because I feel perfectly well, and I wasn't sick before you sent me here, so please come to take me home before it's too late.

Your daughter,
Marie Mazza

June 5, 1938

Dear Mother,

Papa came to see me yesterday. He asked the doctor if I could go home and the doctor said I have to stay here a while longer. It seems silly about you letting them keep me here, the doctor has no real reason for keeping me here and I feel as though I am getting sick from being here, instead of getting well. The way you say well, you'd think I was sick, but I'm not sick and will be very glad to see you when you come so I wish you'd arrange for them to send me home as have been here a pretty long time and staying here isn't doing me any good so please try to get me home as soon as you can, the only thing I care about now is to get home and I don't care about anything else. If I'm left back, you needn't wonder why. It won't matter anyway.

Your loving daughter,
Marie Mazza

P.S. I'll be waiting patiently.

During Marie's first years in Camarillo State Hospital, her family visited at least once a month. Her parents brought along a picnic and Marie's four siblings. To the family, already familiar with Marie's behavior, Marie seemed far more normal than the other residents of the women's barracks, as though she didn't belong in the hospital at all. Bizarrely childlike adults approached visiting families, asking, "Got any candy? Got any cigarettes?" The residents stole each other's belongings, formed conspiracies and broke them, hoarded curious treasures, seemed to know nothing about each other, seemed to know everything, woke suddenly with a shriek from apparent reveries, danced to inaudible be-bop, picked endlessly at their ragged hair or pocked faces, exuded innocence easy to believe, and were impossible to trust.

Marie may have been drugged. She seemed quieter some visits than others. She did, during those first years, ask to be taken home. She always knew her family, never believed they were spies or demons who'd come to hurt her. But she had no friends among the patients, causing her sisters to wonder how Marie acted when the family wasn't visiting, what weird things could she do to these other "crazies" to cause her to have no friends, or did she want no friends other than those only she could still hear talking to her?

On the big lawn that was part of the Camarillo grounds, the family took Marie outside for picnics. Sometimes they took her off the grounds to the beach, until she could no longer be restrained from following men, often at a run, calling out "*Hi!*" They also couldn't take her to restaurants. Her erratic behavior magnified when she was out of the hospital. She might argue loudly with an invisible antagonizer, get up and leave through the kitchen as though she had business there, or ask strangers not to look at her. By this time, even to her family, she seemed to have a vaguely peculiar appearance, an oddity difficult to pin down or describe. Perhaps it was an effect of some drug, perhaps her fellow residents' neurotic behaviors were easy to imitate, perhaps the look in her eyes when she spoke to imaginary friends and enemies was strikingly unlike direct eye contact when one real person speaks to another.

After a few years, Nana decided to take Marie home. None of her strange behaviors were any better, most were worse. She would wander away, talk to the people only she could hear, demand that her sisters or their friends stop staring at her, go into stores and walk out with whatever she chose to take. Finally, for whatever imaginary infraction family members can now only guess at—being touched, being asked to brush her hair, being asked to move aside so Nana could use the kitchen sink—or perhaps for no infraction at all, but connected to those voices and noises she heard, Marie chased Nana out of the kitchen with a butcher knife. Neighbors had to call the police, and Marie went back to the hospital. This time for good. Marie was "committed," became a ward of the State of California.

Nana and Grandpa had never signed the first consent form for Marie to be sterilized. Now, two or three years later, perhaps because her hospitalization was undeniably going to be permanent—or perhaps because she'd officially became a ward of the state—Marie did get that prescribed treatment: she was sterilized. After that, as electric shock had already proved unsuccessful, nothing was done except to use drugs to control her behavior.

Basically warehoused, Marie's days were structured only with meals, bedtimes, and the once-a-month visits from her family. One by one her siblings went to college or got married, served in the war, had children of their own, started careers, and stopped accompanying Nana and Grandpa on their monthly sojourn to Camarillo where they rarely attempted to take Marie on outings away from the hospital. If they did—just to a nearby drive-in to treat her to a milkshake—within an hour Marie requested, "take me back."

I never thought to ask my grandparents about Marie—children in my family were not encouraged to initiate conversations, especially on topics that would be considered adult business. But even when I was in my twenties and Nana, newly widowed, was temporarily living with my parents, I didn't think to ask. I realize now that she might have liked to talk about Marie, especially since during my grandfather's illness and after his death, Nana's visits to Camarillo had slowed to an infrequent interval. She had never learned to drive, so she could now only get there when one of her children had the time to take her.

Nana was the embodiment of that candid unconditional love we seek from pets. Four foot six inches of selflessness. She chuckled softly when Grandpa shouted and criticized as they prepared a meal together, and when her grandchildren corrected her reading as she recited the Sunday comics. She gave us silver dollars and anisette biscotti and let us win at Old Maid and canasta. She sang to us as she rocked whoever still fit on her lap in the rocking chair: *I lost my leg in the army, I found it in the navy, here I come with a rusty gun to shoot the German army.* She, who had killed and eviscerated poultry in her Brooklyn backyard, tried to comfort me in my late teens when a neighborhood dog killed one of my pet hens. And she never (except that once) lamented aloud about her lost child. Every month she would write *Camarillo* on her calendar, on the day she would go again to see her daughter. Through the 1940s, fifties, sixties, seventies, and into the eighties, as Marie turned thirty, forty, fifty, and neared sixty. Each trip to see Marie, Nana must've feared, could be the last.

But no one thought to ask Nana anything about it, from what had happened, to how she'd carried the tacit grief for almost fifty years. Recently my aunt said, "We should've asked Mom about all this." Because now no one remembers or even knew in the first place if Marie had the opportunity to paint, draw, write, sew or knit, listen to music or sing along, mold clay or bake cookies. In her adult life, her family never saw her read or have a book. I'm not rhapsodizing about the "pleasures of life" Marie missed, but speculating on activities she could've learned, something she could've *done*.

By the 1970s, politics had entered Marie's life. Ronald Reagan, governor of California, along with governors all over the country, initiated cutting funds for state mental institutions. One reason given to the public for these cutbacks was the 1950s development of psychotropic medications, enabling some patients to function more normally, therefore allowing them to live (less expensively for the state) in group homes or even in their own apartments. But the economic reasons for the cutbacks, especially those after 1970, were far less oriented to the well-being of the mentally ill patients: There is a federal law, labeled the IMD exclusion, that excludes Medicaid payments for people in institutes for the mentally disabled. What this means for states is that if a person with mental illness is a full-time patient of a mental institution, the federal government will not pay any of the costs of their hospitalization. If, however, those same patients are released from the institutions, the federal government will pay half the cost of their (outpatient) treatment and care. The 1991 "Harvard Mental Heath Letter" notes that "about 250,000 people with schizophrenia and manic-depressive illness are now living in public shelters, on the streets, in jails, and in prisons; only one fourth as many live in state hospitals."

Marie would never have been one of those statistics on the street or in jail. With a large family—growing larger as Marie's nieces and nephews grew up—no one would've allowed her to disappear. But this possibility was never faced. Perhaps because no drug had ever brought about anything resembling lucid adult behavior, perhaps because of the length of her residency at the hospital, perhaps even because of her gender—Marie was one of the more fortunate schizophrenics in Reagan's infamous purging of the mental hospitals. In her fifties, after over thirty years of institutionalization, Marie was transferred to a halfway house. It was not a move that helped her discover independence or identity—at least not healthy independence or identity. She continued to stray on aimless excursions, usually either shoplifting or engaging in sexual activity. The family is not sure if Marie was being raped or willingly entering into sexual intercourse, but the frequency of her sexual encounters was such a problem that it resulted in her repeated deportations back to the mental hospital in Camarillo.

Marie bounced back and forth between halfway houses and Camarillo, group homes and Camarillo, even a private home and Camarillo for the next twenty years until the closing of Camarillo State Hospital meant that her residency at a halfway house had to work. By this time in her seventies and crippled—atrophied from her body's lack of use—Marie was not able to wander away or engage in sex. The last communication between Marie's caregivers and her family concerned her knotted-together hands. Unable to separate her hands, caregivers were incapable of either washing her hands or trimming her fingernails. With the danger that her fingernails would begin gouging into her palms, they wanted permission to cut Marie's hands apart by severing tendons.

AROUND THE SAME time that Marie was bouncing between halfway houses and Camarillo, I was steadfastly performing treatment on David's muscles and tendons and on his social behaviors, toilet training and self-feeding. Because the IMD exemption didn't apply to the profoundly retarded and acutely physically impaired, state-funded treatment continued in the third wing in the small convalescent hospital in Lemon Grove. Every so often we underwent an assessment to determine if there had been sufficient improvement as a result of the therapies. With a significant absence of improvement, a ward would be removed from the ranks of the "worthy" and go back to receiving mere "basic care." In this self-fulfilling cycle, therapy meant funds, funds meant there could be therapy. In the middle of the circle, the kids themselves, and the question: Was the therapy doing any good?

There were always signs of cracks in the system. The most obvious lapse involved a fifteen-year-old boy who weighed a mere forty pounds and was rigidly fixed in a mummylike position. In fact, he more than a little resembled an unwrapped mummy: skin shrunken against bones, hands clenched and arms fixed in a crossed position over his chest, legs with protruding knees extended and unbendable. The only *un*-mummylike characteristics were his head turned sharply to one side, a fleshy pink protruding tongue, and slowly rolling eyeballs. This patient was scheduled for a type of "recreation therapy" that would teach him to turn in the direction of a sound. Much of recreation therapy seemed to be supplying a patient with a range of aural, visual, and tactile stimulation. In some cases the rabbit fur, burlap, and silk we brushed against arms and cheeks, the music boxes and bells, and the bright mechanical mobiles *did* elicit giggles or smiles or groans of pleasure from immobile patients. In the case of the mummy boy, however, there was never a response — and no wonder. His medical chart told me he was blind and deaf.

But these glitches didn't, of course, apply to a kid like David. On my days off I brought David on field trips to my parents' house to see the tree full of colorful hanging birdhouses I'd made from gourds we'd grown on the property; to Spring Valley's Eucalyptus Park that was often empty of other people and had the tallest swingsets I'd seen; and to K-Mart to let him smell the persistent scent of popcorn and to wheel him past the rows of bright toys and clothes. Meanwhile at the hospital during his therapy and bracing schedule, we'd started using a vertical contraption to establish him in a standing position at a table where he could work on his fine motor skills by putting blocks and beads through a hole cut in the plastic lid of a coffee can. That he would rather throw the block across the room suggested to me not defeat, but that David was a boy.

One day when I arrived at work and went immediately, as usual, to find David and make sure the day shift aide had left him in his braces as the schedule required, I found David in the therapy room on the mats receiving range-of-motion therapy from a man dressed as though for the Peace Corps in khaki shorts, boots, and white shirt.

With the confidence of one who has always completed her homework, I inquired, "How's he doing?"

"Oh, pretty good, getting these hams and gams stretched, the ligaments are more difficult, but they're coming along too." He remained kneeling, hovering over David, continuing the range-of-motion exercises on the little pipecleaner legs.

"Yeah, he's tolerating his braces much longer now, we can even do some of his other therapy while he's wearing them."

"So the standing table is working out?"

"Oh yeah, it's been great!"

"Good, I didn't think that would be much of a problem."

Practically breathless by this time, I blurted, "And when will he walk?"

The man stood. David rolled to his belly, slapped the mat with his good hand, swiveled his head to search for his beloved rubber ball. "David won't walk," the man said matter-of-factly. "He hasn't the physical tools nor the mental capacity to learn."

Just one of those head-on collisions when reality shatters the windshield while we're en route to another place we'd thought was just as true. With an I-knew-that shrug and nervous laugh, I picked David up and took him to his room to change his diaper.

Was that moment another chime in the death knell for my maternal instinct? I doubt it, but if so, it wasn't conscious. Still, unlike David's mother—and unlike Nana—when I left employment at the hospital after three years, I never returned to visit.

David was a nine-year-old who still crawled on his belly on the floor, batted a ball and followed it, gaily chirped his three words, screamed for attention and laughed when tickled. Working there, even though there were girl patients as well, was like having my boys' town all over again; I could make up personalities and futures for all of them. But I'd allowed myself to conceive of who they would *become,* instead of, as in the geriatric section, imagining who they had once been. With real people, imagining who they *were* can't be taken away. But inventing who they'll become *can.*

In reality, if he's still alive, David would be somewhere around thirty-five years old, still in diapers, still saying *mama* and *ball* and *hi-there,* still crawling on the floor unless, as an adult long past receiving state-funded therapy, he's been strapped permanently into a wheelchair and has became rigid with spasticity, those hams, gams, and ligaments once again, and even more severely, shrinking and retracting.

IN GRADUATE SCHOOL, I tried, then gave up writing a story enacting the daily life of nurse aides working with profoundly handicapped children. Over the next few yeas, I was able to recapture the geriatric portion of the hospital in my first novel, *How to Leave a Country.* But it was almost two decades after I'd left my part-time job at Lemon Grove Convalescent Hospital before I was able to make effective fiction using my memories of the kids' ward. I gave the starring nurse-aide role to a woman who did not go to college, who had a child as a result of date rape, and subsequently that child she'd never wanted chose to live with her father. So in my alternate reality, while writing the novella, I tried to play the part of an empty-hearted mother filling her own perplexing void with a severely retarted ward of the state. So I did reexperience my reversal from covert sanguinity to skeptic, and made a better story of it by employing a character with a more complex life than mine had been at twenty years old. Some might say that in writing the story, I could've been trying to test myself: asking again, was my care for David the last call of my atrophied (or mummified) maternal instinct? But I still don't think so. He was my pet, and I'd wanted him to accomplish what we were in training to fulfill. It was my grandmother who knew the real despair of a mother whose child's need for help could not be answered with a Charlie McCarthy doll.

Part 2

HOW FAR SHE CAME

SYMPHONY EX, EX-SYMPHONY

In the winter of 1998, the San Diego Symphony was preparing to end a sour silence. A month after releasing a final plan to bankruptcy court, the orchestra would present its first concert in over two years, a ceremonial event to proclaim the reestablishment of a symphony in San Diego, with a new full season set to start in fall 1998. In the two years since filing Chapter 7 liquidation bankruptcy, various groups—from musicians to board members, from patrons to constantly shifting management—had worked, together and separately, to change the bankruptcy to a Chapter 11 reorganization, to save the concert hall and music library from the auction block, to negotiate a labor agreement with the musicians' union, to install a new board of directors, to raise almost $5 million from donors, and to wade through the quicksand of logistical and legal delays that, throughout 1997, repeatedly revised intended dates for the resumption of classical music. At long last the music would resume. When this festivity happened, however, my applause and ovation would be private and from afar. I was a former symphony spouse of that former symphony, and there would be no similar gala event, planned or otherwise, between my musician ex-husband and me to celebrate the end of our secluded silence.

The relationship between city and symphony, between management and artists, and the dissolving of that relationship . . . is it only to me that it's all eerily similar to intimate personal relationships and divorce? Or perhaps an earlier decade of crisis for the San Diego Symphony was so snarled with how my marriage to a musician failed that I tend to personalize the difficulties that performing arts groups have with those closest to them: their cities, their supporters, their patrons, their audiences, their artists.

ONE AT A time, my sisters and I finished our college educations, left the ranch house on Hartzel Hill in Spring Valley, and gravitated to one of the places kids growing up and moving out in San Diego County in the sixties and seventies could afford: North Park, Golden Hill, Normal Heights, or Hillcrest. One sister lived with her husband in a one-room trailer—not a mobile home, a trailer—with a bed at one end, sofa at the other, and table in between the two, nearly touching the tiny sink and stove originally intended for vacation "camping." The other sister rented what must've been a converted chicken coop in Normal Heights. Behind someone's much-larger white clapboard house, right across the street from a cardboard box factory, the thin-walled shack was divided into three rooms: A kitchen big enough for one person to stand and reach the stove, sink, and small counter; living room about the size of most tract housing's smallest bedroom; and bedroom big enough to jam a double bed against two walls, leaving a two-foot-wide aisle around the other two sides. Our abodes were furnished with whatever patched-together or three-times-handed-down furniture we could accumulate, plus the requisite bricks-'n'-boards and wooden grocery crates (which fit record albums perfectly). One plywood chest of drawers started in the Salvation Army in the fifties, then my parents used it in their master bedroom furniture. After that it passed from child to child, until it was moved out with me. It changed color from natural wood to green to phony "antiqued" chestnut to glossy black. My sister made an area rug by collecting unfinished carpet samples and sewing them together like a patchwork quilt. It was fun to piece together the accoutrements of "adult life," and what we managed to scavenge or renovate or build or refurbish, we treasured. The reason our first combined yard sale in Normal Heights was such a flop was that if *we* didn't want something any longer, who would? Few stopped to buy from our junk lined up on the parkway.

My own converted chicken coop was in Golden Hill, again a shack in someone's backyard, an alley running close past the bedroom window. More likely it was an example of quickly assembled World War II military housing that the private sector had provided, seeing the opportunity for patriotism and profit combined. Without insulation, with walls covered in phony wood paneling, of course without an air conditioner nor any kind of heater, the place was torturously hot in summer and nose-chilling cold even in a California winter. I could push nails into some interior walls with my thumb. The windowsills were adorned with old termite trails, worn smooth into fossils. The kitchen floor undulated. The tiled shelf by the sink looked as though it had experienced its own private earthquake. Decorated with wooden crates and bricks-'n'-boards, an old sofa covered with an older bedspread, a desk made from a cast-off dining table leaf stretched across two pieces of what had once been a fifties-era "vanity table," posters on the walls, Ken Cinema schedule on the refrigerator, and plenty of houseplants. Into this hideaway, my new husband and I settled, after spending the first few months of our marriage in a North Park cottage that was above our means: $350 a month when his symphony salary was roughly $360 every other week, while I was still a graduate student. We had one car between us, foraged in thrift shops for cool clothes, did laundry at the Laundromat on 30th street right up the alley, bought groceries at the farmer's market downtown between K and

L Streets. For dining out, there were a few Mexican cafés on 30th Street, or we ventured to City Heights where Nicolossi's and Little Italy offered "Italian Feasts" for $6.

But on weekend evenings, he dressed in white tie and black tails, and we went to the symphony concerts.

IN CHILDHOOD, WHEN I made many rash promises as to what I would someday do—write novels, show dogs, run a chicken ranch—one of the first proclamations I remember is that I would marry a man who wore a black suit and white shirt with a black tie to work. My color scheme was only slightly off. Male symphony musicians do wear black tie with tux coats for Sunday afternoon concerts. But for evening fare, the dress is black tails and white tie. Female musicians don ankle-length black dresses, somewhat plain, usually with long sleeves. Until the twentieth century, women were not allowed to play in most professional orchestras. In fact, in the late 1990s a symphony in Switzerland finally voted to allow women among its musicians. Adding women in long black dresses, however, didn't alter the traditional clothing of the male musician, nor has the advent of tenured contracts, recording residuals, summer music festivals, pops orchestra extravaganzas, or membership in the national musician's union. And it is significant that, for musicians in a majority of professional orchestras, white tie and black tailcoats remain, unquestionably, the appropriate uniform. Evolving from eighteenth-century sportswear (the frock coat or cutaway), black tailcoats became the traditional working attire for nineteenth-century male servants. Butlers, valets, manservants, any male domestic wore black tails. In the eighteenth and early nineteenth centuries, when any respectable family of wealth had as many servants as they could support, musicians hired for parties were also among the servant class. When one had a formal soiree, the musicians playing in the corner were as unnoticed by the guests as the servant with the tray of finger napkins, as unconsidered as the stereo at a contemporary society-page cocktail party. The music was enjoyed, danced to, or talked over without a thought given to the men producing the sound on stringed and woodwind instruments. When women joined orchestras, it would have been in keeping with tradition if they had been garbed in the body-length white aprons over black dresses worn by housemaids.

Subtle (and not-so-subtle) vestiges of the classical musician as servant still remain. A symphony concert is considered "highbrow" entertainment. Lincoln Continentals and BMWs pull up to the parking attendant, a bejeweled matron waits for her door to be opened before stepping out, the master hands his keys to the attendant, the car is whisked away from them while they join the others in glittering formal wear in a plush lobby, sipping champagne until the subtle flicker of the house lights. Then the dull murmur of conversation shifts somewhat, the aristocracy enter the theater, settle into their seats, cough discreetly and applaud graciously—a steady, equitable volume of patting hands without catcalls—as the conductor (also in black tails) comes on stage. The patrons are out for an evening of pleasure and entertainment, while the musicians are, after all, at work.

Echoes of the musician-as-servant also remain in public and governmental, as well as the symphony's own management's, sensibilities—attitudes both general and individual, cognizant and careless. When a city loses its symphony, most of the media spin concerns the city's image: how a major city loses credibility without its own symphony; how businesses seeking to settle in a particular location do consider conditions such as the cultural atmosphere in the city; how quality-of-life ratings include availability of classical music and the health of arts organizations like symphonies, operas, theater, and dance companies. The symphony itself, the very word or idea, is considered an entity, as though it were a historic building, a sewer system, attribute of the landscape, or trolley system, instead of being a collection of people who play instruments. Civic leaders and the general public as well only want to view "a symphony" as a commodity a city must have, like a convention center or ballpark or library. Rarely do editorialists, either professional or amateur, seem to recognize that without the group of musicians, there can be no symphony.

Musicians are people earning their living with a skill they have trained ten or twenty years to actualize, and yet on this level the attitude toward them is also often curiously cavalier. When they unionize, when they collectively hold out for a salary higher than $20,000 for full-time work, the public's commentary is frequently along the lines of "Well, if they don't want to play music, they don't have to," or "Isn't it their hobby to play their instruments?" Or "For gosh sakes, they're just doing a two-hour concert three times a week!" Or "Why don't they agree to play for less, if it will help keep the symphony in San Diego?" Certainly an attitude that still suggests a musician's servitude to a wealthy master.

Even the verb used to describe what they do with their instruments must have some significant background: They *play*. Like professional athletes who have taken games to the level of career, musicians are essentially taking for their livelihood what was—again in the seventeenth and eighteenth and nineteenth centuries—an art learned by young ladies to prove their gentility, to fill their leisure time with enjoyment, to entertain and woo suitors. This seems the opposite of the musician-as-servant, if the gentry themselves were making music. And the gender division complicates the picture (or explains the contradiction): It was an essential part of education for the female children of gentry to play an instrument, usually harpsichord, piano, or harp, and to sing. But the servants who produced music on stringed, woodwind, or (later) brass instruments were all male. Perhaps the word "play" used for creating music on an instrument is more related to music as a leisure-activity tradition, rather than the poorly compensated servants who anonymously sat in a corner cranking out an endless tape-loop of waltz and minuet. And because musicians "play" their instruments, the public asks why they won't provide concerts for less money, and blames the greedy musicians for stopping the music.

When employees of a factory are laid off, we think of their hardship, their struggle to provide for their families; we don't dwell on the clothes or shoes or cars that won't be manufactured. But when classical musicians lose their jobs, those who care enough to respond will often think first of what the city won't have, the smudge on our cultural reputation, and the musical performances we personally will miss out on, rarely giving thought to what will happen to the individual musician. It feels more like our loss than theirs. Perhaps that's in part because when employees of a factory leave their jobs, the factory is still there. But when those men and women in black tails and long dresses get up from their chairs and leave the stage, there's no thing called "orchestra," empty or hollow and waiting to be staffed, left behind. When the people leave, there is no symphony. Like a marriage. So we want to blame someone. It takes a while to turn the pointing finger back toward our own chests.

IT WAS MOSTLY a benign union, not based too much on either passion nor security. We joked that no one would look for security marrying either a musician or a fiction writer. On the passion side there were problems. My problems. Even though with him, for the first time, I'd sustained an adrenalin-thumping euphoria for several months, my body's history of sexual anxiety had not been alleviated by marriage. But we (mostly tacitly) handled our secret difficulty without hostility or rebuke because the ratio between passion and friendship tilted way over toward friendship.

There are moments that represent our marriage more completely than our distressing and eventually sexless bedroom. On at least two occasions—but probably more than that—he sat beside me for hours, holding my hand and reading *Sports Illustrated* while I vomited every twenty minutes. I'm prone to violent and profound motion sickness as well as dizziness and nausea not directly associated with a car, plane, or boat. The first time, I'd just had some minor surgery in a outpatient clinic and afterward was kept on a narrow gurney in an ordinary doctor's exam room because I had reacted badly to the anesthesia. Every time I rose to the surface of consciousness and embraced my hospital-issue U-shaped plastic bowl, I would groan, "Honey . . ." and he would answer mildly, "I'm right here."

Another, earlier, time we were taking a bus from New York, where I was a graduate student, to Nashville to visit my sister. My first ride on a jet the previous August had been a nightmarish six hours of turbulence, vomiting in a middle seat in the center row of five, nausea that lingered for my first four days in New York. So taking a bus to Nashville was my avoidance of a return to that hell. My mistake was in not being certain the bus I chose was an express, which would've stayed on the interstate freeways, a mode of travel I'd learned to cope with. The local Greyhound stopped every hour or so, at gas stations and cafés, along state routes and rural U.S. highways, zigzagging its way south from New York. For twenty-four hours my husband of one year sat beside me with his magazines while I retched and puked.

Most of the time we traveled by car—actually, a mini pickup with aluminum shell. One trip east in December, a cold front extended like a blunt wedge down as far as New Mexico and the panhandle of Texas, the point of the front invading from the north just as we were coming through from the west. The truck's heater a pathetic sham, we stopped at a Wal-Mart and bought blankets. Each of us was wrapped in our coat plus a blanket, but we still had to spread an unzipped sleeping bag across our laps and chests, up to our chins and tucked around our shoulders. We huddled together with the dogs, coats and fur, blankets and sleeping bags. The one driving had towels wrapped around his or her hands. To distract us from the chill, he sang Beatles lyrics in operatic style—each *yeah* and *woooo* in "She Loves You" delivered in a full-throated, classical baritone, and the cracking-up laughter warmed us some.

Unlike the common stereotyped depiction of "egghead" classical musicians, he enjoyed television, and seldom switched to PBS. The TV was almost always turned to sports or sports news while he practiced endless exercises, scales, and etudes meant to strengthen the muscles used to play his trombone. For general watching, he preferred baseball and football games, *Star Trek*, and reruns of *Kung Fu*. His favorite movies were *Star Wars*, *Indiana Jones*, *RoboCop*, and *Terminator*. But in his own life, he didn't crave adventure, special effects nor drama. All he wanted was to earn his living doing what he'd been training for since elementary school, follow his favorite sports, and to share it with a devoted best friend, preferably one he could be married to at the same time. He made no opposition to the other interests dragged into the relationship by his partner, which included dogs instead of children, and baseball. He'd always been a football devotee, and when we met, baseball was something he neither liked nor understood. Within two years, he was one of those walking baseball-statistic encyclopedias, fervently analyzing other teams and what the hometown, always lowly Padres should or could do to beat the odds. Then came 1984.

George Orwell's "futuristic" year was a prosperous one for us, for me, for the Padres, and for the San Diego Symphony. I started the year with a new puppy, the one that would go on to become my first obedience trial champion, dam of champions, and grand-dam of more champions. I found her name in a Gershwin tune the symphony played at a winter pops concert: *Strike Up the Band*. That same year my first novel, while still in manuscript, won the PEN /

191

Nelson Algren Award for fiction. I flew to New York and was courted by agents and editors. No longer living in the converted chicken coop on an alley in Golden Hill, we had moved "up" to a 1.5-bedroom prewar era cottage in Normal Heights with its own converted chicken coop (complete with struggling musician inhabitant) in the backyard. The symphony also moved up: Leaving its status as tenant in the Civic Theater by acquiring a full downtown city block that included the historic Fox Theater. And the San Diego Padres had the best 1984 of all of us, their first batting-title holder, their first division title, their first National League pennant. During the playoffs and World Series, we could hear the clamor of the crowd in Jack Murphy Stadium from our Normal Heights front yard. In a seesawing game four of the playoffs, when the Cubs were ahead, a musician friend from Chicago called for a sportsmanlike posttournament handshake, consoling us with his congratulations on a fine season and his assertion that it had been an exciting series. When Steve Garvey hit his celebrated home run to win game four, doors up and down the block were flung open and people burst into their yards to join the reverberation coming from Mission Valley. The friend did not call back.

But did a mysterious hex caused by Orwell's dire predictions attach itself to many successes garnered in 1984? In the next ten years two players from the '84 champion Padres were dead, bankruptcies and embezzlements plagued others, a starting pitcher lost his arm, and the pennant hero retreated from the public eye in personal disgrace. Meanwhile, after falling $2 million short in renovation fund-raising, the breathtakingly restored Fox Theater (renamed Copley Symphony Hall) and the new Symphony Towers constructed over and around the former vaudeville and movie theater were tilting dangerously close to falling into creditors' hands. My award-winning manuscript, abandoned by the courting agents and editors when they discovered it to be "not commercially viable," searched for a publisher for eight years before being "discovered" by an independent press. In June 1985, while the Padres struggled in vain to repeat a division title, and while musicians sat in the stadium watching a game before their annual postgame symphony concert, one of San Diego's worst wildfires devastated our Normal Heights neighborhood. Our house was not involved, but before leaving for the baseball game, as the flame-whipped wind blew ash down our block, we loaded our truck with manuscripts and the dogs and moved them to a friend's place. Seated in the upper deck of Jack Murphy Stadium, we stood and turned away from the field to see the blackened hillside rising up from Mission Valley, and the houses along the rim with frantic arms of flame reaching from windows and embracing over roofs.

NOT TOO LONG before 1984's advantageous (and, I believe, wise in principle) real estate move by the San Diego Symphony, trouble had already been brewing. In 1981, what seemed at the time the welcome gift of an idyllic three-month summer vacation with my new husband before I would travel 3,000 miles to pursue graduate study, was actually the first time symphony management canceled a portion of a season and left the musicians to get by on unemployment and whatever freelance jobs they could find. So "vacation" was to splurge on potato chips and watermelon (then cut away the hard green skin and use the white rinds in stir fry); to take our kittens on leashes down the block to the canyon that dissects Golden Hill and South Park; to walk up to the North Park business district, get an "energy bar" from the natural foods grocery and browse in Controversial Bookstore; and to listen to the Padres on the radio until a players' strike put a hole in the middle of the season.

The musicians were not on strike, but, like the athletes, it was not *their* fate that was decried by the media—it was the summer entertainment the public was living without. The symphony's sum-

193

mer season had always been a success. Before establishing a permanent summer site near Mission Bay, the summer orchestra had toured the county, playing at stadiums and parks. Families would spread blankets on football fields or park grass, bring portable barbecues and Frisbees, and the symphony would entertain with a light fare of classical music, popular tunes, big band arrangements, Sousa marches, and finale fireworks blockbusters like music from *Star Wars*. Always popularly supported with large audiences, the summer pops concerts were supposed to help financially sustain the symphony's more formal winter season. But similar to baseball owners' assertions, the demand for big-name guest artists began to plague these summer concerts when the fees for guest artists outstripped any profit the symphony could hope to collect from "family rate" entertainment. Appearing with the summer pops symphony were names like Doc Severnson, Benny Goodman, Rosemary Clooney, Roy Clark, and Ethel Merman.

Classical instrumentalists everywhere have chafed under their fate to perform pops in the summer. This would be similar to a publisher agreeing to publish a serious literary novel only if the author also produced a few pulp romances to offset the cost of production for the novel that wouldn't pay for itself. Perhaps that's why that first canceled season in the summer of 1981 did not bring about as much distress to the musicians of the San Diego Symphony as forthcoming cancellations would. Everyone tightened belts and looked forward to a new fall season of substantial music performed in a concert hall without the difficulties of outdoor weather conditions affecting the instruments, fireworks raining ash into the orchestra, children running and laughing during the performance, audiences clapping along but unable to maintain a steady beat, the smoke of wayward barbecues drifting into performers' eyes, the acoustically grotesque necessity for amplification when playing in stadiums, and the awful white dinner coats worn by male musicians instead of tails. One musician celebrated the end of a summer season by setting fire to his white coat while others cheered.

Whiners. Crybabies. Spoiled, snobby, elitist stuffed shirts. The musicians knew this is what the public would say of them if or when word of their disdain for the pops season became public. Accepting the unfortunate necessity, no musician refused to play pops concerts, but the conditions for summer rehearsals and performances often became sticking points in contract negotiations, as musicians wanted the outdoor orchestra stages to be covered to protect them from ash, wanted heaters in the backstage areas for chilly summer nights by the harbor, wanted ear protection for the musicians seated too close to the speaker system, wanted assurances that outdoor daytime rehearsals would not be held when temperatures rose above ninety — this to protect sensitive instruments, not sensitive musicians. For some musicians their instrument is an investment as substantial as a house, and some own instruments in lieu of real estate.

A precursor to major trouble, the canceled summer season of 1981 was the first visible symptom of the symphony's slow decent into what we called "the crisis." While I was in New York in graduate school, symphony management had trouble meeting the payroll in spring 1982. Paychecks came late, paychecks came truncated, paychecks were skipped and promised later. A contract was being negotiated between musicians and management. Was the payroll problem during negotiations a coincidence? By the time I finished school in summer 1983, a new contract was in place and management had found a (temporarily) smoother road for symphony operations. The purchase of the Fox Theater, plans for Symphony Towers, and an agreement with the Port Authority to establish a permanent summer site for the Symphony Pops concerts on Mission Bay were going to usher forth a new era. The new sum-

195

mer site improved conditions for musicians and audience alike, creating a cabaret atmosphere with tables and food-and-beverage service, while continuing to provide family picnic areas as well as bleacher seating and family-rate packages. The fireworks were detonated from the tip of a jetty behind the state—far enough from the now-covered orchestra shell so that burning hair or spontaneous combustion of wooden instruments was no longer an issue.

Then there was the Fox Theater. Some time in the late sixties, my family had come there on one of our rare outings to a first-run movie. The Fox Theater is where I sat agog and watched *Mary Poppins* and thought Dick Van Dyke was the handsomest man in the world. This was also around the same age I vowed to marry a man who wrote a black suit and white shirt to work. So my husband dressed in black tails and went to work at the new symphony hall. Still wrapped, nearly buried, in scaffolding and construction fencing, the interior had been returned to its grand days as a velvet-draped, gold-adorned vaudeville theater, but with newly engineered acoustics.

Once a week after concerts we would join other musicians and spouses (or spouse-musicians) and go to one of downtown's trendy restaurants, Piret's or La Gran Tapa, trooping in with instrument cases and formal wear but largely ignored by other late diners, many of whom were symphony patrons also out for a late dinner after the concert. Rarely if ever did anyone ever come to the musicians' table to offer congratulations on a concert well played. Once again relegated to servant status: the several tables jammed together to accommodate the musicians may as well have been in the kitchen. Our budget allowed my husband and me to share an appetizer, and one glass of wine was enough for the two of us. Sometimes the after-concert event would be a party at one musician's house where the music might be jazz, the food potluck, the conversation anything from sports to politics to children's braces to dogs (ours) to the debate over whether the new CD technology would be better or worse for classical recordings. And the dress was, as always, formal. My husband's tails were purchased secondhand when a tux rental company cleaned out its closet to make room for new styles (likely all those powder-blue tuxedos kids would be wearing to proms in the seventies). By the time I met him, the worn-out lining in his tails coat was hanging in ribbons. Not much of a seamstress, I still dutifully sat one evening and pieced the lining back together by hand, so at least it wouldn't flutter from the bottom of his tails like streamers. A new tailcoat might've cost most of his biweekly paycheck.

IN JANUARY 1985, my third dog, Bizzy, was born into my hands and took her first breath, a literal gasp, clearly relishing her first seconds of life. A week later I began teaching as an adjunct lecturer in the San Diego Community College district. My monthly pay was $600 to $700 for three classes. My husband also played in the San Diego Opera Orchestra, four to six operas per year, each opera production netting $700 to $800 in salary. The reason our budget didn't allow for necessities like new tailcoats or pleasures like each of us ordering an appetizer after a concert, was that we were saving for a down payment on a house. A year after the symphony's real estate purchase and renovation was completed—but still during the construction of Symphony Towers—we bought our two-bedroom house in East San Diego.

It was spring of 1986, just about time for another multiyear contract between musicians and management to be pounded out for the start of the 1986-1987 symphony season. Interesting that the failure to meet the biweekly payroll kept popping up in contract-negotiation years—as it would again in the nineties. In 1986, the payroll failure was announced with an "emergency fund drive." The symphony had to raise several million in donations in three or four weeks or else "the future of the 70-year-old musical institution was in jeopardy" said the typical release from management to the media. The fund drive was immediately center stage on the local classical radio station (which, itself, now no longer exists). Musicians and the music director manned phones and gave interviews.

This emergency fund drive was launched after we'd found our new house and while we were in the process of applying for a mortgage. The cheerful loan officer had indeed heard the news of the symphony's financial distress, but apparently current news about an employer's problems doesn't sway the mortgage process; only our credit report, record of tax filings, and current "status" of employment seemed of interest to her. She did, however, inquire, "Can't you just transfer to Los Angeles or something?" causing us to exchange tired, weak smiles that stood in for outright exasperated sighs. As though "symphony" were a corporation with branch offices in every major city. There would be more, and worse, ignorant or just plain mean-spirited comments from the citizenry of San Diego County.

The emergency fund drive ended—I don't think the goal was met—escrow closed without a hitch and we moved in. The spring season drew to a close and summer pops approached. But no announcement of the winter 1986–1987 season, including guest artists, programs, and special packages, was made by management. Negotiations dragged on. My husband, responding to the general cynicism and pessimism beginning to heat up among the musicians, applied to graduate school at San Diego State University. He only needed course credits to finish a master's degree—started in Boston and abandoned when he'd become a professional—in order to be qualified to teach.

It was a long, hot, tense summer. The deadline for adjunct professors to request summer school classes had passed before the financial crisis had hit, so my income was reduced to collecting on the unemployment insurance I'd contributed to during the academic year. I wrote in the mornings, trained my dogs in the afternoons, worked in my new backyard in the evenings while listening on the radio to the Padres floundering, just two years after their championship season. At the summer concerts, we sometimes arrived early with other musicians, ate sandwiches on the grass behind the stage, then lay on our backs, still listening to Jerry Coleman's tiny voice describing another baseball game from a transistor radio my husband carried in his pocket. Seldom did anyone bring up the contract negotiations or management's silence regarding the fall season. Later, nearing the end of the concert, I would wander back behind the stage by myself, once again lay flat on the grass, and watch the fireworks that were fired off from the tip of the point—so perfectly, amazingly timed with the music, even though each rocket had to be launched seconds or minutes before it splashed in the sky.

The rank-and-file—those musicians not on the negotiating committee—were not privy to what went on during negotiations. The negotiating committee had been advised by the union lawyer not to discuss the details of the negotiation process with the membership. So as far as who said what to whom and the tenor of discussions—raised voices or terse retorts, methods of intimidation and/or passive-aggressive concessions, heated disagreements, or shared jokes or exchanged pleasantries or stern game faces—the majority of musicians hadn't a clue what was going on in the fruitless sessions. The musicians were occasionally called to meet so the committee could report on the status of the negotiations, or if the committee had deemed it was time to bring an offer to the membership for a vote. Meetings like this occurred whether or not the committee itself was satisfied with the offer. It was necessary to update the anxious membership on the progress (or lack thereof) in the negotiation, to show the membership the "best and final" offer currently under discussion or one that had ended talks for the time being.

I was even one more step removed from precious information. Families were not allowed in union meetings. This didn't mean the musicians could not go home and recount contract offers to family members. Thus, thirdhand, I know an essence of the negotiations that the media found too insignificant to report—that, like most contracts, salary was not the only issue, and that management could strive to bury the entire process in an avalanche of minuscule details. In one contract offer, management took the old contract's provision that "every musician shall be provided a suitable locker" and removed the word "suitable." Every indication pointed to management having no intention of bringing these negotiations to a contract, no intention of having a 1986–1987 concert season at all.

This is not to say that salary was not a major issue. But when it comes to salary and compensation, again the public only hears that the musicians are turning down a base salary, and that they want a higher minimum and they want a longer season. The general public, whether symphony patrons or not, will only notice the amount of that minimum wage, for example, $700 a week, and exclaim, "that's plenty for what amounts to part-time work or a hobby!" What these people don't realize is that it's $700 a week *only* for the number of weeks in a season. If the season is thirty weeks, it's a yearly salary of $21,000, for work that's not part time at all when one considers the three or four concerts per week (five in the summer), and three or four rehearsals per week. To this the average citizen replies, "Well, if they don't like the pay, they don't *have* to be musicians."

But it's not really my intention to argue the pros and cons of letting the arts live or die in a free-market system that places value on products according to demand. My interest is the people I used to know, the men and women who sat on stage with reeds in their mouths or bows of horsehair in their hands, clutching chin rests between jaws and collarbones, or emptying spit out of valves, doing what they had trained since childhood to do, supporting their families doing it. And how a history of contention with management can (and did) affect life offstage.

In 1968 a wage dispute with the musicians of the San Diego Symphony brought about a canceled season of concerts. The musicians were demanding more than their $1,500 annual salary. In 1974, musicians again went on strike, then accepted a yearly salary of $4,200. Wages and length of the season grew mightily in the following decade, to approximately $22,000 to $30,000 annual salary, not counting certain highly paid principal players, for a twenty-eight to thirty-six-week season. But then in 1986—months after management had already let pass the usual spring announcement of the 1986–1987 winter concert dates—stalled contract talks with the musicians were blamed for the cancellation of another entire symphony season. The musicians never called for a strike, never even took a strike-authorization vote. They were locked out. With over $2 million in debt, the symphony management had known all along it could not afford to keep the symphony active in 1986–1987. The contract talks with a demonized union—feigned and prolonged since spring, through summer and into the early fall—were a good excuse and a good way to deflect the public's focus from management's debt to the musicians themselves.

The musicians—a rather motley crew except when on stage playing a complex Mahler or Stravinsky—mobilized. There was the phone tree (in pre-email days) to get information out to the membership quickly. There was a fund established by the union from which members could take no-interest emergency loans. There was the picketing committee that prepared and repaired the signs, set up picketing teams, and scheduled the demonstrations. There was the musicians-helping-musicians roster where individuals listed their skills for service or trade to other musicians, from hair cutting to sewing to lawn mowing to handyman to baby-sitting to caretaking of elderly parents. Official word from the union that there was no strike enabled musicians to file unemployment claims. The negotiating committee took on the task of handling media reports. Press conferences and rallies took place on the steps of Symphony Hall, with musicians dressed in full formalwear. Members of visiting ensembles like the Philadelphia Orchestra, booked to use the empty concert hall, joined the San Diego musicians in picketing the theater before their own concerts.

Many musicians were married to nonmusician spouses who held at least comparable, but often better-paying jobs. These musicians were no less involved in the mobilization and solidarity efforts, their hard-won careers no less threatened, their identities and credibility no less shattered. For those musicians who were single or married to other musicians—or married to dancers or singers or artists or writers—financial concerns compounded the impact of realizing that what they'd worked their entire lives to become could evaporate with little notice. For some, no amount of advance warning could be enough to prepare them for any kind of viable alternate employment. In situations like this in the corporate world, when the media reports the personal story of a "downsized" manager, public sympathy rushes toward the suddenly obsolete former executive so unfairly robbed of his livelihood and his future. Whether it was because the musicians were in a union in a union-unfriendly town, or because management had successfully deflected blame for the lockout onto the musicians' refusal to agree to a contract that called for a shorter season with a smaller weekly minimum—successfully drawing the public eye away from their own budget deficiencies and huge debts—there was little public sympathy for the musicians. One person even said to me, "Well, they don't really provide a *necessary* service, they're getting paid *enough* for what they do."

My monthly salary for teaching three courses at San Diego Mesa College was just about the same as our monthly mortgage bill. My husband's unemployment covered utilities, gas, and grocery necessities. We did not use credit cards nor tap into the union's emergency fund; instead we notched our belts still tighter. Every other week, the phone tree reported where we could go to pick up a box of government surplus food. At the distribution point in the courtyard of a church, boxes of surplus food were stacked on folding tables. There was always a five-pound block of American cheese, a five-pound bag of flour, a five-pound bag of white rice, a pound of real butter, a loaf of white bread, a pound of pasta, a dozen eggs, and a half-gallon jar of thousand island salad dressing. Then each time there were miscellaneous items that must have achieved temporary "surplus" status: three kiwi per family, one bag of chocolate cookie mix, a head of lettuce, a box of Jell-O or instant pudding. Unbelievable as it may seem, it's difficult to live on these supplies. I guess I could've baked a cake every day. We had many more cheese sandwiches with salad dressing than I care to remember; the remainder of the cheese helped the rice to make casseroles, or was used as dog-training rewards. The accumulating butter and flour became my donation to family Christmas cookie baking. And my parents' bountiful three-quarter acre was another source of "surplus" food: the last of the summer eggplant, green pepper, and squash, and the winter tangerines and oranges.

As a means of sustaining morale through reducing isolation, the symphony musicians held potlucks twice a month at the union hall. Musicians' Local 325 is located in a rather overlooked part of San Diego, across the freeway from Mission Bay, on a strip of road housing tire and body shops and car stereo stores. Behind the union hall was a lumpy, badly paved parking lot butting up against a straggly hillside. The hall was equipped with folding tables and chairs, just about as homey and comfortable as the waiting room at the unemployment office. Here, twice a month, we brought home-cooked creations we'd made from the government surplus food. It became a game to see who could come up with a creative dish from the free supplies. Casseroles could consist of just about anything, from the requisite rice and pasta to oatmeal and cornflakes—and of course, lots of cheese and eggs. Salad dressing made a funky topping for meatloaf. Loaded with kiwi and apples, Jell-O and pudding undulated and shimmied on the unsteady folding tables.

But after the exclamations and laughter over the prepared dishes, we had to sit down across the table from each other and think of something to say. Something besides: Had anyone won an audition for another symphony? Was the music director locked out as well, or was his paycheck still issued on time? When was the next bargaining session scheduled? Were key principal players being paid under the table to encourage them to not audition elsewhere? Had someone really taken money from the emergency fund to buy a new television? Where was that lawyer who was supposed to be helping handle negotiations? What's going on? What's *really* going on?

It was similar, maybe worse, on the picket line. Since families were invited to join the picket lines, on at least one occasion I brought the dogs downtown to picket with little signs that hung over their backs. There were signs comparing the executive director's salary with the base musician salary, signs decrying refurbished offices and board-of-directors meeting room, signs saying, "Honk if you love music." To avoid the disconcerting topics of conversation, we waved to union comrades in work trucks sitting at the traffic light on B Street, and gave cheerful greetings to pedestrians, even the slickly dressed personnel entering the theater building. Payroll not being as difficult to make with musicians locked out, many on the support staff were still working, but the symphony's clerical and management employees never passed through the picket line—they used an entrance from the parking structure on the other side of the building—so those entering the building through the picketers could be anything from ticket-window clerks (now selling tickets to

Barry Manilow or the Philadelphia Orchestra) to employees of another business altogether. Symphony Towers had begun to rent out other suites in the theater building.

We had vague notions of when important meetings were to take place, so the picket lines were usually organized to be present at such times, as well as during performances in the concert hall which management was renting out. We understood how far in advance any act—whether symphony orchestra or solo singer—books venues for touring shows. So how long ago had management been making arrangements for these uses of Symphony Hall? How long ago had they known the musicians would be out of work for a year? And at lunchtime when catering trucks parked in the loading zones (usually wherever the picket line *wasn't*) and large deli trays were swiftly whisked into the building, we wondered: was this how management had cut back on operating expenses?

And what about the membership—why were certain people never present for picketing, for potlucks, even for union meetings? Was the musician who recently married the music director getting her paycheck? Had *she* come to any meetings, and would she tell her husband what the negotiating committee or union lawyer was planning? Whose side was the music director on; was he in the union; was he still being paid despite his $100,000-salary reported to be among management's debts?

Still, it was easier for us to face those questions among the continually dwindling group at the "morale-boosting" potlucks, or among the dogged ten or fifteen picketers, than it was to face them alone together at home. After the end of the baseball season in September, we'd stopped our subscription to the newspaper—part of the belt-tightening—but any time the phone tree called with news of an article or editorial, we wasted no time in driving to 7-11 for a final edition, all the while knowing there would be no information given to the media that would tell us anything new, anything hopeful or anything helpful. And there would be no answer to the "what're we going to do?" that I asked too many times between his sessions of practicing for auditions that hadn't been announced in superior cities that supported their symphonies, or as he sat on the sofa with a musicology textbook from one of his graduate classes, the irrelevant words blurring on the page before he tossed the book aside and picked up the last newspaper that hadn't yet been collected and dumped.

"How can they do this?" I asked.

"They obviously can. They did it."

"But what'll we do?"

"I don't know. Stop asking that. Just wait and see."

"But you can't do anything else."

"I know, I'm worthless."

"I don't mean *that*, but it's not fair, after your whole life practicing and taking lessons, you'll end up pumping gas or selling sodas to kids after school at 7-11."

"And getting shot."

Variations on a theme, the conversation played itself out almost every day, until he begged me to stop asking.

Feverishly, I looked for outlets to release the anxiety in other ways. In our small backyard, I prepared plots of ground and planted as many winter vegetables as I could: cabbage, brussels sprouts, onions, and lettuce. I sent my résumé to every other college English department in the county, seeking additional adjunct courses. I conditioned prospective show dogs for other people and gave private training lessons.

I had always been the one who made sure bills were paid and balanced the checkbook, but the lockout intensified my supervision of our budget. In fact, it intensified my supervision of many unrelated daily activities: when and what we ate, how much gas to put in the car, when he should practice his instrument, when we could make a long-distance call, how often should the laundry be done or the toilet flushed (this was during a drought). And I oversaw his exercise routine: which exercises he did, when he did them, how many repetitions. These were things I could control.

"How are you doing?" I would call from another room or from the screen door with feet too dirty to come inside.

"Horrible."

"Don't you feel good about doing them?"

"No, I'm sick to my stomach."

No hypocrisy in my exaggerated behavior: besides my teaching, gardening, conserving, and decreeing, I remained disciplined when it came to keeping my butt in a chair in front of my typewriter and maintaining the dogs' training schedules. *Some*thing had to feel like it was continuing, progressing, plugging away toward a result, a next step, a dividend. Likewise, I acted as "manager" of my husband's graduate school career: reminding him to do his reading, asking when his next deadlines were, asking him to describe his term paper project, inquiring if he needed to go to the library, going to the library with him, reminding him to work on his rough draft, setting up the portable typewriter on the coffee table so he could pick at it during a football game or between practice sessions, then finally typing the final paper for him—adding footnotes and correct documentation. I can make it sound like a dutiful, supportive wife. But all of these words—"reminding" and "asking" and "inquiring"—could be replaced with "hounding."

"There's plenty of time," he would say, "I'll get it done."

"Okay, when?"

"When I decide to do it."

"Don't you just want to get it done and over with?"

"It doesn't *need* to be done yet."

"Well then don't come to me to type the damn thing the night before it's due."

More tyrannical supervisor than supportive life-partner, I made sure I knew the deadlines for scheduling his graduate recital, for lining up a faculty committee, for reserving the hall, for hiring an accompanist; I knew the requirements for the degree, the substitutions he could make based on his previous courses, the deadline for applying for graduation. While the future of the San Diego Symphony—his profession, his pension and medical benefits— was gyrating so wildly out of control, and while my writing career seemed to be endlessly treading in deep water while the lifeguards called out, "It's not commercially viable," his graduate degree was something I could influence and direct. Consequently, he was treated more like my ward than my partner.

Both of us feeling utterly helpless, we reacted in opposite directions. My method for satisfying my need to be in control tipped our relationship into a dominant / subordinate mode. But in addition, perhaps abdication of control is a condition some professional musicians have become accustomed to: He'd spent nearly ten years being a dependent of a management that held all the power, instead of seeing himself as being the very reason there was a management in the first place. Many musicians have adopted the stance of hat-in-hand gratefulness that management provides them a symphony to make music in. This is, of course, exactly what management wants. Rather than seeing themselves as a support staff for the artists who produce the performances, management seems to view itself as the creator and the musicians as the raw material management is compelled to use. There are certain publishers who prefer to print and market only works by deceased writers to avoid having to deal with questions, suggestions, and ideas from an author. Likewise, I'm sure there are symphony managements who would favor putting on concerts with androids playing the music instead of real human musicians. I don't know how I could've or should've helped my husband toward a more assured, independent view of himself as a musician, but I should not have treated him in exactly the same style of domineering control that symphony management had always taken.

It's not such a psychological stretch to see that what I wanted, besides to feel in control again, was an authority figure of my own, someone to say *Just follow me, I'll take care of you.* And my autocratic veneer did occasionally crack. The August before the lockout (when we should've seen it coming and didn't) I had Bizzy, my youngest dog, bred. She whelped two puppies in October, and I had both sold before they were ready to wean. Not intended as a money-making prospect, the $300 per pup just about offset the stud fee and vet bills. Breeding a show bitch accomplishes not only "proving" her, but, after she finishes weaning then sheds her depleted coat, she'll come into a beautiful "bloom" and be ready for the show ring. As Bizzy began to come into the promised post-motherhood "bloom" and was winning best-of-breed at every practice match we entered, as the lockout dragged from fall 1986 into winter 1987 with no contract talks scheduled and my husband's unemployment benefits dwindling, I asked him, "Do you think we should sell Bizzy?"

"*Sell* Bizzy? Why would you ask that?"

"She's a quality bitch, proven producer, ready to be shown, she could be worth—"

"She's *ours*," he stated. "I can't believe you would say something like that."

"I was just trying to figure out if there was something else we could do. . . ."

"We're not selling our family."

Odd, even profane I realize, to speak of our dogs as our family when other families had children with braces and college educations to worry about. But he took a stand that day, and I recognize now that it's what I wanted: For someone to inform me that I was not going to make such an emotionally consequential decision just for the temporary feeling that I was doing something constructive. Wolf packs may, without remorse, send adolescents off on their own when it's become difficult to feed the whole pack, and that day I needed to be reminded we weren't a wolf pack. He made this pronouncement without even having the knowledge that in the long run the gesture would've been financially insignificant. The regret would've lasted indefinitely.

But my moments of seeking his lead or council were few and soon forgotten in the face of how decisively I attempted to carry, push, or pull both of us to the other end of the lockout tunnel—the 1986–1987 season—even though there was no assurance that the end of this season would bring about a new one, with a contract agreement, concert schedule, and budget. The music director had resigned (so, we surmised, he *hadn't* been paid), but as far as anyone knew, no guest conductors had been booked for a possible 1987–1988 season.

Long before the summer of 1987, I had locked myself into a five-course load for fall, two at University of San Diego and three at Mesa College. I also requested as many summer school classes as they would give me at Mesa, then secured two additional summer evening classes at a community college in the east county. The first eight weeks of summer I remained in maintenance overdrive, keeping a vegetable garden plus teaching and grading papers. Also during this summer an independent donor sponsored a series of concerts billed as "The Musicians of the San Diego Symphony" (both "San Diego Symphony" and "San Diego Symphony Pops" could only be used if there was a contract with the current symphony management). The concert series did not pay substantially, but by this time contract talks had resumed, and we felt we had "made it." The finish line of a marathon approaching, the last bell in a one-sided boxing match about to sound, the first gas station in 100 miles of desert finally in sight. By the time my summer classes were completed, a new contract had been negotiated, and a new concert season announced.

There were some immediate visible consequences of what management wanted to call "the hiatus." Many of the ensemble's principal players had won auditions in bigger, more secure orchestras, in some cases leaving gaping holes to be filled, yet management boasted of $1 million in donations collected during the crisis. But some lethal blows take longer to kill.

Under a new contract with musicians, a fall concert season was launched in Symphony Hall in October 1987. During that 1987–1988 season, my first book, *Animal Acts*, was accepted for publication. Bizzy, who I'd offered to sell during the lockout, won a best-in-match (over all breeds) and high-in-match (highest obedience score) at the same event. My husband finished his degree, played his graduate recital in the fall of 1988, and I was offered a prestigious position as writer-in-residence in Tennessee. It was a one-semester post. Since our marriage had begun long-distance with me in New York at graduate school, and because our distress in the bedroom had been accentuated by lack of trying until we now never attempted, I didn't hesitate to accept. But our unspoken view of my stint in Tennessee was as a trial separation. Similar to management's lockout, spring of 1989 was a lockout in our marriage. From which we would not recover.

WHILE WRITING MY novel *Dog People,* which contains a subplot about a dance company experiencing bitter contract negotiations and a possible lockout, I learned that dance companies are often founded and run by choreographers or former choreographers who are themselves former dancers. In dance, performers, former performers, those involved with creating the performance, often also have their hands on the reins of management. Symphony orchestras are seldom if ever (I'd like to say *never*) run by former professional musicians, but by businessmen, hired managers, and executives, and by boards of directors made up of wealthy patrons. This difference may be significant in how the performers are treated and in how the performers view themselves. Compared to other large performing arts organizations—operas, theater groups, dance companies—musicians seem more likely to be dealt with as subordinates, incapable of management decisions, treated with an attitude that administration is not only beyond their ability but none of their business, still related to those musicians-as-servants who didn't question the way the master ran the estate. In *Hamlet*, when a group of independent traveling actors arrives at the castle to entertain the royal family, Hamlet expounds with some envy upon the lives of these thespians. But in *Gone With the Wind*, every party scene has a live ensemble of musicians providing the music: servants—sometimes slaves—who play their instruments for the pleasure of the guests, with little acknowledgment and without stopping.

The disintegration of our marriage paralleled the motif of the unhappy musician-management relationship. The symphony's financial crisis, management's use of contract negotiations to lock the musicians out for a year, and how we individually reacted, all worked to magnify, even distort our preexisting personality traits. So when a storm hit us, we battled in opposite directions, as though leaning into two separate winds. I didn't treat my husband as a servant. Still, I did not treat him as a partner but as a person I had to take care of and make decisions for, as though he were incompetent to manage his own life.

The 1986–1987 crisis and lockout landed a (seemingly) lethal blow on the San Diego Symphony as well, but this was an even slower retrogression, a wound that pretended to heal while hiding the festering gangrene beneath the surface. With debts supposedly wiped clean in 1990—the mortgage notes on Symphony Hall forgiven and the hall renamed Copely Symphony Hall—the orchestra management went back to business as usual. By 1991–1992 there was nearly a million-dollar deficit in the operating budget. The 1994–1995 season itself netted a $1.5 million shortfall. Two familiar-sounding emergency fund drives were not successful. Once again paychecks were late and/or truncated. In 1995 the executive director, on the job for less than two years, resigned, asserting that making the biweekly payroll—that is, paying the musicians for their work—was killing him. Now with more than $3 million in debts, half the nonmusician staff was laid off, contracts with guest soloists were canceled, but musicians—perhaps servants-no-more—did not agree to renegotiate their contract and accept a cut in pay. In answer to the musicians' stance, management announced plans to file bankruptcy in January 1996. A successful threat, the board's vote to file bankruptcy resulted in a short flurry of negotiations with donors while the musicians were, in effect, out of work. The bankruptcy filing was delayed. Announcing that donors had contributed enough for the orchestra to resume its season in March, management and musicians ratified a waver to the labor contract, calling for eight weeks of service with a minimum salary of $870 per week, and a lump sum payment to each musician due April 15. ($870 was also the minimum weekly salary in the contract under which the musicians had already been working for the entire 1995–1996 season. The lump sum was to make up for earlier skipped and/or reduced paychecks going back to the previous November.) But within a month management reneged on the lump-sum payment of back wages, the musicians declined to rehearse, the remainder of the season was canceled, and management once again put out a call for donors to cover operating expenses. By the end of May, a Chapter 7 liquidation bankruptcy petition had been filed.

Again, media spin tended to blame the musicians, who "refuse to rehearse," and "refuse to re-negotiate their contract," all but calling them greedy or stubborn. Yet no comment was made about a professional management that votes to file bankruptcy, a month later announces that donors had contributed enough for the orchestra to resume its concert schedule, and another month later admits that it had only secured donors for a endowment fund but not for the day-to-day operating expenses—nasty little details like paying the musicians.

With what seemed to be the decisive death of the symphony in 1997, several years after my divorce was final, what I felt was not relief that I didn't have to go through it again, nor that any kind of "justice" had been served as payback for the pain of ending the marriage, nor any gloating that my ex-husband was now an ex-member of an ex-symphony. I did not feel anything but my own delayed grief.

HOW FAR SHE CAME

Many people don't leave Arkansas, but he went to Boston and then to Brazil in order to become a trombonist, which was all he wanted, except to avoid the draft, which he did by taking a psychological test and saying he would rather arrange flowers than drive a taxi and the reason he didn't want to have children was they would probably be better than him at sports. In a hypothetical class photo, when asked to choose his best friend, he didn't pick the blond (practically glowing) football star but pointed to the cliché dork with buck teeth in too-small checked shirt and black-rimmed glasses with ten pens in a breast pocket. The diagnosis was neurotically immature, which certainly wouldn't play in Vietnam. He was Arkansas' first, or maybe premier hippy, his name kept on file by the FBI because he'd visited a "known commune." Proud of his D in ROTC, which he had to pass before graduating from college, and at one time he knew how to take a rifle apart and put it back together. Then he moved to Brazil where winter is summer and security guards carry automatic machine guns and half the classical musicians in Rio are frustrated Americans. He taught Brazilians to say "How big is your weenie," carried a purse, grew his hair and sideburns, became a vegetarian, learned Portuguese, dodged dirty water thrown from doorways, and stepped over burning sacrifices set out on the sidewalks. When he decided to come home, he left in the summer and came back where it was still winter, except in the Southern California city where (what else?) he got a job playing trombone. He went to parties and stood at the buffet table eating, sometimes reaching two directions with both hands, and someone once said he looked like a prisoner of war because he had narrow shoulders and weighed 125. He cut his sideburns and his hair, pierced his ear, got a new purse, wore black jeans instead of tuxedo pants with his tattered tailcoat, carried his white tie in his pocket until the last second before going on stage, and he fell in love. With baseball. He listened to games while he practiced trombone or with headphones at rehearsals, in the wings during concerts he huddled with the stage crew around a tiny television. They had huge bellies and bald heads and thought he was a fairy, but they asked him about obscure rules and what was the pitcher's ERA and where did this second-baseman play last year. Then for a year a dispute with management kept him from working, so to finish a graduate degree, he gave a recital for solo bass trombone and one row of seats was filled—those he called his friends which now included his wife—and they made him take five curtain calls. The final time, he came out on stage without his trombone, arms folded, foot tapping, then flashed his distinctive smile—maybe the first time in months, who was keeping track?—flipped up his bedraggled tails, and bowed. But one day realized he was in his late thirties and hadn't yet been to Europe— an ex-pat in Brazil at twenty-four somehow didn't count as *abroad*. Upper thirties and hadn't gone *On the Road*—car trips home to Arkansas didn't count. Hadn't even been to see a play in too long— *Oh Calcutta!* when he was twenty-six didn't count. He helped two lesbian friends through their disastrous affairs and offered his home as their haven and made them tea or yogurt milkshakes and asked them how to make love to women but it didn't help much in his anxious marriage. Daily life had been static for a while, a long while, immutable and inert and he didn't know why. But he could play near master-level chess and keep score of a baseball game on a complicated chart and recite Hall of Fame statistics and do Tai Chi moves and use his Arkansas accent for southern jokes and sing Beatle songs operatic style and Simon and Garfunkle Vegas-style and sing to his wife's dogs in a Bing Crosby voice that made them lick his mouth. And he could play the trombone.

SOME YEARS AFTER, bailing out on secondary school teaching, before I'd ever started—having logged four more years of education; having gotten published and married; having given up the fanciful he-works-as-a-musician-and-I-write way of life; having survived through the year management locked out the musicians and canceled the symphony season; having spent several years as a "freeway flier," one of those part-time instructors of composition at two or three colleges who receive no medical benefits nor retirement plan, no opportunity for promotion or pay raise; having won a distinguished national award for fiction and completed a prestigious one-semester writer-in-residency—another prospect materialized. I could be a college professor. With this verdict, I had to accept that (1) I would be looking for work outside San Diego, probably outside California and (2) my classical-musician husband would not be coming with me. The agreement: he would accompany me on the cross-country drive to the interviews, and we would get a divorce as soon as I got a job.

One of the rites in seeking a university tenure track position is the Modern Language Association (MLA) annual convention, always the week between Christmas and New Year's Day. During the three and a half days, university and college English departments conduct their interviews for prospective new faculty. Before getting invited to an interview, a candidate has already made it through a screening process, one where the search committee may have considered over 300 résumés and dossiers. Later I would learn that a dossier is a formal enterprise, apropos of an academic milieu. Not a person who even uses the word *milieu*, I didn't know that dossiers are files of pertinent documents kept for job seekers by a central agency; that writers of recommendations send original copies of their letters directly to the applicant's dossier file where professional clerical employees (possibly in latex gloves) keep the papers in ready-to-send packets, in a colored folder with the applicant's name computer-printed on official labels; and that this file-keeping agency sends the dossier directly to prospective employers who request to see it.

When job announcements requested a dossier, I used a dictionary to see what it was they wanted—*a collection of papers or documents pertaining to a particular person (from Old French, bundle of papers having a label on the back)*—then set about compiling my own. Firstly, xeroxed letters of recommendation I'd collected (some a year or two old—I called the authors and asked if I could white-out and change the dates). I also included copies of unofficial transcripts from college, computer-printed graphs of student evaluations given me at the schools where I was an adjunct, and xeroxes of advance publicity for my first book (a document I created out of the jacket mock-up, since there was no actual advance publicity). Paper-clipped together, my résumé on top, a brief letter of interest on top of that, a few xeroxes of stories from literary magazines, and my application materials were complete. Not to mention completely homemade.

Likely I was forgiven my oafish attempts at academic application protocol because I was responding to calls for a fiction writer. Eleven colleges and universities called me to arrange an interview at the MLA convention in Washington, D.C., two more scheduled phone conference interviews, and one arranged to meet me while I was en route to D.C.

Most participants at the MLA convention are academic professionals. Almost as many more are academic hopefuls who come to hazard their future on an interview less than an hour long. Wannabes and chosen alike, they stay at the three, four, or five downtown hotels reserved for MLA members. Although the vast majority of conventioneers flew to Washington DC—unless they took trains from Boston or New York—I would not fly to the convention, and I wasn't staying in these hotels. My husband and I drove 3,000 miles with two dogs in a mini pickup with a heater only competent enough for a California winter, huddled with the dogs under blankets through subzero temperatures in New Mexico, Texas, Oklahoma, into Arkansas. There we spent an uneasy holiday with his relatives who never inquired about our reason for pushing on to D.C. through a snowstorm the day after Christmas.

We drove into downtown Washington on the morning of my first interviews and parked in a high-rise hotel's underground garage. I changed clothes in a bathroom, then had to leave the dogs in crates in the truck—my weary husband staying with them, reading the paper or sleeping stretched out across the bench seat—while I went to four or five interviews. Since the conventioneers were distributed between at least three big hotels, my schedule often had me hurrying from hotel to hotel, sometimes blocks apart, slipping into rest rooms in the lobbies of each to see if (as my mother had more than once fretted) I looked like an orphan. During longer breaks between appointments, I returned to the garage to exercise the dogs. That night we went to a Motel 6 outside D.C.—far outside, in Maryland. We had to be back in the city before nine the next morning for a repeat of day one, and would be leaving to head west to California right after my last appointment in the afternoon.

The interviews are held in hotel suites. Four or five academically attired English department colleagues sit clustered around room service hot beverages on a coffee table. Candidates arrive at intervals, announce their presence with a timid knock on the door. The halls are quiet, trays of dirty dishes waiting on the rug beside the meditative candidates who ignore the others like themselves dotted here and there. Meetings timed to last exactly forty-five minutes, rarely does one candidate see another coming out the same door he or she is waiting to knock on at precisely the minute of the scheduled interview.

Downstairs in the hotel lobbies, those with a half hour or more until the next appointment congregate and fortify themselves. In a ballroom-size space of arm chairs, coffee tables, and settees arranged in dozens of intimate groups, candidates' anxiety can be both lulled and sharpened by the muted conversational din spiked with academic lingo.

The chair was worried about the ramifications on our undergraduate colloquium . . . Oh yes my book came out from . . . They're looking for a Victorian deconstructionist . . . presented a paper at the Joyce symposium . . . She's a postcolonialist with a specialty in urban narrative . . . panel discussion on medieval feminist theory in . . . There are post-structuralist roots in early modernity . . . and an essay of mine appearing in New Directions caused someone to ask . . . seeking to add a multicultural angle to our rhetoric and literacy line . . .

Computer-printed name tags on every chest, leather shoulder-strap portfolios on their laps, propped beside chairs, flopped open on coffee tables. They also dress in academic formal wear. Men: suits — gray or black — tweed coats acceptable, vests optional, slacks and sport coat satisfactory; usually, since it's winter, an overcoat, wool, tailored. Women: calf-length skirts — gray, black, brown, plaid, or tweed — and boots; on top a blouse and tailored blazer. Business suits with shorter skirts also admissible. Pant suits, if tailored, allowable, but not anything gossamer, frilly, garish, or polyester. I went with the midlength skirt topped with a sweater. My only coat was a denim parka. That's okay, I could shed it in the lobby and leave it behind.

That's where we waited, the morning of the second day. The dogs safely in the garage in the truck in their crates, my husband, needing a new *USA Today* and a doughnut, came in with me. No notes to pore over, I'd memorized an ambiguous one-liner about deconstruction and a list of five titles for the standard "what works do you teach" question. Had already faced the prototype dubious professor inquiring what I would do with the fresh-faced farmgirl who's come 500 miles from her small-town high school to go to college in the big city. Had already fielded the trick questions and veiled insults, not only about my writing but about my home state: "You sure you'll be able to leave all the beaches in California?" (If the interviewers had known about the dogs in the pickup and receipt from Motel 6, instead of seeing the San Diego address on my résumé, they might have asked how I could leave California's year-long summer. I tried to make long, intellectual statements that meant "I need a job.")

Sighing, I looked up drearily from the dog-eared list of my appointments. My husband was sitting across from me, a newspaper folded to football statistics in one hand, the napkin that had held his doughnut still waded in the other. We'd left the motel room early; he'd packed the truck while I'd showered and dressed. His disheveled hair had not yet been combed, his sallow face shaded by a day-old beard. His black suede jacket, sprinkled down the front with doughnut sugar, was still zipped to his neck, covering a plaid flannel shirt whose collar was awry and sticking out the jacket's neckband. Of course he had shed the padded gloves he'd worn while packing the truck, but he'd tucked the gloves wrist-first into the two breast pockets of his jacket, so the palms and all five fingers faced me, like two extra hands emerging from his chest waiting to catch a basketball.

"Know what?" Eyes down to my own rumpled lap, the cotton gauze skirt material as usual fuzzed by dog hair, then back up to meet his, dismal and heavy. "We don't belong here," I said. And his bloodless, winter-dry lips actually smiled.

WITHSTANDING THE ELEMENTS

I moved east. Moving east is, in a way, bucking a time-honored romance, a long-accepted heritage of how Americans "settle." Although there have been (and still are) steady migrations into the United States from South America and from Asia, and from our own rural south to the big northern cities, there's considerable truth in popular history's point of view that the chronological development and settlement of this country moves geographically from East to West. When people "pioneered," or "blazed new trails," or "uprooted and resettled," it was simply understood that they were moving West, whether it happened in the 1860s or 1950s. Those who couldn't thrive, who gave up and moved back to original homes or where family still remained, were returning East. (In the western half of the country, the term "East" is rarely used without a "back" in front of it.) So it is to the West where people came to dream, to build, to breathe. But I moved East. Perhaps as a Californian should, I pushed off against an established current.

It's interesting, however, that when "western states" have a writing contest, California writers are not listed as eligible. When "south-western states" have a fair for "southwestern books," California is not invited. In the continental USA, there's the East Coast, New England, the South, the Midwest, the Pacific Northwest, the

Southwest, the Western States; and—a land of its own (or on its own)—there's California. It's appropriate, then, as Richard Rodriguez pointed out in his essay "True West," that for native Californians, "the West" is somewhere east of the Sierras. (In addition, to a Californian, "back east" seems to be anywhere east of Denver. So, in 1993 when my packed-to-the-rafters mini-pickup crossed the Colorado River, was I at first, in a skewed California way, actually *following* a pioneering tradition—moving toward and through the *West*? Well, maybe if I'd ended up in Laramie or Billings or Fort Collins. In that case I couldn't make the claim that I'd made a gesture of rebellion against the romance of moving West, a "romance" that is still swallowing and digesting California into slabs of concrete and planned housing developments. But soon after crossing the Colorado, I also crossed the Mississippi. I went the wrong way through the "Gateway to the West."

The rebellion is easy to claim after the fact. Simply, I moved to the Midwest because that's were I got a job. I'd done temporary residencies for the same reason: once in Tennessee, once in Pennsylvania, and a stint in Brooklyn to finish college. Did I want to leave California? Not particularly. Did I dread it? Didn't occur to me. Did I think it would make or break my career as a novelist? Not in the slightest. Each time, my going away from California was colored by a different implication, from the clichéd claim of adult independence to the need for an alternate life where I could temporarily remake myself to tacit self-imposed banishment.

But without exception, people in these new places presupposed I would be intellectually happier, creatively more stimulated, perhaps suffer from mood-altering light-deprivation syndrome but make up for it by experiencing the exhilaration and inspiration of "a true change of seasons." Thus painting California, by assumption, as an invariable place of blinding sunlight, which, along with the inescapable banality, is artistically suffocating, paralyzing, and anesthetic.

Grudgingly, the rest of the country may sometimes admit that despite our intellectual limitations—our supposed tendency toward etherealism, sun-fried brains to match the sun-dried tomatoes— Californians do predict cultural and social trends, good and bad, from the psychedelic summer of love to elimination of affirmative action. But, after fifty years of easy relocation and television that have managed to homogenize the country, non-Californians tend to resort to less imaginative forms of reproof than our regional quirks and customs. So while snow-bound easterners watch a golf classic or the Superbowl played in San Diego on a dazzling seventy-degree January day, perhaps they're able to resist that familiar urge to migrate (thank god) with a new round of criticism. Among the other raps on California—that everyone has to be able to speak Spanish, that cults will steal their children—they say we have no seasons.

SPRING. NO CENTRAL heating, our houses still too cold for us to hold pencils or tap keyboards, so we lie in the yard fully clothed, ignoring the doorbell—kids walking home from school craving tangerines they've spotted over the backyard fence. They leave peels and their spelling papers in the gutter. Eventually the last child goes home from school and in comes the coastal stratum, the haze, the fog, the overcast, the marine layer, June Gloom. Ironically signifying: *Tourist*. The word for everybody before they pick up and move here, complaining it's not as sunny as during the Rose Parade or Superbowl on TV last January, but they'll cluster like the aphids sucking our green pepper plants or leave trails like snails who've discovered our potted strawberries. We know the beach is still cold, but they want to baptize their long, white bony feet in the Pacific. Sometimes it's the celebration fireworks that seem to sear the seaboard soup away, and people call this the start of summer. No thunderstorms to wash away the dirt of each fun-filled day, just hot winds come August which topple shallow-rooted eucalyptus onto powerlines and start the: *Fire.* We go to a baseball game the day half our neighborhood burns, turn backward in our seats now and then, as the crowd cheers, watching yet another house on the hill spray fire from its doorway, roofs falling in geysers of sparks. We'll be encouraged to resist flushing our toilets, nurturing our gardens or washing our cars, until: *Rain.* It comes eventually to kill the fires. The same roads flood every year, every year a different former tourist from a different former hometown steps out of a stalled car and is washed away like the mud on burned hills which slides, sometimes along with showcase homes, into the gutters.

MISUNDERSTANDING AND CRITICIZING each other's weather must be part of how we cling to some regional differentiation. From the California earthquakes of 1989 and 1994 to Atlantic hurricanes Hugo and Andrew, from the eruption of Mount St. Helens to the mysterious El Niño, from the midwestern flooding of 1996 to the eastern seaboard ice storm of 1997, weather strikes fear into the hearts of those who cling to the environment they're most familiar with. Midwesterners speak with awe (and an ingenuous belief they can't hide with irony) of California heaving a final cataclysmic shudder, the ground opening like the mouth of hell, then crumbling into the Pacific. Californians (at least those who were born there) view the Midwest as a place where drab one-room farmhouses are routinely swept away in colossal black twisters that scour the flat fields of wheat and corn. Most people east of the Rockies wonder (before they eventually move to California) how anyone can endure the boredom of so much sun, day after week after month, without variance. After they move here, they're the ones going to dinner in sunglasses, shorts and flipflops, even after they're compelled to put on a jacket. Meanwhile, native Californians, or those who've been there long enough to have forgotten, shiver bitterly as they imagine half a year of incessant blizzards, ice storms, and temperatures routinely below (gasp!) 40.

Seasons in other regions are more traditional, perhaps more honest, and only blend a little at the ends. Snow may arrive in autumn before the vibrant red and yellow leaves have dropped from the maples, or in spring after the grass has greened and tulips have surfaced. And I admit, there's serene symmetry in the faithfulness of midwestern seasons. It makes sense. The same kind of innocent order as the agricultural transition I've passed through while driving west from Illinois via Iowa, Nebraska, and Wyoming: About the same time the cornfields give way to cattle rangeland, red-winged blackbirds marking territory on fenceposts every hundred yards along the sides of the road are replaced by white-winged magpies.

The California seasons, neither faithful nor traditional, incur major overlaps, sometimes have to be declared "open" by those whose job it is to know. How do we divide a year? From the viewpoint of the terminally sports-minded, *football* and *baseball*, to the economy concerned, *holiday* and *tourist*. Besides the commonplace *fishing* and *hunting* seasons, I've known seasons called *flea* (May to December), *marching* (coincides with football), *symphony* (same as an academic year), and *Santa Ana* (roughly August through October). In my father's yard there were seasons according to what was ripe: oranges and tangerines in December and January, strawberries begin as early as February, artichokes in March. Loquats, boysenberries, and raspberries in late May or June; then apricots, plums, and peaches follow in slightly overlapping sequence, and figs in August. Quince, avocados, and apples start in September, pomegranate and persimmons in October and November. Nothing here to lure a storm-follower, one who strives to surf in the eye of a Florida hurricane or saunter in the wake of an Arkansas tornado. And yet sensation and drama do prevail when the conventional standards of meteorology, *rain* and *drought*, bring the climate's seasonal consequences, *mud-slide* and *fire*.

Tell me I'm not experiencing a shift in environmental conditions as winter's highest tides and torrential breakers crash over, across and through beaches, beach houses, piers, restaurants, and coast roads, breaking apart concrete beach walls and streets, pulling asphalt, pier pylons, restaurant furniture and beach sand alike back into the ocean. Or when the searing Santa Ana winds swoop through from the east, often with temperatures over 90, parching grass, complexions, even the oily eucalyptus leaves, toppling the thickest trees, power lines, and TV antenna alike. Or, in the most dramatic of California seasons, when what seems a plague of crickets and grasshoppers begins to flee past in a knee-high current of celluloid wings and clicking legs while I stand in hot breaths of localized gusts, whipped up by the flames of a brushfire.

CERTAINLY CHICAGO HAS known the efficacy of fire. Fires that ravage nursing homes and seminaries full of Catholic schoolgirls, fires that suffocate whole families in unventilated tenement apartments, fires that impel people to splatter themselves on the sidewalk rather than face being burned alive in a highrise where the fire escape ladders are rusted into unserviceable condition. And one very famous fire that consumed half the city then left a legacy: not only in a law that stipulated houses could not be built from wood, but in sports teams and university mascots—the University of Illinois at Chicago *Flames*, the Chicago *Fire* soccer team. The Chicago fire was actually responsible for the city's nickname of "The Windy City." During the physical reconstruction of the city, a simultaneous campaign was undertaken to renovate the city's spirit and reputation. The city's media machines generated so much publicity (disguised as news), the overt bragging was dubbed "wind," and thus the nickname. But these city fires are pure accidents, human mishaps that burn cheaply or poorly produced man-made structures. California's wildfires—whether started inadvertently by kids and firecrackers, by the wind downing a powerline, or spontaneously by a lightning strike—are actually an inherent part of the landscape.

People just happened to build their houses, communities, towns and cities in a place where *fire* is one of the natural seasons.

An earthquake "season" could be said to exist as soon as the last brick tumbles: the resulting loss of power and water, the fires caused by loose powerlines and severed gas mains, the aftershocks for weeks thereafter, the piles of rubble for months, the scaffolding and safety fences block after block and building after building, the flurry of freeway overpass retrofits to make them earthquake-proof, and the graft attempted by construction companies to get the retrofit contracts then skimp on the actual work. But there really is no time of year, no temperate condition, that is favorable to producing earthquakes, as there is for tornadoes and hurricanes. A lack of warning, then three minutes of instant devastation. No sirens, and no interruption of television shows with ominous beeping tones followed by the storm caution scrolling across the bottom of a police drama or football game broadcast from sunny Florida or Arizona. It's no mystery why earthquakes have, especially during the six months following a big one, reached near hysterical phantom-killer status. Still, even though nonseasonal and almost unpredictable, non-Californians fear the wrong phenomenon. Earthquakes in California, at least those that do damage, occur less frequently than killer tornadoes and far less frequently than brushfires.

Brushfire. The word is so much more benign than *earthquake.* A brushfire is something my father convened in the backyard to get rid of a pile of branches and dried weeds he'd cleared. I admit, we called this event a *bonfire*, not a brushfire. But *brush* being burned sounds so inconsequential. Who cares?

But *brush* is the original flora of coastal Southern California. Coastal scrub or semi-arid chaparral, indigenous California is a place of waist- to shoulder-high vegetation that stays green only as long as the ground is wet, which may be a week to two months.

Wild oats, tumbleweeds, sage, buckwheat, foxtails, the nonnative wild mustard and anise, grow and mature quickly, then turn brown and scatter their seeds. The cycle may complete itself two or three times in a year, depending on how much time goes by between significant rainfalls. The perennial larger bushes—among them laurel sumac, lemonade berry, coyote and sugar bush—thrive and proliferate in other ways. Laurel sumac in particular has a survival characteristic suggesting that fire is natural to this region. The sumac, with drought-resistant leaves that are characteristically thick and dark, maintains at least half its growth underground in a vast root system. These adaptive roots are capable of drawing nutrients from poor soil, even when no energy-producing photosynthesis is occurring through leaves. So when fire consumes all the branches and leaves from above ground, the sumac doesn't need to wait for scattered seeds to reproduce; each still-living root system is immediately able to send up new shoots. The laurel sumac is often the first regrowth after a brushfire, even before grass, so that the bushes can, within a year, become head-high and big around as cars, part of a natural scheme that purges, then quickly revegetates the hillsides.

When you consider that every year, somewhere in California, there's a major brushfire, scorching at least hundreds but usually thousands of acres, then it shouldn't be too far off to say that occurrence of a major brushfire in Southern California should be as normal and seasonally anticipated as a blizzard in the Midwest. The difference is that snow, even a ferocious whiteout, doesn't demolish a house and send it into the sky in the form of a stinky black cloud. Similar to towns that were foolishly built in river flood plains, almost everything in Southern California was built in fire's territory. The tragedy left in a California brushfire's wake is never charred earth or the fate of native flora and fauna, it's the houses, sometimes dozens or hundreds, not just devastated but devoured.

When we first moved to Spring Valley, to a house near the top of a round bluff, easily a square mile of undeveloped scrub ran downhill from our backyard to the creek at the foot of the hill, and that was just the territory *directly* below us. At least half the hill was undeveloped, crisscrossed with unofficial trails, matted with many years of grow-and-quickly-go-to-seed foliage cycles. And with regular frequency, a small brushfire would come thundering and billowing up the slope, but was halted and snuffed by the one paved road that circled the side of the hill, or by the dirt aqueduct easement right below our property. Maybe once or twice my father threw a hose into the pool and stood ready to drain the pool's water onto the brush just off his land, but he never had to do it.

For us, the sense of excitement was without trepidation. First there would be the possibility of lizards and king snakes taking refuge on our cool lawn, making them easier to catch. There was the strident and astonishing sense of drama as the fire whipped up wind and the wind filled with grasshoppers and crickets with snapping legs and papery wings. There were the fire trucks, sirens piercing ever closer, crowding onto Lakeview Street, then dozens of men in boots and thick yellow jackets swarming over the hillside. Then the aftermath, just as nature planned it, when the matted covering was purged so that new growth had increased nutrients and space to spread out, and when kids could poke around in the dirty ash to discover treasure—soda bottles worth ten cents or rusted pocket knives with blistered handles—previously hidden in the underbrush.

Small one- or two-alarm brushfires near our house were practically a yearly occurrence. It's also a yearly occurrence for there to be at least one major wildfire somewhere in Southern California. Three of these major blazes that scorched areas of San Diego County are significant in my memory. In 1996, a fire burned thousands of acres, including up to 120 houses in the North County, many of them within a few miles of where I lived during summers I still spent in California after I'd moved to the Midwest. It was

October, one of California's fire-season months, and I was enjoying a tranquil Indian summer in Illinois. Out in California, in the house I shared with him May through July, a man stood at his dark kitchen window with binoculars trained on the hillside across a small ravine from his house where not two, not four, not six, not ten, but dozens of houses burned simultaneously. Yet in this unusual instance the burning houses were not all adjacent or being consumed by one big blaze. Sometimes five to ten unignited houses remained dark and quiet between those falling into piles of ashes. The actual wildfire was a few miles to the east in undeveloped brush, but the Santa Ana winds were so aroused, and the flames so whipped into a frenzy, not just sparks but bits of flaming debris flew from the burning acreage, landing indiscriminately on some roofs, leaving others in the placid gloom of an evacuated neighborhood, so some houses burned while their neighbors stood. The man, in a flat-roofed, wood-paneled Corbusier-style house, wondered if he should leave and what he should pack if he did. Of course his dogs and the small parrot in her cage. Also the photo albums and scrapbooks with his dog show records and ribbons, the plaques on his walls. Everything else — cars, furniture, appliances — was insured, but what about the programs and tickets from sporting events he'd saved over thirty-five years, what about tax records and his complete collection of *Road and Track*, what about the scale model of an 1812 U.S. frigate he'd toiled over for two years? His rooms were filled with the smoky smell of burning brush and acrid eucalyptus, and the charred stink of blazing walls, curtains, furniture, plastic floors and countertops, paint, wallpaper, and other housing effects. His neighbor was outside watering his roof. The man stayed in the dark, as though keeping the lights off would stave off the flames, mulling over what he would pack until the urgency to leave was proven to be unwarranted.

Twenty-six years earlier I knelt in the dining room of my parents' house on Hartzel Hill and used the windowsill to balance the huge Nazi binoculars my father had acquired while stationed in Germany in the months following World War II. I was focusing on the glow coming from behind Dictionary Hill, like a localized sunrise occurring only behind this one hill, but it was after eight P.M., ten hours from dawn. On a portable radio beside me, a station was devoting air time to fire coverage—interviews with firefighters who'd come from the front line to rest or law enforcement officials who were carrying out evacuation orders, news updates from reporters at the site, and phone calls to or from anyone else who might have pertinent information. One interview was with an administrator from the phone company who mentioned that evacuated people were calling their home phone numbers, hearing the ring signal and assuming this meant their home was still intact, but in fact this signal was not generated from their house but from a connecting terminal, and the house could actually be a pile of smoldering ashes. I could see the lights and hear the sirens of firetrucks going down Spring Valley's Central Avenue, Sweetwater Road or Jamaica Boulevard, coming from other jurisdictions to join the fight. A reporter had a story about rural homeowners who had defied the evacuation as long as possible, staying to empty swimming pools or even, on older property, their wells onto the roofs of horse barns, on the dust of poultry yards, searching for frightened and hiding cats, then stuffing sheep or goats with their dogs into the back of a station wagon or the bed of a pickup truck. He said some residents had hidden from police who were clearing the area, choosing to stay because of missing pets or livestock too big to move. Others, down behind the road barricades, wept, either with guilt for leaving or in hope that the fire wouldn't reach their yard. Sometimes, through the binoculars, I could see the tips of flames in the orange glow which was bright enough to illuminate the coil of smoke joining the dense cloud spreading over Spring Valley. The next morning, Saturday, the cloud had created a scorched-smelling overcast above Spring Valley, but the temperature was hot—a September Santa Ana, as is so often the case during a fire, still fanning the flames and breathing its hot breath on the participants of the local Lemon Grove Parade. If it weren't hovering in the nineties, we would've thought it was snowing. Sweating in my wool band uniform, I brushed ashes off my shoulders.

My own turn to contemplate choosing what was important enough to save from fire came in 1985. It was, unsurprisingly, a hot day in an unusually hot June, just about the time fire season is declared to have started. In my unairconditioned bungalow in Normal Heights—an old neighborhood northeast of downtown and extending to the bluffs above Mission Valley, named for San Diego's normal school, which hadn't existed for seventy-five years—I had already, weeks ago, covered all of my west-facing windows with aluminum foil to block the glare and heat of the afternoon sun. Sometimes my husband and I slept wearing only underwear, lying on top of the sheets, with wet washcloths on our stomachs and a fan blowing over us. Picturing us this way, side by side like two cooling corpses, should be one of those funny details from young adulthood when the accouterments and comforts of life are makeshift. But this hot summer was, unknown to either of us yet, still incubating a chill concealed in the marriage. Sex was our problem. It was my problem. The 1985 inferno that roared up the canyon walls from Mission Valley and set Normal Heights ablaze was not a metaphor for our passion. No tension had as yet arisen from this condition. Instead, our passion was shared in baseball. This particular summer, our Padres—who had won the National League pennant the year before and had started the season firmly in first place again—had started to let their lead dribble to the Dodgers. Now, appropriately, one wall of Mission Valley was burning, and Mission Valley was the location of the stadium, and the stadium was our destination that day.

The fire—which had quickly reached the top of the canyon and was already burning dozens of houses (it eventually destroyed 80 and damaged more than 100)—was six or seven blocks away from us. Ash blew down our street and smoke rose to hover over us like the black clouds of a summer thunderstorm, which San Diego almost never expects to entertain. Ordinarily people with tickets to a ballgame could easily decide to forgo the game if their neighborhood was on fire. But in this case, the symphony was scheduled to play a concert following the game, so my musician husband's presence, at least by the time the game was finished, was required. The condition influencing my decision to accompany him to the game was that the burning houses were almost exclusively on streets and cul-de-sacs on the rim of the canyon, the few exceptions being close neighbors of those houses whose roofs had caught burning debris. We were directly south of the burning area—between us and the fire was not easily combustible brush but paved streets, sidewalks, and stucco houses. It was implausible that the fire would spread south across lawns and palm trees before firefighters could stop it. But, in fact, the radio was reporting that firefighters were encountering a devastating lack of water pressure and if certain circumstances continued or arose—a stiff wind, dry conditions, lack of water—the fire could conceivably blaze a trail south to the first major four-lane street. Our house would be within this projected path of soot.

Still, this seemed preposterous. I would go to the game. But not without protecting my valuables. My contemplation of what was valuable was different in 1985 than it would have been if I'd been in California during the North County fire of 1996, because I had no homeowner's insurance, no renter's insurance, and no computer with manuscripts saved on disk. Of course my dogs would go—I arranged for them to be at a friend's house while we were at the game—and my husband's trombone would already be along with us. The only other valuable essential was my body of work. I filled two or three document boxes with manuscripts and notes, then paused, remembering a box stashed up in the closet holding an eight-inch-thick stack of letters my husband and I had written to each other while I was away at school in New York. We'd written every day, me on my new electric typewriter, him on my old portable. Letters recording every activity no matter how minor during the hours up to seating ourselves at the keyboard, and, more important, words of embellished passion and desire that had then never been demonstrated when we were reunited in the spring of 1983. I made one more check of the smoke rising above the palm-tree-and-telephone-pole skyline in the north. It seemed less dense, and billows of white showed where water was having an effect. An old airplane buzzed close overhead, a helicopter hovered. Reporters on the radio hadn't made a dire prediction for an hour, and, in fact, were now only reporting on the fire during the scheduled news. The dogs went to the friend's yard in another neighborhood, the manuscript boxes went into the covered back of our truck to sit in the parking lot during the game, but the letters stayed home. They still, as far as I know, have not disintegrated. They were packed in a trunk in the house in the North County where the 1996 fire could've threatened them. But they've never really come close to burning. Unless I decide to strike the match.

THE WORD *SEASON* as a noun means a term, period, time, or division. But as a verb, it means to age, to accustom, habituate, or acclimate. This was the process which caused friends and new acquaintances alike to grin, anticipating that my transition to "real" winter would be a rude awakening. As though I would show up to work in January wearing a tank top, shorts, flip-flops, and a fannypack, or that I'd singe my eyelashes while sleeping with a ring of space heaters around my bed. But my acclimatization to winters other

240

than Californian, already largely consummated before ever arriving in Chicago, had been more than a form of speeded-up biological evolution. *Cold* was more complex than goosebumps and a red nose, more profound than mere discomfort.

Many houses in Southern California, especially fifties-era slab suburbs, have no central heating (and no air conditioning). In my East San Diego bungalow, I had to go outside to get warm in January. I lay on my lawn under winter sunshine wearing a sweatshirt. Inside, in my study, I wore cotton gloves with the fingertips cut off so I could work at my typewriter. There was one gas wall heater with a thermostat in the living room, but if I tried to use the heater to warm the bedroom or study, the thermostat would've had to be cranked so high it would've turned the living room into a sauna.

The heaters in the Spring Valley ranch house where I grew up didn't even have thermostats. They were metal coils that glowed red-hot, one unit installed in the wall of each room. Freshly out of the bath, we flicked wet fingers to make the coils sputter and sizzle. Then my youngest brother, three years old, had a better idea: just pee into the glowing coils, you get a *better* spit and hiss. And a stink. It wafted out to where my mother was reading me a before-bed story. First there were sporadic interruptions as my mother questioned the smell. But as soon as my father investigated, Babar was left motherless or Laura Ingles's Pa stayed lost in the woods, and general pandemonium took over. The heater in my brothers' room had to be immediately disabled, and soon after that my father tore out all the electric heaters—somehow they all seemed to stink, even though they weren't linked to each other. We spent a winter or two wearing sweaters indoors and sleeping under extra blankets on nights dipping into the forties.

Thus I was already conditioned to being cold *in*doors. I bundled up during December vacations in California, in my friend's ultramodern house with no duct system and no connections for natural gas, once again just electric wall heaters, one per room. But because my nearly 100-year-old Illinois cottage does have central heating, with a single furnace in the basement (replacing the coal furnace), being cold indoors in Illinois isn't the problem it was in California. Instead I had to acclimate myself to static electricity that dries my hair before I'm ready to pick up the blow-drier and makes the dogs' fur snap and shock my fingertips.

My first winter in Illinois was the worst in decades. For ten days straight in January of 1994, the temperature never rose above ten degrees below zero. It was too cold to snow during the arctic blast, but a foot-deep layer of snow already covered a sheet of ice. Lethal icicles grew to two and three feet, hanging from my eaves and front porch. People died, were found frozen to basement floors and curled up dead in icy beds. Old houses and apartment buildings burned, killing entire families, when electric space heaters—not infrequently the dwelling's only source of heat—shorted out. People suffocated from using gas ovens for more heat. Vans roamed the streets downtown offering the homeless rides to the shelters. Dead cars dotted empty parking lots after midnight. Crime dropped to near zero. Retail sales nose-dived, except for salt and other ice-melting chemicals. After the temperature resumed normal levels in the twenties, two or three blizzards hit one after another. Future political careers were ruined for aldermen in wards that weren't plowed quickly enough or where salt supplies ran low. A man on a downtown sidewalk was killed by a chunk of ice falling from a skyscraper.

Meanwhile, one of my California-born dogs found the snow to be nothing but a wonderland. For Bizzy, new powder was a psychedelic drug inviting her to flounce about with her butt in the air, then plunge her face down into feathery drifts. Once the temperature rose enough to reduce the danger of frostbite, Bizzy, despite an arthritic back, trotted effortlessly through eight-inch snow with her wedge-shaped face and long muzzle plowing a furrow. Or she

242

would swing her head back and forth, snapping mouthfuls of clean snow from where it was piled just off a plowed sidewalk. She never pulled up lame and confused when ice balls formed between her toes and encrusted on the fur between her pads. To Vixen snow was just another thing you ran through to chase squirrels, but for Bizzy snow was the reason to go outdoors in the first place.

If the deep freeze of '94 was my baptism into the "real world" of winter, then the final initiation would have been my leading role in the icy pileup that temporarily closed I-80 during an April lake-effect snowstorm. But, subtly and gradually, winter and I had already come to understand each other on another level.

Before moving to the Spring Valley house, when we'd lived in a suburban tract, there was no fireplace for hanging our Christmas stockings, so on Christmas eve, we hung them on the knobs of the kitchen drawers. While we slept, our mother filled the stockings then made snowy bootprints across the kitchen floor, using a can of aerosol "snow." But she made a snow *outline* of Santa's bootprint, as though while walking, the falling snow would cover everything except where the boot was. I didn't learn for thirty years that she should've used a bootprint stencil and *filled-in* the print with snow: that's how it works on the sidewalk in front of my house. If I don't clear my walk before someone tromps past, then when I do shovel, the concrete comes up clean except where the white frosty boot prints remain visible. But preventing bootprints on my sidewalk isn't the reason I'm often the first on my block to be out shoveling snow, even shoveling during the storms. Waiting for the storm to drop its full load might make the shoveling too difficult, so I'll go out two or three times while the snow is still falling, removing four inches each time, rather than trying to clear twelve inches all at once. But that's not the whole excuse either. In the same way we can reminisce on periods of abject despair with near nostalgia, shoveling snow at night during a silent storm produces an odd serenity. I'm the only person in a deserted town, the only sound the scrape of my shovel, snow flickers down past muted yellow street-lamps, someone else's icy boot prints still show on my sidewalk.

1989, CLARKSVILLE, TENNESSEE. A one-semester position as writer-in-residence was giving me a forced time-out from the farce I'd made of my marriage. The whole application and interview process had been a rehearsal for the near future when the outcome would more permanent. The move to a log cabin in Tennessee was both a recapitulation and foreshadow of long-distance evacuations and non-California winters to come.

The cabin, reputed to have been a haven for Andrew Jackson on some military excursion, had two rooms downstairs (not counting the kitchen, created out of what may have once been the porch), and two rooms upstairs, equipped with no fewer than seven beds. Usually used as a honeymoon suite, vacation lodging, or weekend getaway, the cabin was owned and operated by a woman who also owned (and was the primary cook for) a private-party-only restaurant. The restaurant, my cabin, and one other smaller cabin shared a piece of property bordered on one side by a busy highway running into Clarksville, and on the other with woods. Naked woods. A blizzard of branches and limbs and boughs and offshoots and sticks and twigs. The leaves formerly attached were, by the time of my arrival on New Year's Day, a thick, crunchy, earth-colored groundcover.

The first few weeks were spent in near total isolation. I wrote daily letters to my faraway husband and received nearly the same number in return. I began a novel. And I walked with my dogs in the completely earth-toned woods, but hardly the peaceful, con-templative activity one would normally imagine during an "artist residency." I was constantly yelling *(screaming)* for them to come back to me, my eyes trained not to ponder nature but only to police them, fearful of losing them not only because they were insane with joy over this newfound expression of their animalness, but because their brown-and-mahogany fur was perfect camouflage. The first time we saw whitetail deer, I did manage to grab their collars before they could bolt in pursuit. We stood together, staring, our breath coming in gasps of fog, our hearts beating in our throats, and I may have still been shouting, not at the dogs but just *something*.

When the college semester started, I joined a group of professors and students photographing the winter landscape. The letters moving steadily between San Diego and Clarksville slowed and stopped. I continued providing my dogs with new sensations they'd likely never again see or savor, but I stopped training, stopped competing. I spent as much time in the darkroom as I did at my typewriter—both considerable—slept less and didn't mind, and never complained of the cold. I was able to shift the focus of my frenetic forays into the woods with the dogs—first to awareness of, then appreciation for a distinctly un-California landscape.

My aroused awareness of my new surroundings was enhanced when I met the other artist-in-residence who was also a Californian (albeit an easterner transplanted in the sixties). We immediately shared exclamations over the turbulence of details in Tennessee's terrain. There were no sweeping picturesque views, no valleys, no distant skyline of trees. There couldn't be—everything was up close, every tract of land that wasn't tilled for tobacco, corn, or beans was crowded not only with trees but with waist- to head-high bushes, vines, and brush, a briar patch of twigs that, even without leaves, could not be visually penetrated.

But we did discover there was more than this dormant brown kindling. We moved closer for a better look. We found crystals of ice pushing up from beneath frozen mud, mist rising from water in peaks to touch a hovering fog, remnants of turn-of-the-century farms decaying in the underbrush, a surreal frozen puddle where a stick under the crust of ice was swirling in a current, etching a fingerprint pattern on the underneath side of the ice. And simultaneously we reveled in the exotic excitement of late-winter and spring thunderstorms. So it could seem predictable that there was another new region for me to discover: my formerly stern, unresponsive body.

Thunder was our code word for the erotic. An incoming thunderstorm starts almost ethereally, with darkness and often a silent increase in wind, a gentle quickening of energy. The approaching lightning may not yet be visible, and the faraway thunder is a soft blurry throb, a moan easier to feel than to hear. The rain may arrive before the storm raises in pitch: suddenly a swish in the trees, a pattering, a purl of liquid movement. As the storm grows in intensity, fork lightning appears and disappears like fanciful snakes in the sky, seconds before each thunderclap, until finally the two are simultaneous and full-blown thunder cracks the sky open. It passes over and withdraws in reverse order. By the time the heartbeat pulse of thunder is once again barely palpable, the loudest sounds are dripping branches and ripples of temporary brooks.

We watched and felt storms from my mini pickup, pulled over to the side of a country road. As the only customers in a Nashville restaurant, we watched as a storm advanced in the distance and a waiter in the foreground gathered the flapping tablecloths and extinguished the candles on the patio. And in my cabin we enjoyed storms that evolved after midnight and subsided before dawn. If we'd been displaced southerners sharing an alternate life in California, we might've eroticized earthquakes or fires.

If my winter and spring in Clarksville was a time warp, a temporary alternate life, then it ended as a life ends. Not necessarily with drama or tragedy, but with finality. And grief. The next fifteen months brought half-hearted marriage counseling, the decision to divorce, then another exhaustive national job search . . . a resumption of dog training and the completion of the novel I'd started in

Tennessee . . . frenzied matting and framing of photos I'd made while in Clarksville . . . daily long walks, not through serene woods but with a cassette player and headphone on the streets of the reputedly growing-more-dangerous east San Diego. Meanwhile I had another new hobby. I was poring through the cupboards and closets of our house, through boxes stored on shelves in the washroom, through drawers and pantries, then making weekly trips to a Salvation Army bin to toss bags of formerly cherished (or necessary) belongings. At one time I'd delighted in constructing my adult life with other people's castoffs. I'd grown up in a family who scavenged; my father still picked up "usable" items, broken chairs or worn-out garden tools, left on roadsides beside trash cans. My grandmother had supervised a Salvation Army store and had foraged through the second-hand goods as they came in the back door. But the full-circle irony was lost on me at the time.

My husband had lived his own alternate life during winter of 1989. We both were aware of the other's experiences—I was unwilling to call either one a transgression, admittedly in my own defense. But while he tried to consider the situation likewise, he felt betrayed. I can't repudiate the validity of his feelings.

My punishment, another banishment from California, began in fall 1990, in Meadville, Pennsylvania, where I'd been offered another job as writer-in-residence. This one was supposed to be a permanent job, for as long as I wanted it.

I rented a two-story, two-bedroom, wood-frame farmhouse that had actually never graced a farm. It was part of a cluster of like houses up the side of a hill, on streets with letters instead of names, and a bronze historic marker at the entrance, denoting this as the country's oldest public housing project. At the end of each street there was a row of spider-webby dirt-floored garages, like a string of barn doors, one for each house. Inside my four rooms, I lived in austerity on dusty unpolished wood floors. For the first three months I slept upstairs on the floor on an air mattress, with some bricks-'n'-boards stretched along one wall. The second bedroom was never used other than as a place to keep my suitcase and some empty boxes. Except a small desk for my typewriter and, later, a futon to sleep on, I didn't buy furniture. Eventually I put the futon downstairs in the living room with the bricks-'n'-boards forming a bookcase headboard, so both upstairs rooms were empty except clothes in one closet. If I'd put mirrors and barres on the walls, it would've resembled the media's invention of an idyllic bohemian dancer's loft. No table in the kitchen, instead I stored the dogs' training jumps between the refrigerator and stove. Until winter actually arrived, I carried the jumps nearly every day out the back door into the large backyard—fenced temporarily with chicken wire and bordering some woodland—and trained Vixen on the uneven, bumpy excuse for a lawn, soon so covered with leaves I was forced to buy a rake.

But it may as well have been winter for nine months in Meadville. Located in the snow belt east of the Great Lakes, the sky was consistently shrouded with lake-effect overcast which more than frequently produced snow, and the snow remained on the ground, more than a foot thick, December through March, even into much of April. I wasn't cold, and I had only my own three porch steps to scrape clean. I didn't have to drive twenty miles at ten-miles-an-hour through falling snow on a congested urban expressway to get to the school. And the weather wasn't preventing me from fulfilling anything I would've otherwise been doing—no boat, golf clubs, bicycle, motorcycle, or hang glider languished in my garage. My days in my college office were largely spent turned away from my door, looking out the windows onto a street that ran through campus and the sidewalks that spiraled off through the snow toward other buildings. On a pad on my desk I wrote dialogue for stories, and random sentences noting what I saw out the window.

Everyone assumed I was a Californian going through light deprivation syndrome, that I didn't have the depth to maintain a vigorous, productive outlook simply because the sun was rarely seen, trees and bushes were bare, and grass under the snow was brown. Too consumed with my own solitude and self-imposed exile, with relationships I'd ruined and opportunities lost, in the winter half of that academic year—in three months—I wrote only one three-page short story called "First Year in Meadville."

No curtains on my office windows, unfrilled view through the storm glass, my feet on the ledge, chair tipped, head barely visible to those in the hall, remarking, "You spend a lot of time looking out your window." But I'm working, just like the man in plaid shirt and knit hat, still raking leaves in March. I watched him plow the icy sidewalks last month—snow turns to mud, but leaves don't go away. He's still raking. Maybe tonight his wife will press her face to his beard and inhale the scent of leaves and grass and oily tools and him, and their bodies will be lit like soft neon, like the brewery signs in Otter's Pub where they'll go later for a beer, and neither will need a sleeping pill when they set the alarm, turn down the heat, sigh, and shut their eyes, not afraid to lose their lives until morning.

MY SECOND YEAR in Meadville was not a year. I gave up the empty two-story house, put my entire teaching schedule into one semester, and took a room in the dorm for only the winter. Winter kept the dorm quiet, *dormant* as the name implies. As though a snowpack had sound-proofed the walls. As though winter's cold had put me on hiatus, had numbed the past enough so it could be broken off with less distress, and had set aside my future—on ice—and kept it from spoiling before I got there. My intermediate realm was muffled, snug, guarded by the snow itself. By the time I heard ice melting outside my windows, dripping from eaves, plopping from branches, trickling in rivulets, I knew I would not return to Meadville. But not because of winter.

I returned to California again for a year. To welcome a different kind of solitude — one I'd chosen. To train my dogs outdoors year-round in sunny, eucalyptus-scented parks. To complete a novel set largely in those parks where people with dogs set up jumps then shout, run, and throw balls, ecstatic to win ribbons at weekend shows — you'd never know they've failed at sex therapy, at marital therapy, at group therapy, even failed at starting over.

The next time I packed my mini pickup and left California, a moving van followed me out of the driveway. There would be no more empty houses to wallow in.

TELL ME

The last twelve hours of 1999: a flight from San Diego to Chicago, a fitful nap in the startling dryness of my heated bungalow in the western suburbs. Then a drive through lucid, breath-taking, still-December night air into the city, north on Lake Shore Drive to a lakeside park, an orderly line of cars filing into the lot. The winter-angry chop of Lake Michigan not visible from here, just the tree skeletons on the grassy banks where a crowd of people was gathering. Not thinking anything except, "Here I am. I'm here."

Fireworks began precisely at midnight. Shot into the black sky from the beach, it was every fireworks "finale" from every outdoor symphony concert I'd ever lay beneath on a silky summer evening beside Mission Bay in San Diego, collected into one winter night in Chicago. The sound through the speakers had switched to a medley of passionate classical climaxes, but the music was nearly buried in the shrieking, the Gatling-gun rattle of pops and big-boom detonations, and the exclamations we couldn't control. Continuing without pause for over twenty minutes, a war of color and flash and sparkle and glitter on a wide-angle black screen over our heads—with two or three other fountains of color down the lakeshore we could see from here, tiny like toys compared to the huge simulated-battle of sparks directly overhead, an entire ceiling of erupting embers. A celebration of the future made out of the technology that invented firepower and explosives. But the smell of gunpowder was heady, the smoke cloud unnoticed. Every flying, falling, arcing spark of color became a 2000 through cardboard 3-D glasses.

For a few hours, as the 1900s turned into 2000, I was in parenthesis—didn't feel the potent optimism the festivity was begging for, but neither did I open the door to the pall the new year had promised. At home, at the start of the year 2000, Vixen, my sixteen-year-old competition partner and companion, slept comalike as her failing kidneys poisoned her body, and Bizzy's big heart, seemingly full of robust canine health at fifteen, would almost literally explode before the new year was forty days old. Meanwhile, out in California, my mother couldn't say my father's name.

WHEN DECEMBER 1999 began, two situations were simmering, seeming to settle then threatening to flare again. In November, just after turning sixteen, Vixen's appetite had abruptly waned, and she stopped displaying any signs of joy when attached to a leash for a walk. She could no longer come up the stairs from the basement and had to sleep down there at night because of the frequency of her urination and (very soft) bowel movements. Blood tests continued to suggest her organs were functioning enough to sustain tolerable life, and finally steroids restored some appetite and quieted her inflamed bowels. How long did I think she would live like this? I didn't ask. Every day that I could entice her to eat with baby food or homemade cuisine was another day she remained my dog.

The other consequential event in the fall of 1999 was my mother's heart attack while she was visiting Maine. It was the first time she'd been back to Maine in two decades, and it was a small attack. She became slick with sweat and short of breath during the first day's requisite harborside stroll, before the real business of visiting lighthouses could begin. So she lay down on a grassy dune, just to rest for a while, she said. But she also thought she knew what was happening, took an aspirin, and didn't argue when my brother hurried back to the rental car and drove her to an emergency room.

While my father and my brother's family continued their planned excursions—embarking on a day's work with a lobster fisherman or ferrying to oddly named Cuckolds light that stands alone on a rock island near Southport—my mother spent a week in the hospital in a small town not too far from Southport's craggy coves, where a century and a quarter earlier her alleged adopted ancestor had floated ashore in a featherbed during a storm. A week later, I received a pastoral postcard in the mail: showing a placid blue harbor with quaint colorful fishing dinghies, boardered by a green park with meandering pathway. My mother drew an arrow pointing to a place on the grass and wrote on the card, "Here's where it happened!"

She finished her vacation—a week of watercolor classes farther north in Maine—and flew home at the end of September. The HMO scheduled her for an angioplasty in early December, so I assumed danger wasn't imminent and did not revise my plan to remain in Illinois for the holidays.

The angioplasty, however, immediately indicated that bypass was inevitable, so the more serious procedure was scheduled for the following day. Then twelve hours after triple bypass surgery, my mother only had enough energy for depression over the extent of the trauma this common surgery has on a body. They'd cracked open her chest—sawed her breastbone and spread her ribs with the medical equivalent of a tire jack—stopped her heart, sliced her leg, and pulled a vein out from shin to groin. They'd removed cardiac arteries and sewn in the replacement pieces. Perhaps they'd even handled her heart with latex fingers. The bruises, wounds, and swelling are certainly more than skin-deep, and somehow more than physical, for every bypass patient. The prospect of eventually being more robust and capable of increased activity seems little consolation in light of their ravaged bodies immediately afterward.

On the phone the day after the surgery, my mother's dull, weak voice wondered if she would ever feel better.

"Of course!" My bedside cheeriness boomed across seven states.

"I hope so," she murmured. Instead of "I will."

The *I will* did not come back to her for a while.

THERE'S ANOTHER COMMON side effect possible after bypass surgery. A study in the early nineties, subsequently published in the *New England Journal of Medicine*, validated a long-held speculation that "neuralgic complications are a common risk of coronary-artery bypass graft," and that bypass surgery carried slightly more than 6 percent risk of "adverse cerebral outcomes." Neuralgic complications and adverse cerebral outcomes are commonly known as stroke, or, the National Stroke Association's appropriately scary nomenclature: *brain attack.*

Like a heart attack, where a cardiac artery is clogged with plaque or a blood clot, depriving the heart muscle of the oxygen it needs, stroke has been redubbed *brain attack* because an artery carrying blood to some part of the brain becomes clogged and the brain is suddenly starved for oxygen. Brain attacks are a risk to coronary patients because plaque due to coronary artery disease, or a blood clot formed in an impaired heart by arterial fibrillation, can break free and be carried to the brain where it becomes lodged in a narrower artery. So bypass surgery can either accelerate that risk, or can *cause* the risk: A blood clot forms because of the distress of interrupting the heartbeat—slicing, dicing, and sewing traumatized tissue—then, within days of the surgery, just as the patient starts to be able to sit up and walk across the room, perhaps just as the sheath of depression seems to loosen because some small headway has been attainable, half the body goes slack or numb or the head hurts like it may explode or legs and arms have gone back to infancy without enough coordination to walk or hold a cup or vision is suddenly blurry or completely lost or a simple request to go to the bathroom comes out as gibberish.

My mother's brain attack, also, was small. There was no loss of consciousness, no paralysis, no blindness, no drooping, no slurring. But, with one of my brothers present, she was uttering an unintelligible alien language, then she shut up and refused to speak. The report to me was: Something's happened and Mom can't talk. In truth, she could talk: she could make noise with her vocal cords and form the sounds of vowels and consonants, grouped as words, with her mouth. But what she wanted to say, tried to say, the things she was *thinking* were not the sounds coming out, and in fact the sounds coming out were not any words anyone had ever heard before. So, scared, she stopped.

It seemed to take a while for an actual doctor to have an opinion. She was sitting in a hospital but no one seemed to know what was going on, nor if a doctor was making an assessment and doing any treatment. Reports came to me from cell phones via siblings who managed to get through to nurses: maybe a seizure; a stroke or a seizure; they don't think it's a stroke; no one knows if this was caused by medication or if she's been given any medication for whatever this is. (There are drugs that can immediately break up a clot and restore oxygen to the brain before too much brain damage has occurred—hopefully before permanent brain damage.) Then a more hopeful report: she's talking again—She just said "What's going on?"

We later learned that some restoration of the brain may come quickly, within minutes or the first thirty-six hours. Further restoration may take six weeks. And some of the damage may not be restored at all. For my mother, the outright speaking-in-tongues was gone in a few hours.

There were only voices connecting me to the scene, one at a time or in conference calls, but the picture in my mind didn't remain a white cubicle with echoey, disembodied voices coming from inside it. There had to be a hospital bed, looming large with thin white linen, cranked partially upright, polished chrome side rails, at the metal foot perhaps a removable chart for notation of meal delivery and medication. Above the head of the bed, on the wall, a bulletin board with my mother's name—computer printed in red with clip-art flowers—not to remind her who she is, but for the nurses and aides, so each caregiver could enter the room with a cheery, "Hello, Ellie, how're we feeling this morning?" The bulletin board is also for instructions, quaintly in first person, "Make sure I wear my support socks to prevent blood clots," "Make sure my meals are low sodium," "Phone calls from my family are OK before 8 P.M." Beside the bed, a nightstand with plastic water pitcher and cup and, in the drawer, a bedpan. My mother's glasses are also on the nightstand, and the *Reader's Digest* she was reading the afternoon of her stroke. There's a tray table whose wheels can slide under the bed while the tray slides over the patient's lap for eating meals in bed; plus wheeled IV stands with plastic tubes running from the bags of fluid to her bandaged arms and, starting the next day, a nutrition bag will be hung there and attached to the feeding tube running down her nose, because the stroke has partially hampered her swallowing muscles.

This is generic, I know, until I add my father, only five foot two, dressed in his cheerful red Christmas vest, his voice booming in forced enthusiasm, making puns and grimaces at hospital food, glasses glinting, hands in his pockets or on the foot rail of the bed, one hand going frequently to his bald scalp as though mopping sweat. And my oldest sister, Lee, sitting in a yellow vinyl chair beside the bed and holding my mother's hand; red-rimmed eyes and nose as though she came from her own sickbed, but smiling, eyes darkly glimmering, holding on, and holding onto her smile. And my brother, Ralph Christopher, three years younger than me — he lives in North Carolina but was on a business trip to Los Angeles when my mother went into the hospital. Only four inches taller than my father, dressed in a business suit, he looks like more of a grown-up than I'll ever be, with his cell phone and laptop, keeping in touch with his company while he also keeps tabs on the doctors, what they know and still refuse to admit. The room doesn't (yet) have any pictures or flowers or cards, except a stack of mail my father remembered to bring that morning, before he knew of the stroke. But there has to be a window. A big one, with southern exposure. It has to be southern exposure because this is December, the sun nearing its lowest angle, not passing directly overhead but leaning south. California winter sun is reassuring, is faith, is what warmed me when I lay in my yard fully clothed in jeans and a sweatshirt after working all morning in my chilly slab-house on a novel I had no presumption would ever see the light of publication. There has to be a block of winter sunlight reaching into the room, passing across the objects as morning moves toward afternoon, spotlighting one wall then the foot of the bed then bathing the IV stand then the nightstand in genial radiance, glowing on each person's skin if they choose to seek its energy. Including my mother, in the bed, propped up and leaning toward her daughter's breast, short colorless hair awry, not wearing but covered by her new cream-colored fleece bathrobe, alternately crying and lying deflated with eyes shut.

A neurologist finally came, with an entourage of medical students. This was no television doctor imparting mentor wisdom to his acolytes while administering comprehensive yet personal care to a scared patient. He spoke to the students instead of to his patient, and spoke to them *about* his patient, in front of her and her family as well. While it's true she was failing to process incoming language as completely as she was failing to produce it herself, she understood his expression, the negative shake of his head. The doctor asked her who "these people" were. She said, "They're okay." Perhaps his brusque manner made her think he was asking her if they were strangers, if she wanted them out of the room. More likely, she was covering, not wanting him to know she didn't know their names.

Then the doctor showed my mother his keys and asked her what they were. He showed her his watch. He showed her his pen. She opened her mouth. But she could feel that the sound about to come out was something else, the wrong word, or not a word at all. She closed her mouth. She needed more time, but he turned away, toward the students, shaking his head. "I know," she either said or tried to say.

As soon as the neurologist was gone, my mother pointed to the stack of mail my father had brought. He moved the stack to her tray table. She didn't want any of the cards, just an envelope, the clean back of an envelope. Her hand made a writing motion, so my sister fished in her purse for a pen. My mother quickly and deftly sketched out a drawing of a key, a watch, and a pen. She passed the envelope to my brother. He took it and looked up. She was also passing him the pen. "Tell me," she said, pointing to the drawings. He wrote the three words under each picture. Then my mother held the envelope again, and they all said the words together. *Key. Watch. Pen.* She put her finger on each word, as though through touch her brain would process the information more clearly. Key. Watch. Pen. She said the words.

"Take with them man next year," she said. "She not mean I'm stupid."

She practiced with her envelope and the three drawings, said the three words over and over. Covered the printing and tried to say the word that labeled each drawing. She waited for him to come back, but the neurologist would deliver his diagnosis to her admitting physician and she would never see him again.

THE ONLY RESULT of my mother's stroke was aphasia. Sometimes aphasia is a catch-all term for a variety of language problems, including a brain that can no longer trigger the speech-making muscles to move properly but is unimpaired in writing, reading, or understanding. Although my mother showed a slight tendency toward a muscular involvement with isolated words, most of her aphasia involved nonphysical language impairment. Aphasia's language impairment symptoms—always caused by brain injury— may be as severe as a patient who is able to generate only a few words and is completely incapable of understanding much, if any, spoken or written language. On the other end of the scale, aphasia could be as mild as not being able to come up with significant nouns and verbs but retaining fluent sentence-making capability and whatever ingrained use of grammar was present before the brain injury—symptoms we all think we suffer from occasionally. Well-meaning people would tell my mother they knew what she was going through because they *always* forgot words and people's names. But no one can really know until language is taken away from them.

Understanding aphasia is almost proof that language is a mediator between what we're thinking and what we want others to understand—that we don't actually think in our spoken language. Spoken language is just one of the available methods of delivering meaning, but it's the one most of us have come to rely on exclusively. There are several classifications of aphasia, and sublevels for patients with some symptoms from more than one category. My mother's aphasia was called anomic aphasia, which is mostly the pronounced difficulty finding words, in both speech and writing.

But she had other language-processing symptoms as well. She could read single words and very simple sentences (if she moved her finger along under the sentence as she read). She could understand most speech said directly to her, if said slowly and if there wasn't any background noise or other people talking. But she could not follow dialogue on the television or read a newspaper article, let alone a book. As was demonstrated by the neurologist's sophisticated test, right after the stroke her brain was unable to supply words for things she wanted to say. Her sentence-making capabilities were also radically impaired. Simply put: What was still in my mother's brain—her whole intact memory and intellect, everything she wanted to communicate—had severe difficulty coming out through speech. Plus she had almost equally serious difficulty processing incoming language into meaning.

Clinically, linguists could (and probably do) learn about language by charting patterns of language difficulties after a brain injury. I couldn't help but marvel at what I noticed as my mother struggled to communicate. Pronouns were backward: she consistently used *he* for *she*, *him* for *her*, and visa-versa. Other abstracts that could have an opposite or partner word were also often reversed: *ago* for *until*, *since* for *before*, *give* for *take*, *to* for *from*, *year* for *week* or *month* or even *hour*. Specific nouns that were lost to her were substituted with generic replacements: *the person, the place, the thing.* Lost verbs often became *do, did* or *does.* And then there were nouns indicating family relationships: *husband, sister, daughter, son.* These were a jumble. But out of the jumble, she still ended conversations with her trademark, "you bet," and didn't have to fish to find it. Her handwriting was the same, and her inflections and accent the same, although the sentences came more slowly.

Talk to her, read to her, ask her questions, do anything to get her to talk. This was her prescribed treatment. Of course she was also still in early recovery after heart surgery, so she fatigued easily, her appetite was poor, she was in pain and didn't sleep much, she was advised to do hourly breathing exercises, and her activity level was supposed to be gradually encouraged and increased. *She'll make most of her improvement in the first six weeks*, the diagnosis warned us, *she must get thorough and constant language stimulation and therapy during this crucial time*. It was round-the-clock rehab work, and there were six therapists—her five children, and her husband—working shifts.

First my father and brother came in with armloads of framed photos of children and grandchildren and propped them on the nightstand, the window ledge, the tray table. She was happy to see them, but didn't want to try saying the names. "Yes, all of them. I know some people," she assured everyone. "They're of mine." Then she cried. Fought back the sobs and wanted something else. It was two weeks before Christmas. With the pencil she would've kept tied to her wrist if they'd let her, she motioned for a piece of paper—always those envelopes from the day's mail—and she began to sketch. In moments the scene she was shaping was obvious: an exact black-and-white replica of the Christmas card she'd spent weeks creating, first by painting a watercolor of the three kings on camels, then by having the painting color-xeroxed, reduced, and printed onto cards. The bundle of cards had been sent before her stroke, a personal note inside each, in her vivacious handwriting. She wanted the painting.

When the armload of paintings arrived—the Christmas card and several others—she held each on her lap and reviewed techniques she'd employed to create cloudy or stormy skies, bushes, or trees in the distance, and her constant watercolor nemesis, shadows, and shade. Lee sat with our mother and helped with the names of colors when she used *banana* for *yellow*, *gee* for *green*, *burple* for *purple*, *pond* for *blue*.

Commuting almost daily from Orange County, Lee also brought a frayed illustrated Christmas carol songbook we'd used as children.

It had remained in the bench seat of the Chinese-red piano when it had relocated to my sister's home for another generation's piano lessons. With my mother holding the songbook and Lee sitting on the edge of the bed, their heads leaning close together, they sang carols, soft high voices that gently floated into the hospital corridor and caused nurses to hum *Silent Night* or *Oh Christmas Tree* as they discharged meds or gave sponge baths in other rooms. The melody, coming from another part of my mother's brain, came effortlessly. Again her finger followed the lyrics, sometimes finding a word to sing in chorus with Lee. *Hmmm-hmm-hmm Night. Hmmmm-hmm-hmm Night. All hmmm-hmm. All hmmm-quiet.*

My youngest brother, Walt, the one of us who still lives in San Diego, brought her a children's pictorial dictionary. This book was not organized in alphabetical order, but by category, so on the pages with body parts were pictures of noses and ears and smiles, arms, legs, and feet, with the words, large and bold, beneath each. There were pages for dishes, for clothing, for transportation, for tools, for food, for household items. When the nurses wanted her to dress and go on a walk down the hall, she propped the book on her pillow and looked for the picture of socks, said the word, then put hers on her feet. Found the picture of a robe, said it, and put hers around her shoulders.

Meanwhile the photographs surrounding the bed were an exercise she still wasn't eager to tackle, simply saying "I know," as she looked at them. Unwilling to be wrong with her own children's names.

"Who's this?" Ralph Christopher quizzed, holding a framed portrait.

"Kee." The word that had eluded her when the doctor showed her his keys, one that she'd practiced as she looked at her drawing.

"Close. It's *Lee*."

"Klee."

"Almost." He was matter-of-fact and businesslike, the way he would lead a meeting of executives. "And who's this?"

"My son."

"It's your grandson. What's his name?"

"J—"

"Three of them start with J—Jake, Johnny, and James. Which one is this?"

"The middle say you."

The photo of me they'd selected was a dog show picture taken after Vixen and I had earned the highest score at a trial. "I know him. And his pop— poppy."

"*Her* puppy. Who is it?"

"My sister."

"*My* sister."

"My dau—"

"Good. How about this one, who's this?"

"My honey."

"That's right—that's been my name for fifty years!" Since the head-shaking neurologist, my father could no longer stand by and watch her struggle.

"Ralph," my brother prompted.

"Yes," said my mother.

"Say it."

"Rauuu—" Our father's name eluded her the longest. But besides *honey,* there was always *Dad.* She said "My dad."

"No, *my* dad."

Every morning, with her honey, she sat and read the Christmas cards arriving daily in the mail. Holding the card between them, my father read the printed verse out loud while my mother underscored the words with her finger. Some words she said with him, or like an echo, *merry* and *greetings* and *new year.* Then my father read the personal messages aloud. Most of the cards were from people who had no idea how their season's greetings were being put to use:

"It's to — The man — At the school." A former colleague of my father's from Mesa College. "We haven't been them for — after fifty years ago." Old friends they hadn't seen for five years. "She does the cards." A man in one of their bridge groups.

My brother, listening from the foot of the bed, got the idea to bring a deck of cards to the hospital. My mother took the deck, face down in her palm, one by one turned each card over. "Jack of spade, two club, eight of club, queen diamond." She sounded like our Italian grandfather who'd never mastered English. "Ace heart. Ten of spade." The same number, *ten*, which could easily become *a hundred* when used for *hours* or *years,* gave her no problem in terms of playing cards. In childlike bliss, she tuned out the people in her room, laid out a solitaire game on her tray table, and began to play.

The thing I might've contributed was useless. She'd been waiting for years for "Waterbaby," an essay about her childhood, to be published. When it had sold to a literary magazine, I planned for it to be a surprise, a Christmas gift. But while she could read bold words under pictures of hats and shoes, while she could read the numbers on playing cards, reading dense gray paragraphs, with my idiosyncratic long sentences, would remain unattainable for a while.

Instead, the hospital's speech therapist arrived with an armload of props so my mother could play the toddler level "What's this?" game. Starting, however, with items already in the room, the therapist discovered my mother had been studying with her pictorial dictionary.

"Billow."

"P — P — P — Pillow," the therapist helped.

"Yes, P — illow."

After each answer, she looked at my sister who was trying to stay out of the way in a corner. Lee answered each of our mother's glances with a smile.

"How about this?"

"Shade. Dr—ape."

"Curtain?" The woman smiled, jotting a note on the chart. "Okay, I have some new things here. Do you know what this is?" A hat. My mother's hand on top of her head as she said "hair." A pot. The therapist noted, again, the inversion of the P. "Bot." A whisk broom. "Sweep."

A trophy. "For winning."

"Okay. And this? Isn't this pretty?" A magazine cover of autumn-colored trees in close-to-sunset light.

"Land—"

"Not exactly."

"Landscene."

"Landscape," Lee muttered.

"Oh!" The therapist wrote again in the chart. "How about this?" A map. "The wor—"

"No, try again."

"Worr—world."

"Oh. Okay. It's also a map, isn't it?"

"Yes," our mother agreed.

"So what's this?" A miniature framed painting.

"I know that. Mon—"

"No."

"I come there to hear it. Mon—"

"No."

"—nay."

"Try again."

"She's saying Monet," Lee said quietly.

"Yes. Moe-nay. I came to hear it, at where my mother stays."

The Monet exhibit at the Art Institute in Chicago. Where her daughter lives.

"Oh," the therapist said, smiling toward her paperwork where her pen scratched with apparent zest. Dotted her last "i" with a whole-arm gesture, then she flipped the chart closed, packed her tools, and said her cheerful good-bye.

The HMO decided our mother needed a rehab facility, possibly for up to six weeks. Then it took two days for everyone, even the paper-clogged HMO, to realize the rehab facility had nothing to offer. But before the paperwork caught up and allowed Mom to be discharged, one of her visits from my two sisters — Phyllis had, by this time, arrived from Idaho — featured a violin and clarinet Christmas carol concert. Between songs, my sisters giggled like they had when, as teenagers, our mother coaxed them into playing for relatives; and our mother, alternating between her upside-down smile and wiping tears, sang along when the melody helped provide a word or two. She was released on Christmas eve and gave my sisters directions for how to drive home from the rehab facility.

I DIDN'T ARRIVE home until the evening of Christmas day. I had only spoken with my mother once on the phone, to tell her I was coming home. She cried. I think she was saying "I'm sorry," or "I'm happy," or both, or something else. And I think she did cry for some kind of happiness, or relief, but also confusion and uncertainty and fear. Perhaps the stroke had also damaged the part of her brain that regulates emotion — her bouts of weeping thus triggered by a swirl of extreme feelings she neither understood nor could name or blame. Except she knew she made mistakes and couldn't say what she wanted to. And she desperately wanted to. It made her cry, but it's what saved her. Her vital need to express herself outweighed her mortification over "being stupid."

But every time she cried, two or three of us would fly to her, flutter around her, pat and hug her, smiling and cheerful, to tell her it was okay. Our mother crying had always been a rare but dreadful event. Her skin darkened to an unrecognizable shade, and her features bloated or distorted—no longer the face at the center of our universe, a typhoon descended onto our valley that was supposed to be forever hale and sunny. Her crying meant a nameless horrible thing had happened that we would never understand. It's a sheltered childhood when nonviolent marital disagreements, maybe once a year, result in anxious alarm. A clue that childhood hadn't prepared us for familial crisis.

At the end of the 1900s, it was finally time to grow up. My siblings, raising children, had already realized they were adults, and I *thought* of myself that way: I paid bills, had bought and sold a house, had been married and divorced, had credit cards and life insurance, wrestled with my HMO, scheduled car repairs and dental exams, and twice a year drove the 2000 miles between Illinois and California in three days, alone. But despite having acquired all the accouterments of maturity, the sudden insight that *now* I was irreversibly an adult struck me when I went home for the holidays in 1999. It wasn't tied to any responsibility for my own life, but to the role-reversal with my mother, and the abrupt absence of a safety net beneath me. A net I'd rarely used, but had always known was there.

Christmas 1999 was far more than a you-can't-go-home-again return to the house where I'd grown up: drowsing poorly in the room where I'd pretended to sleep while listening to my sisters discuss high school social dramas, bathing in the bathtub where I'd observed with trepidation my developing adolescent body, plonking together leftovers in the kitchen where my mother used to—whirlwind-like—prepare fresh-ingredient cuisine for seven every evening.

THE SCREEN BACK door squeaked as I came into the laundry room. From the din of voices making merry in the living room, my father exclaimed, "There she is!" Taking the long way through the kitchen—strewn with platters of cookies and persimmon bread, homemade doughnuts left from breakfast, a platter of cheese and

salami and olives, a tray with glistening empty oyster shells—I
arrived at the foyer as though I'd come in the front door. The floor
of the living room was barely visible—boxes and wrapping paper
and ribbon and unopened gifts. Surfaces of end tables and the
coffee table were likewise crowded with newly opened gifts, books,
CD's, puzzles, more cookies, dates and nuts, my father's dried
persimmons and figs. And people everywhere: four of her grandchildren—two kids lying on the floor with Gameboys, and two
others, nearly adult, leaning against each other on the sofa—and
three of her children and children-in-law, also sitting on the floor
or standing. Separate animated conversations boomeranging, the
bubbling beep of the Gameboy, "Let It Snow" swinging from the
stereo, all woven with my father's laughter. With her back to the
foyer, in an armchair, my mother was swathed in pajamas and fleecy
robe. Her thin brown hair, having lost the last of its perm before she
entered the hospital three weeks ago, rose wispy on her head like
down on a chick, or a dandelion. A startling metaphor, even now—
I'd never viewed my mother as fragile. My sisters were kneeling on
either side of her, leaning close to speak slowly into her ears. "Oh?
There—now?" she said, turning, her ashen face not brightened by
the powderpuff texture and color of her robe, nor by the new
emerald earrings, a gift from my father. But the smile, the upside-
down smile, was hers. "Oh, you. You're—there." She swiveled the
chair around and reached to clasp my hands, the last of her children
to return home for this unexpected Christmas reunion. "Thank
you for going to be me."

I don't remember what I said. "You look good," or "It's so good
they let you come home." She was nodding, her voice hoarse from
the breathing tube used during surgery, saying, "I'll go to be—I'll
do—Better next day—I was pretty good—later—"

"She gets tired. She was doing better earlier," a sister agreed,
always, all of us, touching her when we spoke.

My mother was gesturing an arm across the room toward a grandson. "Take now. Take. Of all. All my sisters."

"A picture?" He rose, having been given charge of her camera. My sisters and I gathered behind and around her chair, hovering over her and leaning close.

"All mine. In this place. Sisters all of one—Same hour."

"Yes, we're all here, all at the same time."

But the reunion made speaking and understanding all the more difficult for her. This room was a tempest of conversation, laughter, puns and jokes, brain-teasers read from new gift books, idioms from three generations.

My mother tugged at my sleeve. "Were you at—the place—enough years—before being here—to come to you, my card?"

"Did I get your Christmas card? I did. The first one I got. It was beautiful."

"I did all it—Everything since—this thing." Her hand indicating her breastbone where, under the fleece robe and flannel pajamas, the bandaged incision and stitches from her heart surgery were still fresh and painful.

"You mean you made the card *before* your surgery."

"Yes, yes. And—The one who takes them to me—He worked—you know, with the desks and pooks."

"Books? You mean a teacher?"

"Yes, yes. He teacher with her at—the place. A friend of—hers. My—*Her*." Pointing.

"You mean dad? A friend of dad's from school?"

"Yes, give it on his—machine in the desk—"

"Computer."

"Pooter?"

"Com. Com. Ca—" I was stuck too. "Like, um, *come. Come*-puter."

"Ca—pooter."

"*Come*—"

"*Come*-pooter."

"There you go."

How do you do this, help her without making her feel wrong, without *correcting* her? But they had said: Every time she says something wrong, tell her what was wrong and correct it, she should repeat it back, repeat it several times. But when we started to be able to understand her, as though inventing a new language, we started to answer without editing, the way our father and aunts and uncle used perfect American English in response to our grandfather's half-Italian. Sometimes we handled it this way, just replied to her reassembled language, letting her know we had perfect understanding of what she had meant. Some of us remarked on the "mysteries of the brain," like when she wanted something to drink and asked for Bubble-Up, a beverage that hasn't been manufactured for well over a decade. Occasionally we made light of her mistakes, made guess-what-Mom-is-trying-to-say into a family word game. She would laugh. But some of us, as often as we could, with previously unused levels of patience, laboriously corrected.

When my oldest nephew was four or five, if anyone used the attention-getting gimmick, "Guess what, Bobby?" his earnest response was never "What?" but a staid, "Tell me." These were words my mother might've wanted to say, as she fought to find the names of things and places and people, but she also wanted to do it herself. Instead she would look at me, sometimes as she tried to put together a sentence for my father, her head snapped around, her eyes said "Tell me." Or "Show me." Her eyes not on mine but focused on my mouth, and I shaped the beginning of the word she wanted. *Shhhhhh*, or *Brrrrr*, or *Oooooo*, or *Unnnnn*.

EVERYONE FINALLY LEFT for other houses. After a restless night roused frequently by the automatic sprinkler system and the hot tub filter, I woke in the dorm-style bedroom I'd once shared with my sisters. The red piano replaced by desks and the new computer for which I had gotten my mother a step-by-step guidebook. The three closets now filled with filing cabinets, photo albums, and winter coats. My typing table held the sewing machine, the third bed had been replaced by the upholstered rocking chair—recovered five times over the years that her children had squeezed in beside her while she read aloud. I lay in bed for a while. I didn't have to fling myself into an Illinois winter morning and go down to the basement to tend a blind dog wandering aimlessly, to clean up her several rivers of urine and splotches of feces on the concrete floor, then try to find a delicacy she would eat.

My father's footsteps padded down the hall then made the kitchen linoleum creak. The click of light, the glug of water from the cooler as he filled the coffeepot. When I heard the faint murmur of my mother's voice, my father's louder answer as he came back up the hall, I got up and dressed.

My mother was sitting on the side of her bed in pajamas and robe, unwilling to go on until she could say what those things were she was about to put on her feet. The children's dictionary was beside her on the mattress, open to the clothing page. "Shoe," she muttered. "But—it's something else."

My shift started. Ralph-Christopher had returned to North Carolina on Christmas eve. Lee would have her first day in two weeks not driving down from Orange County—she left us a pot of homemade soup gleaned from the Christmas turkey. My other sister, Phyllis, who'd arrived from Boise four days ago, was on a Christmas-gift-from-grandparents day at Legoland with her family. Walt was self-employed and had to work.

"But this," my mother touched an inner garment, already on under her pajama top. "This is—bud in this. Look. Is this okay?" She pulled the undershirt out from her body and leaned forward. "Is it okay, or is bud going out?"

The garish incision, eight inches down her chest, was dry. I glanced, but didn't stare. Then she unbuttoned her pajamas to show me the faint pinkish spots on the undershirt. "Bud got here. Need new others."

"Blood. But not really blood. And it's just a little."

"Also here." Her hand on her lap. "In my p—pan—pants."

"You're bleeding there?"

"The bills, from heart, give like period."

"Bills? Oh—the medicine?"

"To show bud—easier to go."

"Blood thinner?"

"Yes. Makes me give a period, after hundred years of none."

When I was nine or ten, grocery shopping with my mother, I asked in an unbridled voice what were those huge pink boxes she was always buying and storing in our bathroom cabinet. She said she would tell me later. That night she'd sat with me on my bed and informed me that I would, someday soon, find blood in my underwear, but it was okay, I should tell her and she would show me what to do.

My father was out of the shower now, in the kitchen counting my mother's pills into a complicated pill box, one row for each day in the week, four compartments on each row for morning, noon, suppertime, and evening medications. I made oatmeal, poured juice, stewed prunes. She came into the kitchen, her slippers making the same sandy sound on the floor they always had when she slid from stove to sink, fixing seven grapefruit halves while eggs popped in a fry pan. She named the ingredients of her breakfast, but ate slowly and didn't finish. With one finger, she moved each pill my father placed on the counter, like beads on an abacus, from one side of her bowl to the other, asking my father what each was for.

"So many bills," she said, grimacing, perhaps a sardonic smile. "I never had to do bills."

"No, *I* do the bills," my father boomed, trying to be jovial, but his voice was hoarse too.

"What?" she looked up at him.

"*Pills*," I said. "Like *Pan. P— P— P*ill."

It wasn't just the steady amateur speech therapy she needed. Not just coaxing her to eat and, especially, to drink. She still had breathing exercises, supposedly every hour. She'd been directed to get on her feet and walk, as much as she could. She would have home visitation from field nurses to check the incisions on her breastbone and eighteen inches on the inside of her leg, take blood and give instructions. My mother's medical chart was a notebook that stayed with her; each nurse or therapist who saw her added their own report sheets. My father had been in charge of the pills and notebooks and instructions and appointments, but by the afternoon of the 26th, he was flat in bed with the flu. The house seemed dim, too amber and too warm, the air too syrupy. Outside in the sun, iridescent hummingbirds came to check empty birdfeeders.

"Ming. Ming," my mother muttered, shaking her head. "They need."

I filled the feeders. I put music on the stereo—the Christmas CDs they had loaded yesterday. She followed the lyrics in the songbook then sat listening with eyes closed. I removed empty boxes and bags of trash from the living room. I warmed soup on the stove.

"I'll do in a year," she said of the soup I offered.

"An hour? Okay."

But she wanted to talk. Soft carols in the background, we talked about her sister who would be touring Maine lighthouses with her daughters in the spring.

"My sister and my mother— His mother— No, the girls, children, *his* children. All coming down Maine to find the lights."

About the new watercolor teacher she'd found this year and the difference in his approach from the previous teacher.

"No many barns, he gives water, and much green places."

About a lady on their meals-on-wheels route, who'd moved into a rest home and my mother had tried to visit her every other week.

"He had, like you, a boppy, until he—stop work, no more work a hundred years from now."

About reservations for a trip to Rome my father had canceled after the first heart attack in Maine.

"Maybe in an hour, we will come from it still."

About a cousin I'd only met once, who'd made jewelry and hitchhiked to Boulder in the late sixties, but who now lived with a husband in San Diego.

"He had it in . . . the state, over there, with mountains. L - O - C."

"Oh, Colorado."

She continued to talk while we played cards. She had to remind me of the rules for gin. And she won every hand. The smell of turkey soup drifted in the room. Sunlight left the windows. A few lights with automatic timers clicked on.

WHEN PHYLLIS'S FAMILY returned from Legoland and moved their sleeping bags and Christmas toys into the big dorm bedroom— time, like noise, increased in vigor. It was only a week until I would leave, but we settled into some kind of routine. Three tiny meals, encourage fluids, hand her the breathing exercise contraption. Put her new Dean Martin and Rosemary Clooney CDs on the stereo, play cards, restack the kids' toys that daily became strewn across the floor. Help her put her socks on and trim her toenails, take her to get her hair done then to walk in the mall—down one wing, rest, then back again. As we passed the movie theater, she labored to describe a movie she'd wanted to see, and as we approached See's Candy she said she'd better be well by February so she could go out alone and get my father's box of Valentine chocolates. Days sand-wiched around anticipated visits from the nurse, and, finally, a mobile speech therapist. Mornings we practiced with the work-sheets left by the therapist, like fill-in-the-blank pairs I read aloud: boys and _____, dog and ___, fruit and _____, sheets and _____, knife and _____, paper and _____. This last one had caused puzzlement when the therapist read it.

"Plate," my mother tried. "What else does it? In the cup. Hot."

"You mean coffee?" The therapist was also confused. "Paper and coffee?"

"We call the newspaper just *the paper*," I offered. "That's what *paper* means."

Regular exercise—standard rehabilitation after a heart bypass—was difficult, especially on Valley View Lane and the other county roads nearby, with no sidewalks and too much uphill. Phyllis and I took our mother to Chollas Lake. Practically an inner-city park, this was a place where I'd released my pet duck after he proved to be a boy, and a noisy one. A flock of hybrid domestic ducks and huge white geese share the lake with mudhens, mallards, and cormorants. Fishing is allowed for kids, and a three-quarter-mile walking/running trail circles the pond, with wooden exercise equipment—sit-up benches, pull-up bars—just off the path for complete workouts. My sister's boys were immediately absorbed into the culture of stomping mud, running, swinging, climbing, splashing, and chasing ducks, leaving Phyllis and me to walk the trail with our mother. We held her arms. Continually asked if her chest hurt, if she was out of breath. "I'm okay," she said each time, slightly panting. "Keep on."

But we couldn't. Halfway around, she said "Stop, have to." We stood, needlessly holding onto her, joggers and walkers passing us like busy traffic. "Wait, wait," our mother said, "Just for soon, wait." We spotted a split-log seat and urged her to walk a few more yards. When she sank to the bench, her face collapsed as well.

"Mom, don't cry, it's okay to rest."

"I did everything," she sobbed into her hands, then raised her streaked face. "Never so tired. Not bad like this. I did *everything*."

Phyllis and I spoke in chorus: "I know, and you'll do everything again. It's been two weeks since surgery, you have to get well, then you'll see how much better you feel."

"I don't know. How? Will I ever still be doing?"

"Remember, Mom, *I can and I will*."

"I told it to my sister."

"*My* sister," I said.

"Me!" Phyllis chimed.

ON A QUIETER day, after Phyllis and her family had returned to Idaho, it was time to go buy my mother another bra. Actually a camisole. She couldn't wear a bra until the incisions fully healed.

The summer I entered eighth or ninth grade, my mother had consented to my first two-piece bathing suit—not a bikini, but the kind where the bottom came up to the waist, and the top came down so close to the waistband, only two inches of stomach showed in between. The one we bought had "room to grow," but I never did grow into those stiff cups, and started to avoid wearing the suit in public because the top stuck out so unnaturally, lizard-green and Playtex-looking.

We decided not to park close to Wal-Mart's doors because the walk from the parking lot would be her day's exercise. Our eyes, however, were unaccustomed to judging a slight uphill grade, and we were halfway to the store when her breath labored. "No, keep on, I can," she said, and we inched our way to the entrance. Inside, holding onto a shopping cart, she moved with more confidence, tried to explain to me how odd it was to her to be in a swarming after-Christmas Wal-Mart after so many days in a hospital. "Like I've never gone in this place since a hundred years."

It took a while to find the women's undergarment department, especially with Wal-Mart's knack for displaying merchandise in the aisles that one decides at the moment should be bought or would be nifty to have. Because neither of us could come up with the word *camisole*, she didn't want to ask for help. The consequence of our poor judgment of the parking lot's grade and distance, our poor shopping habits, and our poor undergarment vocabulary, was that my mother was growing overtired.

Painstakingly, with others buzzing past to get to the checkout lines ahead of us, we maneuvered toward the cash registers. But even in a bustling line of postholiday exuberant shoppers, everything remained underwater slow-motion. She said, "I have to . . . stop." We glanced at the front of the store: the ice and soda machines, the manufactured firewood, a lotto machine, an ATM, a mailbox, and a bench. But two women were already sitting there. Why was I mired in glue? Why didn't I take her there and ask them if they could let her sit down? I just kept looking at the occupied bench, unloading our merchandise onto the belt, then she said, "I'll do there." Momentarily broken from inertia, I walked her out of line and to the wall, near the bench. "I'll wait, okay here." The two women on the bench didn't look at us. "Are you sure you're okay?" I asked, more for their benefit than hers, but she answered, "okay." I left her standing beside the bench and returned to my place in line. I kept my eye on her, but did I really?   where was I looking? Suddenly she was going down. Not fainting, not falling. Her knees bent, one arm reached for the floor.

I burst from my place in line. "Mom, are you—?" She was down on one flank, her other leg half extended in front, one hand down on the floor, the other in the air, reaching for something or someone. She was crying. I grabbed her flailing arm. "I can't. You can't do—can't put me up."

"I can, Mom," and together we hoisted her to her feet.

"I just was to sit, then couldn't—knew I couldn't—go up again."

"So you weren't fainting?"

"No, just down—to rest."

Still standing right beside the occupied bench, I finally said, "Could she sit here? She just had heart surgery."

One of the women got up and left without a word. When my mother sat there, the other woman began a dialogue that soon revealed she was on vacation from Maine. Speaking slowly, as though from fatigue, my mother was able to reply, including the name of the island, Southport, where her family had come from, and the lighthouse, Hendricks Head, her grandfather had lived in as keeper. If the people in the checkout line hadn't put the rest of our things on the belt and allowed the cashier to ring up my total, instead of putting me at the rear of the line, I might've given my mother enough time to tell the lady the whole legend of the 1875 shipwrecked baby.

My mother waited at the door while I took the bags to the car and drove back to pick her up. After she settled and fastened her seatbelt, she laughed, mixed with a little more crying, wiped her eyes and said, "Don't tell Dad."

So my mom and I became confidants.

THERE ARE MANY things I never told my mother, the kinds of things girls share with their moms. The last time I'd gone to my mother with a social trauma, I'd been excluded by every group in a sixth-grade puppet-show project. My mother had me call the only girl I knew who was also not in any group. We drove to her house, brought her home, had dinner, then the two of us made our own puppet stage out of a cardboard box. With my mother's artistic suggestions, we made our puppets, our backdrops, and our script—Little Red Ridinghood—and practiced our show. The other groups—using refrigerator boxes while ours was probably a medium television-size box—had spent most of their preparation time painting their cardboard stages "psychedelic," and their shows were unintelligible (or avant-garde) tempests of waving (or fighting) puppets and meaningless shouted dialogue. By the time all the puppet shows were given (and polite applause received for our staid two-person rendition of a children's story), I was probably friends again with my usual buddies. It's disgraceful to remember, though, that I never told my mother when *I* was part of the excluding group, even wrote unmerciful stories about the singled-out girl.

But after that—upon entering the feral world of junior and senior high school—I never again went to my mother to discuss the pertinent events of my adolescent life: romantic longings and disillusionment, social failures and triumphs, jealousies, insecurities, anxieties, and immature behavior that made messes of everything. I never told her that because I owned four pairs of knee socks, for four days I could disappear safely outside the harsh light of junior high fashion scrutiny—while not nylons, at least knee socks were also not anklets that showed my hairy legs—but the fifth day I faced with trepidation. I didn't tell her that the only boy who would dance with me at junior high dances was a kid from the family who'd lived next door when I was three, so he felt I was safe, like a sister. After he found his first girlfriend, but was still shy with her, he continued to dance the slow dances with me because it was okay to touch a sister-type girl (a trend that was taken to greater lengths by other boys a few years later). When the band announced the next song would be the last one, this kid's girlfriend jumped up and down, clapped her hands and cheered, "Please be a fast one!" It was, and she got to dance. While disappointing, it wasn't a moment of absolute dejection, because (I also didn't tell my mother) "fast dancing" was something that inspired other kids to laugh at me. I couldn't undulate my hips the way other girls did. I didn't tell my mother that for several of the after-school dances, I waited all afternoon and never danced. I'm sure I wasn't the only one. Part of me relieved that I wouldn't have to "fast dance" in front of other kids, the other part of me wishing the kid I'd known when I was three hadn't gotten over his aversion to touching his girlfriend so he would still come to me when the band played a slow song. I didn't wear dresses to dances. These events were a reprieve from the dress code, so I'm sure, in the flickering dim lights of the school cafeteria-turned-nightclub, I looked like a boy to any of the roving male population cruising the crowd outside the dance area, determining who would be their next lucky partner.

I didn't tell my mother about the heartless joke I pulled at Girl Scout camp, pretending to be a boy and flirting with girls from other troops until one homely girl developed a crush on me, which I encouraged because I thought I was doing her a favor, making her the chosen one. Boys had that power, to choose us or not choose, and I didn't tell my mother when I got caught shoplifting at Disneyland, trying to impress a boy into choosing me. I didn't ask her to clear up my confusion over how people were supposed to do what the rabbits did when I put the doe in with the buck to be bred.

In high school, where the stakes were higher, I didn't tell my mother that I let my boy buddies practice on me when they were too shy to touch their girlfriends' breasts; nor that when a boy finally was interested in me as a girlfriend, the only things we did "as a couple" was park on the way home from school and play "Can you get out of this one?" I didn't tell her that I thought something was wrong with me when I didn't feel any desire to kiss or have boys rub parts of me, so I thought I'd better endure it so I could "learn to like it" the way I was supposed to. I didn't tell her that in trying to learn to like it, I must have been simultaneously resisting because the second boy who "took me out" used the old cliché and told me I "didn't put out." Was I also called the other clichés, Ice Maiden or Virgin Queen? I wondered and worried to myself if these could be applied to me, but I never asked my mother.

Then, no longer a girl, the list of what I didn't tell my mother grew. I never tried to describe for my mother the disillusionment upon discovering the severely retarded boy I'd "adopted" would never walk. I never told her how I sat trying not to squirm through several weeks of Jehovah's Witness meetings, my mouth barely moving as a moderator led an assemblage through group-readings of a simplistic illustrated proselytizing pamphlet, like a fourth-grade reading circle. I never came close to indoctrination, and that was never my goal. My fearful hope: that my attendance would make the young man beside me decide to be my boyfriend (then *I* could bring *him* back to the world). He pointed to a woman in the congregation, someone he had never met, and said she's someone he could marry. My mother never knew when I went to their wedding a year later.

I didn't tell my mother that long before I finished a four-year degree in journalism, I knew I'd never become a journalist because I would take a hundred-mile detour to avoid communicating with anyone I didn't already know. And I didn't tell her that two days into my student-teaching experience, I already knew I would never enter a high school as a teacher, immediately could admit to myself that I was indifferent toward what the students needed or were expected to learn. I didn't tell my mother that, despite this knowledge, I didn't quit, but let the year play out listlessly — without any concern for the students who were receiving scant attention from an incompetent student-teacher who would rather tingle at her master teacher's flirtations than work out a decent lesson plan. I didn't tell my mother that part of me knew the reason I hadn't quit was because of that flirtatious master teacher, because of the overt sexual tension he took pleasure in kindling between us, and because I wondered if he would help me lose my distressing virginity. Then he took me home to smoke a joint with him . . . and his wife, the same wife he'd been telling me was inadequate to his sexual desires.

A wife who cried on my shoulder after he left the room, asking me if he ever spoke about her at school, and if she'd lost him.

Instead, like so many other incidents and occurrences, I wrote it in a story. I told my mother about it in the only way I could.

So, with too-little practice at intimacy with my mother, there was no chance I was going to tell her that within a few years, my marriage had become sexless. It hurt. I froze. He recoiled. It was easier to not try.

Naturally she knew nothing of the sex therapy, or the joke that was supposed to be sex therapy, where a repugnant man suggested that my parents had taught me sex was bad and dirty. She knew my musician husband was locked out of work in a year-long labor dispute with symphony management, and she may've known the extent of our belt-tightening. But no one, not even he and I, knew that instead of drawing us closer, fear was a growing ledge of ice between us, animals stunned in each other's approaching headlights, hopelessness and sexlessness somehow becoming the same thing.

There was no way I was going to tell my mother of the rash behavior that surged from our disheartenment. Of the lesbian woman who came to live with us for a month, who became meshed with our private lives, our aspirations, fantasies, and fears, and came closest to our innermost secret. There was no reason to even consider telling my mother that my husband's agitation led him to yearn for a threesome: which would allow him to enter *her* life, and her body, through her admitted infatuation for me. Nor that the only thing that held me back from participating was the knowledge that his excuse—that maybe she would help cure me of my sexual demons—was not a good enough cover for the reality that he would use me as bait to allow him to make love to her. I understand his distress, because I acted on my own. Away for four months in Clarksville, Tennessee, my sparse letters to my mother never indicated that I was sexually absorbed with another visiting artist and that, miraculously, the sexual dysfunction my mother never knew I had was evaporating in black nights laced with lightning.

Upon my return from Tennessee, home to California and my husband—looking, one friend suggested gently, anorexic, and acting, she suggested even more tentatively, as though I were preparing for suicide—my mother also couldn't help but notice that something was wrong. So, for the first time, she asked me to tell her. I couldn't. I lied. I said, "Yes, something is wrong," but then I lied. I said I'd made friends in Tennessee and didn't want to leave them. I said I'd lived a kind of life I'd never had before—an intense artistic experience working with students and other professors to make a book of photographs and writings, an exciting new environment of snow and ice storms and thunder—and I'd had to give it up because it was temporary. All lies. All the truth disguised with different details.

She never again asked another question about the inevitable divorce, and all I told my mother regarding the slow death of my marriage, over the year following my return from Tennessee, was that the marriage was ending. I packed up and went to Meadville, Pennsylvania, and other than phoning me and finding a coldly uncomfortable daughter still reluctant to converse, my mother knew nothing.

Ten years later, in the last year of the twentieth century, with an almost lifelong history of not confiding in my mother, there were new reasons for the things I couldn't (or thought I shouldn't) tell her: For fear she wouldn't understand, that her impairment in processing language would force me to tell it slowly, to deliberately hold each horrible word in both hands too long before precisely passing them, one at a time, to her. But also because she had enough to endure, and they were, after all, "just dogs."

I ALWAYS THOUGHT the dogs would tell me when it was their time to go. The reports from Illinois while I spent a week in California after Christmas were, "She's okay. She ate." Enough for me to put it from my mind while I tried to undo what the stroke had done to my mother. The vomiting I did the entire flight from San Diego back to Chicago on December 31 could have been symbolic of how I'd engorged myself with the arrogant notion that I could fix my mother in seven days. Now I was emptying myself to be ready for the next situation I couldn't fix. The nausea lasted until the jet landed at O'Hare. I didn't appreciate that my air sickness resembled Vixen's distress in her last several weeks.

Almost as soon as I returned home, Vixen stopped eating again, her bowels issued only liquid, fluids had to be forced with a syringe, and she threw up at night. She no longer struggled for freedom upon being picked up. Instead she fell limp and immediately slept against my chest as I sat holding her. I knew it was time. I'd thought she'd tell me, but if she'd tried, I hadn't heard until her no-longer-trying was too loud to ignore.

Two days after I got home from California—leaving my mother sitting, in that fleece robe and flannel pajamas, in the Christmas-strewn living room, dim as dusk before the sun rose over Dictionary Hill—I took Vixen to her doctor. She slept in my arms until I put her into her bed, then, just as the first shock of the drug hit her system, she lifted her head and looked at me a last time, her cataract-fogged eyes saying nothing more than they ever had: You're here.

Two days later I packed Bizzy and her beds and her food and her heart medicine into my truck, and we headed south to Alabama where I had contracted several years earlier to spend a semester as writer-in-residence at the university in Tuscaloosa.

I wrote to my mother every week about what I was seeing in Alabama. Described the sprawling eight-room house I was given to live in, furnished with what looked like the faculty's cast-off furniture. It had a big lawn for Bizzy that—I didn't mention—she barely and rarely used. I explained how, on the other side of a tall wisteria hedge, I was across a parking lot from the football stadium and row of college stores and bars, one of which played college fight songs over roof-mounted speakers starting at eight in the morning, so even on Sundays, marching band music chimed across the empty asphalt. I told her of the beauty of an ominous midafternoon black sky and sudden quiet just before the tornado sirens scream, those glittering and gloomy thunderstorms that sent me to the spidery basement where I discovered a laundry room so I could quit hiking to the student Laundromat. Told her about neighborhoods of historic mansions with red flowering camellia trees, and old antebellum plantation houses that now held downtown business or offices. Listed dense pine forests with signs proclaiming the year they were planted, and peach orchards beginning to bloom in the terrible dark light of another approaching storm, and cattle ranches converted into catfish farms with rows of square pools that would be drained and the flopping fish shoveled out. I portrayed old men on the muddy banks of creeks or ponds with four or five fishing poles propped up on lawn chairs, their lines in the water. I described single-wide trailers and three-room shacks in clearings in the woods with vegetable patches bigger than the house's square-footage, elderly black men in overalls hoeing the rows or seated on the tailgate of their vegetable "stands"—usually an old pickup parked at roadside, the bed heaped with cabbages and corn and okra and greens. And these might be next door to a suburban ranch with circular driveway and vast turf lawn landscaped with budding fruit trees, huge trampoline in the backyards but hardly ever a person in sight. I wrote that every small town had a large, privately owned florist and every small town's graveyard was always adorned with fresh flowers on almost every plot, even tiny 100-year-old graveyards containing a dozen graves fenced off in a clearing in the woods. And I explained how you can tell an abandoned house from a lived-in house by whether or not there's a barbecue outside. But I didn't tell her that these things were being viewed on the eighty-mile drive between my house and the veterinary college hospital at Mississippi State University.

Bizzy had been a vigorously healthy dog from her first breath, which she took cupped in my hands. She was my first dog's first-born. When I tore the membrane from the slimy six-ounce newt, she literally opened her mouth and gasped. Fifteen years later, as soon as I was in Alabama, I noticed a change in Bizzy. She stopped her two passions: barking at other dogs and begging for scraps of my dinner. In fact her ration of kibble, usually gone in thirty seconds without chewing, had to sit all day before she finished it— even with stinky canned food mixed in to entice her. I wasn't in Tuscaloosa three days before I received an emergency phone call from my vet in Illinois reporting that Bizzy's last blood test indicated she needed immediate surgery to remove her parathyroid glands, otherwise her kidneys would begin to fail. I drove her home through an Indiana lake-effect snowstorm—for two days a fifteen-square-mile section of northern Indiana was a blizzard while the rest of the Midwest was clear—then brought Bizzy back to Alabama completely shaved from her chin to her chest. She barely ate another meal for the last three weeks of her life. Bizzy's anorexia was her way of telling me. I (still) wasn't listening.

Bizzy's weakened heart, combined with no parathyroid glands to regulate her body's calcium, plus kidneys that had been compromised by the body's fight for oxygen from a malfunctioning enlarged atrium . . . were killing her. But an easier diagnosis was confirmed by the specialist in Mississippi: A broken heart. Literally and figuratively. Bizzy had never been the only dog, alone. IVs gave her temporary dialysis, perked her up enough to lick at baby food. The doctors taught me to administer subcutaneous fluids from an IV bag to prevent dehydration, but if she didn't eat, she couldn't be helped. The first day home from her second week-long stay in the hospital, she began having seizures, each convulsion lasting five or six seconds, head thrown back, legs stiff, she fell to her side, her body emptied itself of urine.

I didn't tell my mother, by letter or phone, about Bizzy's last horrible night, about the Sunday afternoon decision to prolong her life no longer or the electricity-filled storm that brewed as I made arrangements with the local vet. He came to the house that night through a tornado watch, over wet streets littered with branches and leaves, while I held Bizzy on the sofa. A special tribute for Charles Shultz, who'd died that morning, played silently on the TV. I lifted my head over Bizzy's ear tickling my chin and saw a cartoon on the screen: Snoopy on his doghouse with a thought bubble over his head, *A dog is all I ever wanted to be.*

What I was left with—or what I was granted like a gift—in my remaining two months in Alabama was a beautiful emptiness, stripped isolation, calm reclusivity, melancholy turned into tranquil retreat. Strangely, in grief: peace. Allowed a temporary austere life. Finish writing a novel. Read. Feed myself. Watch television. Sleep. Walk and walk and walk. Then drive to see a historic small town or nature trail or archaeological site or lock-and-dam. Feel the genial spring sun on my skin. Smell the spring storms blowing in like warm, moist breath. See the azaleas, daffodils, tulips, dogwood, flowering pear, and wisteria paint the campus landscape as well as run amok in yards surrounding even the smallest shacks. I rarely cried. But I couldn't tell my mother.

I couldn't conceive any way or reason to ask my mother to share or understand the frenzy of my last three weeks trying to save Bizzy's life, nor the stillness of the months that followed. But it wasn't all altruistic, my not wanting to share it. It was selfish. I wanted every minute of it, not diluted, for myself. Didn't want anyone to take any of it from me. Suddenly understood grief and why we're half in love with it when we have it: It's what's left to us of still having what was lost. And we hang on. This slow-motion crash did not have me crying "Mommy." But I was thinking of her.

Would she be able to process any narration of this solemn solitude when I could barely find the language to describe it? Or would I even need to describe it? Wasn't she living her own version?

I imagined her in a dismal, chilly Southern California winter, like those dim days after Christmas when the house was full of food and the floor cluttered with boxes and gifts not yet put away— books she couldn't read, photos of grandchildren whose names she couldn't say—the stereo playing a cycle of five CDs of Christmas carols while she sat in a chair in pajamas with a songbook, following the lyrics with one finger on the page, singing along, softly, just for herself to hear.

In reality, my mother's January calendar was cluttered with doctor visits and speech therapy appointments, and she crossed these days out impatiently until she could begin to go back to watercolor classes, at first driven by my father until she was given the medical clearance to drive alone. She walked daily on her new treadmill and wrote down her time and distance faithfully on a pad beside the controls, pleasing herself with each time and distance improvement. Her speech therapy was still twice a week, then in spring dropped down to once, with a therapist she came to love. To therapy sessions she brought photo albums and letters from her children. She described my father's gardens and their camping vacations in the Sierras. She dreamed of having her therapist come for dinner and conversation as a friend. In the old rocking chair where she'd nursed her five babies, in what had been our big dormitory room with picture window overlooking my father's terraced fruit and vegetable gardens, she sat and meditated. Something she'd never done in the whirlwind activity of her life, something she might've scoffed at if described by our hippy cousin who'd hitchhiked to Boulder, but meditation was recommended by her cherished speech therapist to clear and relax her brain and allow it to slowly look for words it had lost. She went back to bridge groups. Could follow words on TV's *Millionaire* because of how many times they repeated the question and all the time given to the contestant. Followed most of the play-by-play of the Superbowl because she understands the game. And she used her new computer's e-mail:

1/9/00
Got your long letter and will trying to read things. Sory about the terrible sick on the plain. but it was a with Jim for fireworks. I have want to tell you so sorry about Vixon. I now this friend was always dear to your. I am trying this all by my self to live this. I just now you be living Alabama so will not use your address. That is why I am trying e-mail. Trys to sent me pack to e-mail. I love you so much.. Mom

1/17/00
Will try a short note. this morning Dad took me to check on my Heart pacer. We have walked at the fishing place twice. This one we tried around all way. I have also been out to Bently around also. We will try to see your place soon. We love so much to you. Mom and dad.

2/8/00
You have been just good hearing from you that I feel so many times not hearing from you. The speech therapist is helping we my writing We am glad you got safely home and wish that Bizzy will get matter now. I have finish reading from your wonderful Waterbaby and told my therapist I

could read the article taking a slow time! This past Sunday we went to the Symphony. Dad and I celebrating the 49 anniversary by going to dinner at a Chinese restaurant. I am looking for a valentine blouse. I want to gets Sees chocolates but will have to go by myself. I will be glad to finish these doctor times!

4/4/00

I will try a short email from you. We have loved all the southern letters. I am doing better for writing from you. My speech therapist is helping alot for me. She is working now with my writing and understanding other people. Have come a long way but now I still have to help. Hope you understand this email. I love you.. Mom

4/11/00

We are flying to Boise on May 4 - 8. By ladies Bridge is the next day at here. We did found how to attach the clip on the treadmill and I have up to 2.2 speed for 17 minutes which gets me 6.O miles each day for a week. Dad feels he gets enough work in the garden so has not tried the treadmill. Glad to see you soon!

4/16/00

We got your last letter about going to the automobiles. I am saving all of your letters which will be like a book! We look forward to coming to San Diego. Remember Dad and I are going to Boise the first weekend in May. I guess you are going to a dog show that weekend also. So, call me when

you can some date in May. Hope you will see us
real soon. I miss you.. Love, Mom

In truth neither of us was in a dark winter. I was in gentle
Alabama where the daffodils came up at the end of February, and
she in California where my father's strawberries began to ripen in
early March. My southern winter taught me the cathartic beauty of
austerity, and hers at home in California gave her the gist of her
own capacity—power that returned in four words that she had not
forgotten she'd said to us: I can. I will.

10/8/00
Just a short note to tell you we are Home! Walt is
comming for supper a few minutes. Dad went
fishing yesterday. Had a great time with Ralph
and Kate and the girls. Went to the beach on the
Outer Banks and saw 3 of the tall lighthouses. I
made it to the top of Cape Hatteres Lighthouse!
It was some climb!!! Ralph & Dad went out on the
boat fishing and also went clamming. So we ate
a lot of seafoods—steamed clams—cioppino—
clam chowder & baked fish. We swam at the
edge of the lighthouse last twilight & saw the light
go on at dusk.

A native of Southern California, Cris Mazza grew up in San Diego County. She has taught fiction writing at the University of California at San Diego, and was writer-in-residence at Austin Peay State University in Clarksville, Tennessee, then at Allegheny College in Meadville, Pennsylvania. Since 1993 Mazza has lived west of Chicago. She is a professor in the Program for Writers at the University of Illinois at Chicago.

Mazza's novel *Homeland* will be published by Red Hen Press in 2004. She is also the author of *Girl Beside Him*, *How to Leave a Country* (winner of the PEN/Nelson Algren Award), *Is It Sexual Harassment Yet?* and *Dog People*. She is the coeditor of *Chick-Lit: Postfeminist Fiction*, and *Chick-Lit 2 (No Chick Vics)*, anthologies of women's fiction. Mazza was an NEA fellow in 2000-2001.